WITH THE LAW ON OUR SIDE

Also by Brenda Hale

Mental Health Law

Parents and Children

The Family, Law and Society: Cases and Materials
(with David Pearl)

Women and the Law
(with Susan Atkins)

From the Test-tube to the Coffin, Choice and Regulation in Private Life

Spider Woman

WITH THE LAW ON OUR SIDE

HOW THE LAW WORKS FOR EVERYONE AND HOW WE CAN MAKE IT WORK BETTER

BRENDA HALE

THE BODLEY HEAD
LONDON

5 7 9 10 8 6 4

The Bodley Head, an imprint of Vintage,
is part of the Penguin Random House group of companies

Vintage, Penguin Random House UK,
One Embassy Gardens, 8 Viaduct Gardens, London SW11 7BW

penguin.co.uk/vintage
global.penguinrandomhouse.com

First published by The Bodley Head in 2025

Copyright © The Rt Hon the Baroness Hale of Richmond 2025

The moral right of the author has been asserted

Penguin Random House values and supports copyright. Copyright fuels creativity, encourages diverse voices, promotes freedom of expression and supports a vibrant culture. Thank you for purchasing an authorised edition of this book and for respecting intellectual property laws by not reproducing, scanning or distributing any part of it by any means without permission. You are supporting authors and enabling Penguin Random House to continue to publish books for everyone. No part of this book may be used or reproduced in any manner for the purpose of training artificial intelligence technologies or systems. In accordance with Article 4(3) of the DSM Directive 2019/790, Penguin Random House expressly reserves this work from the text and data mining exception.

Typeset in 11.5/14pt Dante MT Std by Six Red Marbles UK, Thetford, Norfolk
Printed and bound in Great Britain by Clays Ltd, Elcograf S.p.A.

The authorised representative in the EEA is Penguin Random House Ireland,
Morrison Chambers, 32 Nassau Street, Dublin D02 YH68

A CIP catalogue record for this book is available from the British Library

HB ISBN 9781847926579

Penguin Random House is committed to a sustainable future
for our business, our readers and our planet. This book is made from
Forest Stewardship Council® certified paper.

To the late, lamented Julian,
a fearless fighter for right and justice

Contents

Forethoughts 1

PART ONE: COURTS ARE FOR EVERYONE 7

Introduction 9
1. Inside the Royal Courts of Justice 11
2. Inside a County Court 20
3. Inside a Benefits Tribunal 34
4. Inside an Employment Tribunal 45
5. Inside the Family Court 56
6. Inside a Magistrates' Court 76
7. Inside a Crown Court 86
8. Inside the Old Bailey 96

PART TWO: RIGHTS ARE FOR EVERYONE 111

Introduction 113
9. Skoolkids Have Rights 115
10. Disabled People Have Rights 128
11. LGBTQ+ People Have Rights 141
12. Workers Have Rights 154
13. Women Have Rights 169
14. Patients Have Rights 186

PART THREE: MAKING LAW FOR EVERYONE 201

Introduction 203
- 15 Making Law in the Courts 209
- 16 Making Law in Government 231
- 17 Making Law in Parliament 244

Afterthoughts 265

Notes 267
Acknowledgements 271
Index 273

Forethoughts

What are governments for? To run the country of course. What should we ask them to do for us? There are all sorts of things we might *want* them to do for us, such as provide us with education, healthcare, welfare benefits, essential infrastructure and environmental protection. But these are all relatively recent wants. There are two things which throughout history we have wanted and needed governments to do. The first is the defence of the realm – to keep us safe from any enemies who might want to attack us and take us over. The last time this succeeded was in 1066 when the Normans conquered England. Since then our governments have been pretty successful in keeping our enemies at bay, albeit at great cost and often with the help of our friends.

But what is the second thing that any government *must* do? It must keep the peace at home. It must have a system of laws which govern how people should behave towards one another. At its most basic, this means that people should not harm one another and should keep the promises they have made to one another. And there must be a justice system to enforce those laws. Where a person has been harmed or a promise has not been kept, there must be a remedy against the person who has done the harm or who has broken the promise. Sometimes the remedy is compensation – reparation for what the person wronged has suffered. Sometimes it is punishment – unpleasant consequences for the person who has done the wrong. And sometimes it is both.

We have had laws and a justice system since long before the Norman Conquest. But these days it can feel as if the government has forgotten how important they *both* are. It likes getting Parliament to make new laws to solve new problems. But it neglects the machinery necessary to make them work. The justice system has been starved of the resources it needs to do the job which we all need it to do. This is true throughout the justice system but it tends to be the criminal justice system which hits the headlines. The task of the police is to prevent and detect crime. This has become more and more complicated in modern times. The resources available to the police have not only not kept pace with the demand but have been cut back. The task of the criminal courts is to decide who has committed a crime and to punish those who have. But many of the local courts which used to do this quickly and cheaply have been closed down. There is a shortage of lawyers and staff to work in the courts which are open. We need lawyers, both to prosecute and to defend. But even when the courts could sit, the numbers of days when they are allowed to do so have been restricted. Huge backlogs have built up, causing delays and cancellations. The prison and probation services have not been properly funded to reform and rehabilitate as well as to punish. There are not even enough prison places to accommodate all the people sent to prison. This is partly because of the delays but mainly because more and more offenders are being sent to prison and their sentences have been getting longer and longer. The Government has set up an Independent Sentencing Review to see what might be done about it. No doubt there are savings which could be made, ways in which the system could be more efficient. But saving money in one place can lead to spending a lot more money somewhere else.

And that is only the criminal justice system. But there is much more to the law than that. There is the civil justice system which provides compensation for people who have been harmed or where promises have not been kept. There is the family justice system which decides what should happen to the family's children, property and finances when things go wrong and how to protect the victims of abuse and neglect within the family. There is the public law system which regulates every aspect of governmental activity in the modern State – deciding what welfare benefits a person is entitled to, where a child should go to school, whether a foreigner should be allowed to stay in the country, whether a person with mental health issues should be kept in hospital, what taxes a person or enterprise should pay, and above all whether a public authority of any kind has acted within the powers that the law has given it, and whether a public authority has violated a person's fundamental human rights.

These last two issues are the most important. It is said that we believe in the rule of law in this country. The rule of law is a two-way street. It means that we, the people, must abide by the law and have remedies against those who do us wrong. But it also means that the government – those in charge – must abide by the law. Their powers are limited by the law and they cannot act outside the powers which the law has given them. If they do, their actions can be challenged in the courts. One of the laws which limits their powers is the Human Rights Act 1998. Public authorities of any kind – including government ministers – cannot act in a way which is incompatible with fundamental human rights. Anyone whose fundamental rights have been violated has a remedy. Thus, for example, a person who has been wrongly deprived of his liberty can be set free; a person who is accused of crime or is involved in a civil or family dispute is entitled to a fair trial before an independent court; no one should be held in slavery or servitude or subjected to torture or other inhuman or degrading treatment or punishment.

Yet it seems that these vital principles are in danger. Government ministers have threatened to disobey court orders which they do not like. They have promoted laws to restrict the rights of people to complain that government actions are unlawful. They have threatened to repeal or restrict the Human Rights Act. They have promoted laws which restrict the fundamental human rights of people they do not like. They have promoted laws which are inconsistent with the international treaties to which the United Kingdom is a party and thus legally obliged to observe. They have vilified the lawyers who are trying to protect the rights of people they do not like. In short, they seem to have forgotten that the rule of law is a two-way street.

These are vital issues which matter to each and every one of us. We may be lucky enough not ever to be accused of, or be the victim of, a criminal offence. But if we are caught up in the criminal justice system, we want the matter dealt with as quickly and as fairly as it can be, by conscientious police, prosecutors and courts. And we are all likely to have to pay taxes and to be entitled to claim a State retirement pension. We may very well be involved in road accidents, whether serious or minor. We may very well have disputes with our employers, our landlords or our mortgage providers. If we run a business, we may have problems enforcing the debts we are owed. If we are consumers, we may have claims for compensation for bad service or faulty products. If we have family relationships of any kind – and the vast majority of us do – we may run into difficulties which we cannot solve for ourselves. If we are sick or disabled, we will want to have our basic needs met and with basic humanity. And we all deserve to be treated equally – not to be treated less well than other people by the providers of work, accommodation, education, goods or services of any kind, because of something we can do nothing about – such as our sex or our race.

This means that we should all care about the law and the justice system. They are there to do things *for* us as well as *to* us. We cannot do without them. They are not just a nice-to-have. They are essential to our functioning and to our well-being as a community and a country. But this can so easily be forgotten – by anyone who is not already part of the system or willy-nilly involved with it, and even by the politicians whose job it is to decide upon policies and priorities. It is shocking that the justice system is not protected in the same way as health and education when public spending priorities are decided. It is shocking that this could be because we do not care about the justice system in the way that we care about health and education, because we cannot see what it has to do with us. Out of sight and out of mind unless we are currently involved.

This is a book which tries to put across why the law and the justice system are important to each and every one of us – why, contrary to popular belief, they are indeed on our side. The first part takes a look at the justice system. I used to be a judge and so I thought I knew how the justice system works. But it always helps to be up to date. So I have been on a little tour, visiting all kinds of courts and tribunals from the lowly benefits tribunals and magistrates' courts to the lofty heights of the Royal Courts of Justice and the Old Bailey, to see what everyday life is like there – to see what kinds of cases come up on a random day and how they are dealt with, to see what all parts of the justice system are like in practice. I tell the stories of what goes on there, stories which will illustrate why the law and the justice system matter to everyone, but also stories which illustrate what is good about the justice system and what is not so good. I may be an enthusiast for the law and the justice system, but that does not mean that I am blind to their defects and deficiencies.

The second part takes a look at the law itself. It tells a different sort of story. Stories which come from real cases which (mostly) I have been involved in deciding, stories about the rights which different kinds of people have – children at school, people with disabilities, LGBTQ+ people, workers, women, and patients. This is to show that everyone does have rights. But it is also to show that it is not always easy to know what those rights are or should be. The law itself is not always clear or uncontested. So I ask you to form your own opinion on what the answer should be before telling you what the courts decided.

The third part follows on from that by taking a look at how law is made. From early medieval times it was made by the decisions of the judges in the particular cases which came before them. They would decide the same cases in the same way. But when a new case came up, they would have to work out how to decide it. They would deduce the principle underlying the earlier decisions and how it could be applied to the new set of facts. They would develop the law incrementally, from case to case, and in small steps. And they are still doing this. So we take a look at the Supreme Court of the United Kingdom, the highest court in the land. We do this because, when the Supreme Court decides a case, the rule that it lays down is binding on all the other courts in the United Kingdom – it sets a precedent that the other courts must follow. The Supreme Court does not have to follow what the others have done. It does not even have to follow what it itself has done in the past. It can make law in a way which other courts cannot.

The second way the law is made is by legislation – written rules. There are several sorts of legislation. At the top are Acts passed by the Parliament of the United Kingdom. It is the fundamental principle of our Constitution that Parliament is supreme. Parliament can make – or unmake – any law. Mostly it makes new laws to deal with current problems. But if it does not like what the Supreme Court has decided, it can make a law to change it. Next come the Acts passed by the Scottish Parliament, the Welsh Senedd and the Northern Ireland Assembly. They cannot make or unmake any law. They can only make laws within the powers which the UK Parliament has given them in the Acts of Parliament which set them up. But within those powers they can do what they like unless the UK Parliament disagrees. Next comes what we call delegated legislation – rules and regulations which are made by government ministers, and some other public authorities, under powers which they have been given by Acts of Parliament. Parliament does have a role in making these rules and regulations: they mostly have to be laid before Parliament; some have to be expressly approved by Parliament; and some can be disapproved by Parliament. Once they are made, the courts can decide whether they are within the powers which Parliament has granted to the person who made them. So we take a look at how government and Parliament make the laws.

There are lots of books telling us fictional stories about the justice system – particularly the criminal justice system. There are a few books telling us true stories about other parts of the justice system and most of these concentrate on a particular aspect, such as criminal, family or juvenile justice. This book tries to give the full flavour of what the law and the justice system are all about. Some of the stories are quite mundane, because the law has to deal with everyday life. Some of them are quite dramatic, because some of the situations with which it deals are quite extraordinary. You couldn't make it up. The aim is to get across to anyone and everyone what the law is about, how it works and why we should all care about it.

Above all, why we should all care. There is so much else to care about – the education system, the National Health Service, what on earth to do about social care, the lack of social and affordable housing, how we transition to net zero – all things which are now regarded as the responsibility of government. But we must never forget that a society cannot function without just laws and an effective justice system. It is time to put justice back on the agenda for all of us.

Part One

COURTS ARE FOR EVERYONE

Introduction

The justice system in England and Wales is in four parts, the criminal, civil, and family courts and the tribunals. The *criminal* justice system starts with the magistrates' courts, where all cases begin and more than 90 per cent are tried. Next comes the Crown Court, where more serious cases (we'll come to what is meant by that later) are tried and appeals from magistrates' courts are heard. Next comes the Court of Appeal (Criminal Division) where appeals from the Crown Court are heard. The *civil* justice system starts with the county courts, where less serious cases (again, we'll come to what is meant by that later) are tried. Next comes the High Court, where more serious cases are tried and some appeals from county courts are heard. Next comes the Court of Appeal (Civil Division) where appeals from the High Court and some appeals from the county courts are heard. The *family* justice system consists of the Family Court, where magistrates, county court judges and High Court judges all sit, and also the High Court, where some cases are tried and some appeals are heard. Other appeals go to the Court of Appeal (Civil Division). The *tribunal* system is separate from the ordinary courts. The great majority of cases are tried in the First-tier Tribunal, which is split into specialist chambers dealing with tax, welfare benefits, health and social care, etc. Next comes the Upper Tribunal, also split into specialist chambers, where some cases are tried and appeals from the First-tier Tribunal are heard. But there are also some tribunals which are outside this system, for example, the employment tribunals and the Employment Appeal Tribunal, which hears appeals from the employment tribunals. Next comes the Court of Appeal (Civil Division) which hears appeals from the Upper Tribunal, the Employment Appeal Tribunal and other specialist tribunals.

At the top of the whole system is the Supreme Court of the United

Kingdom, which can hear appeals, not only from all parts of the justice system in England and Wales but also from Scotland and Northern Ireland. We'll leave the Supreme Court to one side for the time being.

So far so simple, but it is a bit more complicated because there are several different kinds of judge. There are the lay magistrates, who sit (unpaid) in the magistrates' courts. They are addressed as 'Your Worship' or 'Sir' or 'Madam'. There are the district judges (magistrates' courts) who used to be called stipendiary magistrates because they sit in the magistrates' courts but are also paid professional lawyers. They are addressed as 'Judge'. There are the district judges, who sit in the county courts. They too are addressed as 'Judge'. There are the circuit judges, who sit in the county courts and in the Crown Court. They are addressed as 'Your Honour'. There are the High Court judges who sit in the High Court and also try the most serious cases in the Crown Court. They are addressed as 'My Lord' or 'My Lady'. There are the various levels of tribunal judge. They are addressed as 'Judge'. And there are part-time versions of all of these. Then there are the Lord and Lady Justices of Appeal who sit in the Court of Appeal. They are addressed as 'My Lord' or 'My Lady'. And finally there are the Justices of the Supreme Court, who are also addressed as 'My Lord' or 'My Lady'.

I want to show you what is going on in all parts of the justice system in England and Wales, from the top to the bottom. So I have visited two different kinds of tribunal, a county court, two family courts, a magistrates' court, and two Crown Courts, as well as the High Court and the Court of Appeal. I did let them know that I was coming (apart from the Royal Courts of Justice) but otherwise these were perfectly ordinary days' work, nothing special, but always, to my mind at least, fascinating.

1 Inside the Royal Courts of Justice

One gloomy November afternoon I find myself with time to kill in legal London – that patch around Fleet Street and Chancery Lane where the four Inns of Court and the Royal Courts of Justice are to be found, with the Old Bailey not far away. And I think to myself, why not start at the top? Before I was promoted to the House of Lords and the Supreme Court, I spent ten happy years working as a judge in the Royal Courts of Justice. I know the secret passageways behind the scenes along which the judges and their staff can get around this vast and complicated building without ever venturing into the public areas (rather like the mice in Beatrix Potter's *Tailor of Gloucester*). I have hardly ever ventured into those public spaces. I have never seen the RCJ (as we call it) as the public sees it. But where do the courts which sit here fit in the justice system?

The High Court judges hearing civil and family cases sit here – although commercial, construction and technology cases are heard in the modern Rolls Building round the corner. The civil and criminal divisions of the Court of Appeal also sit here. And lurking in a side building is the Central London County Court. So it's a busy place with ninety-odd courtrooms potentially in operation.

I go in through the arched entrance from the Strand, noticing the space behind the railings where demonstrators are often gathered (kettled?) conveniently for the cameras if there is a high-profile case going on. There are steps to get into the building, so help has to be specially summoned if you have mobility issues. Once inside there are the usual security checks, but I am warmly welcomed by the long-serving security staff, who recognise me even though it is now nearly twenty years since I left. They must like working here, which is a good sign.

Just inside the entrance is the Great Hall. This is a truly magnificent space, its stone walls lined with portraits of ancient Chief Justices and stained-glass windows above them just like a cathedral. There is also a group picture of Queen Victoria opening the building in 1882, surrounded by the top judges and other legal luminaries. But this Great Hall is quite unnecessary. It is an echo of the hundreds of years when the Royal Courts – the courts set up by the medieval kings to dispense their justice throughout the realm – sat in cubicles in the corners of Westminster Hall, that ancient building alongside the Houses of Parliament. Everyone – lawyers, participants and public – milled around in its freezing medieval vastness. The architects of the new building in the Strand must have assumed that they would need a similarly grand space there. But in the RCJ the courts do not lead directly off the Great Hall – the most important ones are on the first floor and there is space enough outside them. So most of the people in the Great Hall are simply passing through.

Just through security there is a handsome wooden noticeboard where the lists of the cases to be heard that day are posted. There is also an information desk with friendly staff. But when I ask whether there is anything interesting going on they don't know. It's not their job to know what the cases are and that is scarcely surprising, given the number of courtrooms and kinds of court which sit here. There are also lots of different styles of courtroom. Civil appeals are heard in smart new courtrooms in the East Wing. Family cases are heard in a mixture of grand traditional courtrooms and gloomy 1950s spaces in the West Green and Queen's buildings. Criminal appeals and High Court civil cases are heard in the Main Building where there are very traditional old courtrooms. Most of these are up steep stone staircases. There must be some lifts, but they are not at all easy to find. I meet a young couple with a baby in a buggy on the first floor, desperately trying to find the way out. Being a stranger to this side of the building, I can't help, and it's not easy to find someone else to do so.

The Court of Appeal (Criminal Division)

It is quite late in the day when I arrive, so most of the sittings have finished. Other hearings are being done remotely, a necessity during Covid which is still quite convenient. But it shouldn't be too convenient – there's a lively debate going on about which cases ought to be heard in person and which can be done remotely. We'll see examples of all sorts of hearings in the course of my travels. Today I'm in luck. The Lord Chief Justice is sitting with two other judges in the Criminal Division of the Court of Appeal. So I make my way up the steep stone staircase off the Great Hall and on to the corridor where his court can be found. There is a public gallery on an upper level, but most visitors go in through the doors leading into the well of the court, so in I go.

I don't think that anyone will recognise me, but of course I am wrong. The usher (gowned) and the court clerk (wigged and gowned) clock me straight away as I slink quietly into the back row of benches, behind three rows of barristers and solicitors. If the Lord Chief Justice, Lord Burnett, and the two judges sitting with him, Lord Justice Holroyde and Lord Justice William Davis, do so too, they give no sign. They are concentrating on the case. I gaze around me. It's an enormous courtroom, impressive or oppressive according to taste, with wooden bookcases full of law reports lining the stone walls, and a high lantern roof. I doubt if anyone takes the books off the shelves these days, as everything is on the computers which everyone has in front of them. The three judges, dressed in their scarlet robes and short wigs, sit in grand chairs behind a raised bench 'halfway up the wall' (as Lord Bingham, senior Law Lord, used disparagingly to say), with elaborately carved wooden panelling and the royal coat of arms behind them, the clerk's bench beneath them, and several rows of benches for lawyers and the public facing them. There is a witness box to one side, with a press box beside it, and a jury box and a dock on the opposite side. But there are no witnesses and no jury and no press today. There is also no one in the dock. The five defendants who are appealing against their sentences are all appearing on screen from their various prisons.

No days out to come to court now. Much cheaper and more convenient. No more early starts and long journeys from their various prisons. No more waiting around at court for the prison vans to arrive.

But I wonder how they feel? Would they feel more engaged with the process if they were there in court? Would the judges feel more keenly that they were dealing with real human beings? These questions are obviously important when cases are being tried, but perhaps less so when appeals are being heard – these depend upon legal arguments, not hearing witnesses.

There is nothing to tell me – or anyone else – what the case is about. As barrister after barrister gets to their feet and makes their arguments, gradually it becomes clear. These are all men who have been recently convicted of sexual offences which they committed a long time ago when they were juveniles or very young men. How should they be punished? As they would have been if they had been prosecuted soon after their offences, when they were young and the approach to sentencing for such offences was more lenient than it is today? Or as the people they are today with the approach to sentencing that there is today? Or something in between? The people they are today with the approach to sentencing there was then? Or the people they were then with the approach to sentencing there is today? It's apparent that the Court of Appeal has not always said the same thing in the past, which is why these cases have been gathered together to be heard by the Lord Chief Justice.

Another group of visitors troops in shortly after me. They sit and listen for a while and then troop out. They are foreign lawyers here to learn something about our justice system. I wonder how on earth they can do so when there is nothing to tell them what the case is about. Later on, one of them sees me outside the court and asks me about it. I am at least able to give her a brief explanation, although not what the answer is, because the judges have gone away to think about it and will give their decision in writing later. It occurs to me that visitors to the Supreme Court, the final Court of Appeal for the whole United Kingdom, do at least get a sheet of paper telling them what the case is about and who the judges are. Not much but better than nothing.

We believe in open justice in this country. Not for us the secret courts in totalitarian States where no one – not even the people involved, let alone the general public – knows what is going on. Judges should go about their work in the public gaze. It helps to keep them honest and well-behaved. It also helps to keep the public informed about what is being done in their courts. The courts (mostly) sit in public. Anyone can wander in from the street to see what is going on, as I just did (although you may have to queue for the public galleries in the Old Bailey because it's so popular). But a lot of what goes on in courts is pretty incomprehensible unless you are involved in the case or have some sort of explanation. How difficult would it be to provide one?

Open justice also means that the press and other media should be free to report the goings-on in court so that it reaches a wider public. This used to be far more common than it is now – press reporting is just as vulnerable to cuts as are the courts. But in the Supreme Court the hearings are filmed and live-streamed. Anyone can watch in real time or go back into the Supreme Court's website and watch old hearings. A few are even broadcast on television. Not surprisingly, there are calls to broadcast the proceedings in other courts. Small steps are being taken – for example, broadcasting the judge's sentencing remarks in high-profile cases. I am all in favour. We didn't find that people played to the gallery in the Supreme Court and anything that helps to demystify the law and the justice system is a good thing in my book. But televising the evidence given in trials is another matter – I'll come back to that when we visit some trial courts.

Most High Court and Court of Appeal written judgments are available online these days – something which was just beginning when I was in these courts – another good thing. So the appeals which I watched become a lot clearer some months later when I get a copy of the Court of Appeal's judgment. It has decided that the starting point should be what the sentence would probably have been had the defendant been prosecuted soon after the offence, although there may sometimes be a good reason to impose a more severe sentence (for example, because it has become clear that this was part of a pattern of offending rather than an isolated event, or that the harm done was greater than might have been apparent at the time). But the court cannot impose a more severe sentence than the law allowed to be imposed upon a child or young offender for the offence in question at the time it was committed. Finding out what the law was at the time, let alone guessing what a court would have done, is no easy task because the law on sentencing is complicated and frequently changing. But this is obviously right in principle.

So, for example, a man now aged forty-eight had originally been sentenced to two and a half years' imprisonment for a series of indecent assaults against young children, some committed when he was aged between fourteen and sixteen but some continuing after he had turned eighteen. His overall sentence stayed the same, although some of the sentences within it were reduced. But a man now aged twenty-nine, who was originally sentenced to a total of six years' imprisonment for a series of sexual offences committed when he was aged between ten and fourteen against his sister who was two years younger than him had his sentence reduced to eighteen months' imprisonment. The court's judgment is nearly thirty-one pages long – I wonder whether the defendants read it?

These appeals would not have been necessary if sentences had remained the same as they were when these offences were committed. But there has been an enormous increase in the length of sentences over the past two or three decades. It is one of the reasons why the prisons are full to bursting. What good has it done? Has it really put people off offending? Has it really made it less likely that they will offend again when they are eventually released? Some very senior retired judges and the Independent Sentencing Review think otherwise – the greatest deterrent to crime is the fear of being caught and prosecuted, not the precise length of the sentence.

The High Court (King's Bench Division)

Most of the cases heard in the RCJ, however, are civil cases – where an individual or enterprise wants compensation for a wrong done or a promise broken. So I decide to come back another day, this time to see the sort of complicated civil case which won't turn up in the more humdrum county courts which I am going to visit later (see chapter 2). Again, I wander in at random and again I am in luck. In another grand old courtroom on the first floor, Mr Justice Nicklin is hearing preliminary arguments in a most unusual case. It is basically a commercial dispute, part of which is going on in the Rolls Building round the corner. But part of it is a war about words, and Mr Justice Nicklin is in charge of the list of cases about words – mainly libel and slander, but sometimes breach of privacy (misuse of confidential information), and occasionally malicious falsehood, this case. The essence of malicious falsehood is that the defendant has deliberately told lies about the claimant which have resulted in financial loss or other damage.

The defendants sent a series of messages on LinkedIn and Skype to a number of the claimant company's business contacts. The messages suggested that the defendants had a legal claim against the claimant company for market manipulation, that it was worth many millions of pounds, that others may have had the same problem with the claimant and might want to join a class action against the claimant. These messages are said to be false: there was no class action; others had not had the same problem; the defendants had not brought a claim for market manipulation; it was not worth many millions. The messages are also said to have been sent maliciously. They might have been very damaging to the claimant's business. But what's really going on here?

In the commercial court which sits in the Rolls Building, the claimant is suing one of the defendants for breaching an agreement to use the claimant's brokerage services. The messages were sent while this dispute was raging, not only in the commercial court in this country but also in arbitration proceedings in the United States. So were the messages an attempt to bolster the defendant's case in that dispute? Or is this claim an attempt to bolster the claimant's case in that dispute?

There is a lively debate going on in court about whether it is necessary to know what the recipients of these messages thought they meant. Perhaps obviously, what the recipients thought they meant is relevant to whether the messages caused any loss or damage to the claimant. But is it also relevant to whether the messages were false? The judge seems to think that it is, but the claimant's barrister is fighting back valiantly. As I leave, there is another lively debate just beginning about whether an action can be brought in this country for conduct which took place abroad: the messages were sent from Dubai.

These preliminary skirmishes are due to last two days, with King's Counsel, junior barristers and solicitors on each side. Yet the claimant has been unable to show that it suffered any financial loss. So how much will the claim be worth if it succeeds? Is it really worth the candle? Or is there something else going on which the ordinary observer doesn't know? I learn some weeks later that the parties have settled the case – that is, agreed a solution – so the judge is spared the task of having to answer these knotty points of law. They have settled the commercial court case at the same time. But the terms of both settlements are confidential.

I found all this fascinating, but it is hardly typical of the work the civil courts do day in and day out. The High Court tries all sorts: such as high-value claims for personal injuries, where the injuries are very severe or there are multitudes of claimants (think of the men who claimed to be victims of radioactive fallout from the atomic tests in the South Pacific or the sub-postmasters who claimed that the Post Office had destroyed their businesses and much else); claims about commercial contracts where there is a lot of money at stake (think of an oil rig which was damaged while being towed to its place at sea); disputes about who owns property (think of a boundary dispute between neighbours or challenges to a will); or building disputes (which seem to crop up after every large construction contract); and much else besides. The cases are often complex, with many lever-arch files' worth of evidence and documents. They take a lot of time to try. It also costs a great deal of money. Lawyers who do these cases don't come cheap. And in most cases the party who loses has to pay the winning party's costs (the rules are different in personal injury cases). So there are lots of reasons not to bring a case or to try and agree a solution rather than let a case go to trial.

Every so often, attempts are made to reduce the cost of civil proceedings like these. None has been very successful. The last big reforms were in the 1990s. It seemed a good idea to put the court in charge of managing the case, setting deadlines, enforcing the procedural rules, identifying the issues and the evidence needed, telling the parties what the costs were at every stage in the case, and assessing the costs straight away at the end of the case if this could be done (rather than sending them off for detailed assessment by a costs judge). But it turned out that doing all this could actually increase rather than decrease the costs.

Then it seemed a good idea to discourage people from going to court at all – encouraging them to settle their disputes out of court either by themselves (through their lawyers) or with the help of neutral mediators or in other forms of alternative dispute resolution. But this too can be risky. It is the reverse of open justice. Who knows what goes on behind those closed doors? Is it another way for the richer or more powerful party to win the day? And there is something really troubling about the courts seeming to rubbish the very service which they are there to provide.

But do these thoughts apply to the more mundane civil cases which are heard every day in county courts up and down the country? Let's go and see what happens at the other end of the civil justice system – in the Middlesbrough county court.

2 Inside a County Court

Today I'm off to Middlesbrough, once a thriving industrial town on the south bank of the river Tees, and now trying hard to re-establish itself after years of decline. There is a new Free Port under development nearby and Teesside University is a very prominent presence in the town. There are some fine nineteenth-century buildings and a surprisingly handsome modern Combined Court Centre in the middle of town – so called because it houses both the Crown Court and the county court. The Crown Court hears those criminal cases which are serious enough to be tried by a judge and jury – such as serious sex and violence, robbery and burglary. The county court hears those civil cases which are not worth the sort of money which takes them to the High Court. I get lost trying to find it but when I eventually do so everyone is very friendly and welcoming. The clerk who greets me has worked here for thirty years and loves it. The building is well designed, in a square around a central courtyard, with plenty of windows letting in natural light. It seems to be well maintained and there is a good, solid feel to the courtroom furniture. All in all, it feels like a good place for both the judges and their staff to work – quite a contrast to the world outside and to some of the other courts which I have visited. Quite how good it feels to the public thronging the waiting area on the ground floor is another matter.

I am here to observe the county court. County courts up and down the country try civil cases – claims brought by one individual, business or enterprise against another individual, business or enterprise. County courts are there to put wrongs right rather than to punish people. A lot of this is straightforward debt collecting – millions of cases are brought each year by businesses trying to recover the money they say that they are owed by their customers or suppliers. The debt itself is rarely denied but there can be arguments about how it should be paid – usually in instalments. Some of these cases are really sad, when small family businesses fail or people who have been 'just about managing' find that they can no longer do so as bills go up and incomes go down. No wonder the Citizens Advice Bureau in nearby Darlington has a special project helping people to cope with their debts.

Even sadder is the other volume business of the county courts, which is claims brought by landlords against their tenants, or by banks and other mortgage lenders against their borrowers. The landlord or the lender usually only wants the money that they are owed but as a last resort they can bring a claim in the county court to repossess the property – to evict the tenant or borrower from their home. Very often the answer is a suspended possession order, requiring the tenant or borrower to give up the property, but not taking effect as long as the tenant or borrower pays the rent or mortgage instalments together with something off the arrears. These things can go on for years.

At least public funding for legal services (legal aid) is still available if someone is at immediate risk of losing their home. But often things shouldn't have to come to that. The law is very complicated. A little bit of legal advice and some practical help – making some phone calls or sending some emails – can explain why the arrears have arisen and negotiate a practical solution so that the landlord or lender does not need to bring the case to court. But the cuts to legal aid which the Government made in 2013 meant that this sort of early advice and help is no longer available. The number of court cases has gone up and up – another example of a false economy.

But county courts are not only there to help the businesses, the landlords and the lenders enforce their claims. They are also there to help the customers or clients who claim that they have not been given the goods or services to which they are entitled. And they are there to help people who have suffered harm because of another's wrongdoing (this sort of law is called tort, from the French word for wrong). If I am injured out walking because another pedestrian, or worse still, a cyclist or scooter-rider barges into me carelessly, then I can bring a claim for compensation. But I usually won't do so because it won't be worth my while. The cyclist or scooter-rider (even supposing I can find him) won't have the money to pay me compensation or refund the cost of my lawyers. But it is very different if I am injured by a motor vehicle or in an accident at work. This is because drivers have to be insured against the harm that they may cause to other road users and employers have to be insured against the harm that they may cause to their employees. Many occupiers of buildings or land are also insured against the harm suffered by people coming into their buildings or onto their land, although this is not compulsory. In most of these claims, therefore, the real defendant is not the person who caused the injury but their insurance company. And many of them end in an agreement, so they don't have to go to court.

The money claims which do go to court are classified into small claims, fast-track and multi-track trials, according to how much is at stake or how long they are going to take. Today I am going to see some small claims and some claims for injunctions – orders to do or not to do something. I am going to come back to see some fast-track claims. All entirely typical of what goes on in county courts up and down the country every day.

Small Claims

These days, anything up to £10,000 (or £1,000 if it is a claim for personal injuries) is a small claim. These are heard in private by a district judge. The usual rule that the loser has to pay the winner's legal costs does not apply: the costs which are recoverable are fixed. The procedure is supposed to be user-friendly so that people can take part without lawyers. As it happens, there are lawyers in both the cases I see, no doubt because they both involve motor insurance.

When we go in for the first two cases, it feels very formal. This is because we are in a large courtroom which is used for both criminal and civil cases. There is a glassed-in dock opposite the judge's bench. The bench is high above everyone else (although not quite as high as it is in the older courtrooms). There is a jury box and a witness box which is so tall and narrow that it isn't possible for the witness to sit down, even when everyone else is doing so. This seems to be the one defect in an otherwise well-designed courtroom.

The cases are not the consumer claims that I had hoped for, but apparently they are very common. Imagine that you are in a minor road accident which is not your fault – perhaps you have been run into from behind. You are not hurt but your car is damaged. It will be off the road while it is being repaired. But you need your car to get to work, to take the children to school, to take your elderly father to hospital, and so on. So you get on to your insurers and they arrange a hire car for you. But what if you can't afford to pay for it up front? There are companies which will hire out cars on credit, expecting to get paid eventually by the company which insures the driver who ran into you. But of course their charges are more expensive because they are giving you credit. Sometimes the other driver's insurers refuse to pay them and so the case ends up in the small claims court.

The claimant in the first case is a glamorous young woman, smartly dressed in a shirt and trousers. She hired a car on a credit hire agreement for twenty-one days at £72 a day. The other side's insurance company says that they offered her a vehicle which would have cost £16 a day, a difference of £56, so they are refusing to pay any more than that. Both the claimant and the defendant are represented by women solicitors. The only man in the court is the district judge. The claimant goes into the witness box. As it is a small claim, she does not have to swear an oath. But she is the only person standing up. Even though this is a small claim, there is the usual electronic bundle of documents. And there is supposed to be a paper bundle for the claimant to look at in the witness box but there isn't. So there is a flurry of activity while one is found. Meanwhile the claimant is getting more and more nervous. The district judge does his best to reassure her.

Questioned by the insurer's solicitor, she explains that she hired the replacement car the day after the accident as she needed it to drive to work five days a week. The insurance company says that they wrote to her a couple of days later, offering the much cheaper car. She doesn't remember receiving the letter. If she had received that letter, she could have cancelled the other hire agreement. But it would have been inconvenient to change vehicles – not least because she had to register the hire car with her employers in order to get parking at work.

When the questions have finished, the district judge tells her that the worst is over and she can go back to her seat. The solicitor for the insurance company argues that she can have eight days' hire at the higher rate – time for their letter to get to her and for her to make a decision on it – but the rest should be at the much lower rate. The claimant's solicitor argues that she was entitled to hire a vehicle; she only received an offer by telephone, not by letter; she was not aware of the difference in cost and believed the price was reasonable.

The district judge gives his decision straight away. He explains what the claim is about and what the issue is: even if an accident is not your fault, you have to take reasonable steps to keep your losses to a minimum – it's known as mitigating your loss. Was she reasonable in carrying on with the more expensive car or should she have accepted the offer and changed to the cheaper car? The judge finds the claimant entirely credible and decides that she did not receive the letter from the insurance company. But even if he is wrong about that, the letter (there is a copy supplied by the insurer in the bundle) did not give her enough information to enable her to make an informed choice about whether to accept the offer – such as where the hire company was, what car was available, and so on, nor was it clear that it came from the other driver's insurers. So even if she did get the letter, she was entitled not to accept the offer. She gets her full hire charges plus the fixed costs of the hearing.

In the next case, the insurance company is arguing that it was not responsible for the credit hire charges because the claimant has not provided evidence that he could not afford to pay the standard car hire charges up front, so that it was reasonable for him to enter into a more expensive credit hire agreement. This time the claimant and defendant are both represented but by women barristers who insist on standing up when addressing the court or questioning the witness. Barristers seem to find it more comfortable to stand up when talking, whereas solicitors seem just as comfortable sitting down. The claimant is a middle-aged man, again very smartly dressed in a three-piece suit. He explains that he was medically retired from the Royal Navy. His identity had been stolen several times so he'd decided to close all his accounts and route his pensions and household expenditure through his wife's account, and he didn't realise that they needed this information too. He gives the figures for his pensions and his mortgage. Once again, the district judge finds him credible – he's given a reasonable explanation for the non-disclosure and on the figures he would not be able to pay upfront car hire charges without making sacrifices that it was unreasonable to ask him to make.

I am a little shocked at the time and trouble these insurance companies were prepared to take to challenge such small amounts of money – but of course there are so many similar cases that they will add up to a great deal of money over time. I am also shocked to learn that the engineer's fee for examining the car is not recoverable – some higher court has held that this is a cost of bringing the case rather than the result of the accident and it is not among the fixed costs recoverable in a small claim. But I am enormously impressed with the courtesy and fairness, combined with efficiency and scrupulous attention to detail, with which the district judge handled the proceedings. I just wish they'd been in a rather less formidable courtroom.

Injunctions

The hearing rooms normally used by the district judges are much less formidable. Everything is on one level, with a large desk for the judge and his computers, facing tables and chairs for the people taking part, as in the benefits tribunal (see chapter 3); but unlike the benefits tribunal, there is a low wooden barrier between the judge's desk and the people. This must be because the district judges expect more trouble than the tribunal judges do and there is no one in court to help the judge – no usher, no clerk – so they now have to do everything themselves. The parties have to sit quite close to one another which must sometimes be very uncomfortable. But the judge is expecting these to be telephone hearings and the first two are.

In the first, a housing association landlord is applying for an order against a tenant so that they can gain access to the property for the gas and electricity inspections which it is their obligation to arrange. The tenant has simply not engaged with the landlord at all. Nor does she engage with the hearing. I do worry that it might be one of those terrible situations in which the tenant is lying dead and no one knows it. But there are more probable reasons for her non-engagement. In the second case, a hire purchase company wants an order allowing them to go onto the purchaser's property to repossess a car because she has not kept up with the instalments. The car is worth less than she owes but it is better than nothing – they will probably never get their money. She too has not engaged with either the company or the court. The claimant landlord and hire purchase company join the calls immediately. The judge tries to call the defendant tenant and the defendant purchaser three times but they do not answer. He satisfies himself that the proper procedures have been complied with and grants the orders sought.

These two cases are good examples of things that can properly be done over the phone. But if it is all so straightforward, why do these cases have to come to court at all? The answer is that (as a general rule) no one – not even a landlord or a hire purchase company to whom you owe a lot of money – is entitled to enter your property without your consent or a court order. This is as it should be. The court order is an important check that things are being done properly and in accordance with the law. It was troubling, to say the least, when magistrates were told that they need not bother to scrutinise the energy companies' applications for warrants to enter and install prepayment meters. Some of those warrants should not have been asked for or, if asked for, should not have been granted. The trouble with volume business of any sort is that it is too easy for it to go through on the nod. It is reassuring to see that these two cases do not go through on the nod, even though the defendants are not there.

The next case is more exciting. Another social landlord wants an order to stop what it alleges has been antisocial behaviour by the defendant – causing damage, using drugs, dealing in drugs and annoying the neighbours. There's a statement from the landlord and from a neighbour who says that the defendant threw a stone through her window in the middle of the night. The landlord has already got an order *ex parte* – that is, without giving notice to the defendant – excluding the defendant from the premises, and this is his opportunity to challenge it. The defendant and his mother are in court but the landlord's solicitor is on the phone. The defendant is a young man, casually dressed. He disagrees with the claim – he is not guilty of any of the conduct alleged. The landlord's solicitor asks for an adjournment so that the evidence can be heard face to face. The district judge agrees. He explains to the defendant that the court will want a written statement from him, saying what he agrees with and what he doesn't, exactly why the landlord is wrong. The defendant explains that he doesn't have a computer so will it be all right if he uses a pen – he smiles rather charmingly as he insists that the judge will be able to read his writing.

He also wants the part of the order which bans him from the house lifted – he hasn't been home to see his kids and he is having to pay for other accommodation. He is not the tenant of the house, but the tenant is his girlfriend and he thought that he would be put on the tenancy. They've been together for seven years and have two children, a girl aged four and a son aged one. The judge says that he's minded to amend the order to allow the defendant to occupy the house and the landlord's solicitor says, 'We'll go along with that.'

The judge explains what has happened and what is to happen next. The defendant and his mother leave court quite happy with how things have gone. I wonder how things will go when they come back for the proper hearing, because the defendant won't be entitled to legal aid. He will have to represent himself unless he can afford a lawyer, which seems unlikely. He has done pretty well this time, but giving evidence and cross-examining witnesses is another matter, especially when you are up against a lawyer on the other side. The judges do their best to help, but they have to do so without appearing to favour one side rather than the other, no easy task. Not for the first time, I reflect that cutting back so drastically on legal aid was a false economy, leading to more cases fighting in court and taking longer when they do so.

This case also shows how important it is to come to court and have your say – if you have something to say. The young man wasn't the tenant and the landlord didn't seem to know that this was his home or that he had two young children there. Of course, if he has behaved as badly as the neighbour said that he has behaved, there might be a good reason to exclude him. But that is just the sort of thing which ought to be fought out in person in court. From the judge's point of view, there is nothing like seeing the people in the room, watching their body language as well as listening to their words, and seeing how they relate to one another. There are ways of helping if people are frightened of one another (see chapter 5). This judge is right to insist that this case be heard in person.

Fast-track

Fast-track trials are those which are expected to last for no more than a day. The circuit judge has two in his list today, both claims arising out of road traffic accidents. The first is an in-person hearing in one of the formal courtrooms. Both parties are represented by barristers but no one is wearing robes. It's a typical road accident story. The accident took place at a mini-roundabout in Thirsk, a small market town famous as the workplace of the vet who wrote *All Creatures Great and Small*. There used to be a T-junction, with a street called Stammergate coming into Long Street, a long straight road running north and south, from the west. But the T-junction has been turned into a mini-roundabout because it was so difficult to get out of Stammergate.

The claimant is a corporal in the army. He was off-duty on the day in question. He says that he had his two young sons in the car, one in the front and the other in the back. He is separated from their mother and shares their care with her. He was coming up to the mini-roundabout from Stammergate, intending to take the exit to the right, going south. He stopped because it was difficult to see to his right. He says that he looked both ways, saw nothing coming in either direction, and so moved onto the roundabout.

The defendant is a care worker, who was driving south along Long Street on her way from one appointment to another. So she was entering the roundabout from the claimant's left. In his particulars of claim (the written statement of his case) he says that he was negotiating the roundabout when she changed lanes, cutting across him, and collided with the front passenger side of his vehicle. The photographs show damage to the left *front* bumper and wheel of his car. The damage to her car was at the *rear* wheel hub on the driver's side. The claim is for the repairs to his car (which come to more than £1,000) and damages for the injuries he suffered – pain in his neck and upper chest which resolved after a few days, and 'travel anxiety'.

In her written defence, the defendant says that it was she who was established on the roundabout before the claimant entered it and he should have given way to her. So either it was all his fault or he was at least partly to blame. But she hasn't made any claim for the damage to her car or any personal injuries she might have suffered. She also says that she saw only one passenger in the car and the claimant is therefore 'fundamentally dishonest' in saying that there were two. If he is fundamentally dishonest, his claim must be dismissed even if it is a good one, and he will have to pay the costs less the damages to which he would otherwise have been entitled.[1]

The claimant goes into the witness box. He is very casually dressed in an open-necked white shirt and jeans. It is soon established that he was wrong about the defendant changing lanes: while there are two lanes coming into the roundabout from Stammergate there is only one lane coming into it from either direction on Long Street. He doesn't know why he made that mistake. His recollection of the accident is not very good. But he is adamant that, while he looked both right and left, he did not see the defendant's car coming up to the roundabout from his left. The first he saw of it was when it cut across him 'at some speed' on the roundabout. Nor did he see any white transit van coming from his right and continuing north along Long Street.

He is equally adamant that he had his two sons in the car. They had all been having their hair cut in Thirsk and were on their way back home. It turns out that the 'situational anxiety' diagnosed by the doctor who has provided a medical report for the court amounts to his taking extra care at that roundabout now.

The defendant goes into the witness box. She is a striking-looking young woman with pink hair, studs in her ears and tattoos on her left upper arm. She is wearing a smart black-and-white dress and is carefully made up. She was on her way from one appointment to another but she was not in any particular hurry. She had driven that way a few times before, so she knew there was a mini-roundabout there. There is a give-way sign. She slowed down as she approached it but there was a white transit van coming across the roundabout towards her, so she thought it was safe to enter it. The claimant's car struck hers when she was on the roundabout. When they both pulled up after the accident to exchange details, she walked round the claimant's car and took photographs. She noticed one boy sitting in the front passenger seat, wearing what looked like football kit, with his feet on the dashboard, playing games on his phone. The rear windows were tinted but she could see inside the car and she didn't see a second child sitting in the back.

After the parties have given their evidence and the barristers have made their speeches, the judge gives his judgment straight away. He has first to decide whether the claimant is telling the truth about having both boys in the car, because this will colour his approach to the rest of the case. He thinks that it is much more likely that the defendant is mistaken than that the claimant is dishonest. In his claims notification form he said that there were three people in the car. And as a separated parent, the normal practice would be to have both children with him. So the judge is dealing with two honest witnesses. And he concludes that they were both at fault. The claimant should have seen the defendant's car when he set off and the defendant should not have gone onto the roundabout when her view was obscured by the van. He accepts that the claimant was on the roundabout first, so he allocates 60 per cent of the blame to the defendant and 40 per cent to the claimant. This means that the defendant (or rather her insurance company) will have to pay 60 per cent of the costs of repairing the claimant's car, 60 per cent of the damages awarded for the claimant's injuries, and fixed costs. The judge is not impressed with the claim for 'travel anxiety' – taking extra care at the place where you have had an accident is not a recognised psychiatric injury. It's just common sense. But he accepts that the claimant 'had some gyp' for three days after the accident. The maximum for minor injuries from which there is a complete recovery within seven days is £690 so he awards £400.

Neither party is looking very happy. I wonder what I would have decided. Like the judge, I believed in the white van. If it was through the roundabout but obscuring the defendant's view, then she shouldn't have entered the roundabout. But the claimant hadn't seen it at all. It's tempting to think that he was concentrating on the view to his right and didn't notice that the claimant was already on the roundabout. After all, the damage was to the rear of her car, which is more consistent with her story than his. It all goes to show how difficult it is to decide where the truth lies in an everyday dispute like this. I too would probably have decided that they were both to blame but possibly not in the same proportions. It certainly helped to see both parties in the witness box – the defendant was a much better witness than the claimant, who kept on saying that he couldn't remember. But that's not surprising because the accident was three years ago.

This was a low-value case but a much higher-value case, in which serious injuries were caused, would be decided in the same way – on the basis of any contemporaneous records, such as a police report and photographs, and the recollections of the eyewitnesses, often recounted years after the event. We do expect a lot from people giving evidence. But at least we take what they have to say seriously. People often think there isn't any evidence when they mean that there is no written or photographic evidence. There is still the oral evidence of the people who were there, although we judges tend to say that the most reliable guide to what really happened is any contemporaneous record plus the inherent probabilities – whatever that may mean.

Care costs, repair costs, loss of earnings and other financial consequences of an injury are comparatively easy to calculate. But claimants who have suffered personal injuries because of another's fault are also entitled to compensation for what is called 'pain, suffering and loss of amenity'. This can range from catastrophic injuries like paralysis or permanent brain damage to short-lived aches and pains. How to represent these in money terms? The Judicial College (which provides training for judges) has published a handy set of guidelines giving ballpark figures for a wide variety of injuries, based on the awards which have been made in the courts. Loss of an arm, for example, is worth around £137,000 if amputated at the shoulder, £110,000 to £131,000 if amputated above the elbow, and £96,000 to £110,000 if amputated below the elbow. Damage to the hair from defective hairdressing – perms, tints and the like which go wrong – can range from £4,000 to £11,000 depending on severity and duration. That is why the judge and the barristers knew that the minor injuries suffered by the claimant in this case were worth up to £700.

In the next case, the defendant (or more likely her insurance company) has agreed that she was to blame for the accident, so all the judge has to do is assess the damages. It's an unusual case. The claimant was aged six at the time of the accident. She was injured while riding in the back of her mother's car. Her mother pulled out of a side road into a major road and collided with a motorcycle. It may seem strange, but children can sue their parents if they suffer harm for which their parents are to blame. But this doesn't often happen. The parents often won't have the money to pay the damages and, even if they do, transferring money from the household budget to the benefit of a child, who will not have easy access to it, may not be in the best interests of the child let alone the family as a whole. But it is different if the parent is insured, as all drivers have to be, and this mother was.

Children who are involved in civil claims, whether as claimant or defendant, have to have what is known as a litigation friend to conduct the case for them. This child's litigation friend is her mother's sister. Her evidence is that the child was badly upset and frightened at the time and began to complain of headaches the following day. A paramedic friend advised the mother to give her Calpol, so she didn't trouble the family's GP, but kept the child away from school for two days. After the accident, the child was not her normal bubbly self and fidgeted a lot when watching television. She also had a few bad dreams and often woke up in the night complaining of headaches. She seemed frightened about getting into a car and would sometimes cry and get very upset if she had to go somewhere in the car. Ten months later, the child had made a full recovery from the pain in her head and she no longer seemed worried about travelling by car. The medical report, based on a remote examination five weeks after the accident, predicts that she would recover from the headaches within three months of the accident and the travel anxiety within four.

The hearing is conducted over the telephone from the judge's room. The defendant's barrister argues that the claim is worth £2,000; the claimant's barrister argues that it is worth £2,600, though he admits that this may be 'a little on the high side'. The judge awards her £2,250, plus interest of £40, and fixed costs (which will be a lot more). But of course the money is not to be paid direct to the child or to her mother in trust for her. A district judge will decide whether it is to be paid into court or into a child's ISA or trust account where the interest rates may be higher. No doubt the parties will agree what to do.

Once again I was deeply impressed with the fair and friendly, but effective and efficient, way in which the circuit judge dealt with these cases. They were fast-track cases because the sums of money involved were relatively small. But exactly the same questions arise when much more money is involved: who is to blame for the accident; what financial costs and losses did it cause; and what should be awarded for 'pain, suffering and loss of amenity'? Sometimes the evidence is complicated and sometimes it is not. But as a general rule of thumb, the more money there is at stake, the more evidence is collected, and the longer it will all take. However much is involved, most cases can be agreed without coming to court. But the court is an essential backstop for those which cannot be agreed. Without some cases going to court, and being reported, no one would know what to agree – there haven't been any recent cases about hair damage, for example, so maybe the recommended amounts (which have been updated for inflation) need rethinking.

This is grass-roots civil justice in action. But it is being kept going by the goodwill of the judges and the court staff. There are no frills and the staff have been pared down to the absolute minimum. So have the facilities. There used to be catering in all large court centres like this, for the judges, the staff, the jurors and the public. Everyone had to pay for their meals but at least they could get something on site. Now that has gone. The judges do still get together in the judges' dining room, but they bring in their sandwiches and salads in their Tupperware. Yet government buildings, including the Ministry of Justice, do still have catering on site. No wonder the judges and court staff – let alone the jurors who have no choice about being there – feel that their efforts are not appreciated by the powers-that-be.

But now it's time to see grass-roots tribunal justice in action.

3 Inside a Benefits Tribunal

In the 1980s I was a member of a now-gone body called the Council on Tribunals. Our job was to advise on the composition, powers and procedures of the myriad different tribunals which had been set up to decide disputes outside the ordinary courts, usually disputes between the individual and the State, about taxes, benefits, immigration or the like. The system began with the invention of income tax to pay for the Napoleonic Wars in the early 1800s when general commissioners were set up to decide disputes between the taxpayer and the State. It continued with the proliferation of regulatory schemes during the nineteenth century and the development of the Welfare State in the twentieth. Members of the council used to visit tribunals to inform ourselves of what was going on. So I saw a lot – from a mental health review tribunal in Wales deciding whether a patient should remain detained in hospital (where everyone switched between Welsh and English as seemed most comfortable), to a war pensions tribunal deciding whether an elderly person's disabilities were the result of his having been a prisoner of the Japanese during the Second World War (where everyone spoke in acronyms – FEPOW and the like – but they all seemed to understand).

Tribunals have long been regarded with suspicion by the lawyers in the ordinary courts. This is partly because they are separate from the ordinary courts structure and aim to make lawyers unnecessary. Tribunal members are experts – the person in the chair is supposed to know the law, not to need it explained by lawyers, and there are sometimes wing members who are supposed to know how things really are on the ground. Public funding (legal aid) is not usually available to claimants, so most tribunals are expected to operate in a more informal, user-friendly way than do the ordinary courts. But worse still in the lawyers' eyes, tribunals were usually set up and run by the government departments which administered the schemes of which they were part. So could they really be independent of their sponsoring government department? Wouldn't they be at least subconsciously biased in its favour? That was definitely not my impression of the tribunals I visited in the 1980s – they were much less concerned about the sponsoring government departments than they were about the appeal tribunals which might criticise their decisions. And in those days the sponsoring government departments saw the tribunals, not as a nuisance, but as a way of making sure that the right decisions were made – that the right taxes and also the right benefits were paid.

But the 'system' was very untidy and no doubt the quality was patchy. So in 2007 it was decided to bring most of the tribunals into a single system administered, not by the sponsoring departments, but by what is now His Majesty's Courts and Tribunals Service. There is a First-tier Tribunal, which is divided into specialised chambers – the Tax Chamber, the War Pensions and Compensation Chamber, the Social Entitlement Chamber (which deals with benefits, child support and criminal injuries compensation), the Health and Social Care Chamber and the Property Chamber. There is an Upper Tribunal, also divided into chambers, which hears appeals and some more important cases. The people who used to chair tribunals of all sorts are now called judges. But while some people think that tribunals should become more like courts, others think that courts should become more like tribunals.

Today I am off to visit the tribunal which hears appeals from benefit decisions made by the Department for Work and Pensions – the successor to the Social Security Appeal Tribunals which amalgamated the National Insurance Local Tribunals, dealing with contributory social security benefits based on the insurance principle, and the Supplementary Benefits Appeal Tribunals, dealing with means-tested benefits. I am reminded of a kindly lady chair – not a lawyer – who greeted me with 'I go back to the Poor Law, you know' (the Poor Law which was only abolished in the National Assistance Act 1948). How much has changed?

These tribunals matter to anyone who at any time in their life might claim a State benefit and that must include most of us. It certainly includes me because I claimed child benefit for my daughter when she was young and I am now old enough to qualify for a State retirement pension. They handle a huge volume of cases. In a single quarter of 2023, they received 36,000 appeals and disposed of 31,000, of which 61 per cent were decided in favour of the claimant. Most claimants have to represent themselves, although they are sometimes helped by Citizens Advice Bureaux, Law Centres or lawyers acting *pro bono publico* – for the public good i.e. free of charge. The judges have to be able to work with a wide variety of people who are acting for themselves, who may have limited communication skills, who may not speak English fluently, who may be in a high state of anxiety, and who may well be in desperate need. Disability benefits account for 66 per cent of cases. The tribunal needs expert members to help deal with this. It also has to be easily accessible to people with disabilities. The judges have to know their stuff and this is not easy because the law is very complicated and keeps changing all the time. They have to know what the law was when the claim was made, which may be a long time ago.

There are tribunal venues all over the country, sometimes shared with courts, but today I am visiting the central London tribunal which sits in a modern office block on Gray's Inn Road, conveniently located for public transport. Unlike many more traditional court buildings, this one is wheelchair friendly. There are ramps, lifts and flat floors. There is the usual airport-style security at the entrance and then the claimants go up to the fourth floor where most of the hearing rooms are. There are separate waiting rooms for claimants and for the presenting officers from the Department of Work and Pensions, although I am told that many presenting officers now prefer to appear online. I remember the days when the presenting officers would be sitting in the room with the tribunal when the claimants came in, giving the impression that the tribunal and the presenting officer were all part of the same operation. These days that doesn't happen and in many cases there won't be a presenting officer at all: the tribunal will rely on the file and what the claimants tell them.

The hearing rooms are not at all like courtrooms. They are not designed to intimidate – more to allow a structured conversation to take place. There is no raised bench. There is a large table in the middle of the room. The tribunal sits on one side and the claimant and any accompanying friend or helper sits on the other. There is a little table behind the tribunal for the clerk, who goes to fetch the claimant when the tribunal is ready. There are chairs at the back for onlookers and the public. It may seem odd that benefits cases, which are about some very private matters, are usually held in public, whereas family cases are usually held in private. There is a bookcase with a selection of holy books in case anyone is asked to give evidence on oath (although mostly this doesn't happen). There is a big screen to the side of the main table for people to take part remotely. And there are lots of screens in front of the tribunal and the clerk. No more bundles of paper documents. All the files are now electronic. People can lodge their appeals online. But they can also do so on paper. Their documents will then be scanned and put into the electronic file. But I don't get the impression that the screens get in the way of the conversation.

Disability benefits

Two thirds of the cases in these tribunals involve disability, so it is fitting that today there are several for me to observe. In each case, the tribunal consists of a judge, a doctor, and a disability expert. In the morning, the expert is a wheelchair user. In the first case, a mother has made a claim for disability living allowance on behalf of her fifteen-year-old daughter, Selina. Selina was a normal, healthy teenager who played sports and socialised with her friends – until she was diagnosed with Hodgkin's lymphoma, a very rare and serious form of cancer. She had a year off school undergoing chemotherapy. She has been left with a number of physical and mental frailties. The tribunal's job is to decide whether she needs care during the day as well as during the night, so that she can have the higher rate of the care component of the benefit, and how well she can get about without help, in case she is also entitled to the mobility component.

Mother and daughter come into the hearing room with an interpreter: the daughter speaks excellent English but the mother does not. The judge explains what is going to happen and asks Selina whether she would like to talk to the tribunal. She says that she would and a very good thing it turns out to be. The tribunal can hear about her life directly from her and get a real feel for how badly she has been affected by her diagnosis and her treatment.

The doctor asks questions first. She gently points out that she's read the papers and understands a lot, but she can't know how Selina feels. It's hard to come here and talk to strangers. But Selina is very articulate. She explains how her mental health got bad after her treatment finished. She started to have flashbacks and anxiety, she stopped going out and spent all her time in her room, apart from going to school and coming back. Her friends don't know about her diagnosis and treatment because she doesn't want them to (her mother is crying as the interpreter translates this – she would like her daughter to tell her friends). Physically, she suffers from leg pains, shortness of breath and balance problems. She has had some serious falls because of her balance problems. At school she can walk between classrooms if she can hold on to something but not otherwise. She doesn't go outside because she can't run and she gets embarrassed if she wears PE shorts because of the stains on her back and her legs. She used to play sports and go out alone but now she can't. The mother adds that she doesn't have her old daughter, there's a complete difference between her friends' daughters and her own daughter.

The disability expert takes over the questioning, again probing, but very gently. He explains that some of the questions may seem a bit weird, but that's because of the things the benefit rules look at. He's exploring how far she can walk and her social isolation. He also asks her mother about helping her to bathe and get dressed and undressed because of her problems with balance. Of course, says the mother, I'd like my daughter to be healthy and happy and do everything for herself but she can't.

The judge explains that the tribunal now has to make a decision and would like to tell them the result today. But if they don't want to wait, they are free to go. It has been tiring and emotional. We all leave the hearing room while the tribunal confers. It doesn't take long and we are fetched back in by the clerk. The judge explains that the appeal has been allowed: she is going back to the higher rate of the care component because she needs care during the day as well as at night; and she can have the lower rate of the mobility component because she needs help going to unfamiliar places. When she reaches sixteen, it will be a different benefit (a personal independence payment or PIP) and she should put in a claim herself. The written decision will come in the post. He thanks them for coming and answering their questions. It has been really helpful.

It clearly was. It would have been so easy to think that the mother was infantilising her daughter and exaggerating her difficulties, whether for financial gain or out of misplaced motherly devotion. But that was the reverse of the impression gained from seeing them both together and hearing directly from Selina.

It is a good thing that the claimant is there in the next case too, although he clearly does not want to be, and there has been talk of whether he might become violent (it is not clear what the tribunal would do if he did, other than suspend the hearing and get out of the room, which is what a court would do). Fortunately, he is accompanied by two stalwart women supporters who are able to calm him down. A comparatively young man, he has been very badly injured in a road traffic accident and now suffers from a variety of serious mental and physical problems, although his life was quite chaotic before that, so it is difficult to know how much is the result of the accident. Not that that really matters. What matters is what he could and couldn't do when he made the claim. He insists that the two women with him, Penny and Samantha, are not his friends but his carers, but they sound like pretty good friends to me. They certainly care about, as well as for, him. He walks in on crutches and sits slumped in his chair: 'I don't want to be here right now, I want to go home, I've just lost my dad, just get on with it, I'm not coming back.' He is waiting to see someone from the Maudsley hospital because he keeps wanting to die.

Samantha, a sensible middle-aged woman who has known him for twenty years, explains that there are days when he can't get out of bed or can't get out of the house. She has supported him making calls to the mental health people, because his mental state got a lot worse after his dad died and his seventeen-year-old dog had to be put down. He didn't go to a follow-up appointment with the head specialist last year because they were afraid that he might have a meltdown. He can become very aggressive and things get broken. She tries not to let him get that way, but anything can trigger it. He forgets where he has put things (he hasn't brought the papers because he forgot where he had put them).

The doctor member checks that he would rather that she spoke to his carers about him and he nods. He spends a lot of the time with his head in his hands. Penny says that there have been lots of effects of his head injury – he can see someone across the road and think it is the person who ran him over. Samantha explains that he is not very good at planning, he forgets where he has put his phone or the TV remote control, and halfway through a conversation he forgets what they are talking about. He doesn't go out much, she tries to persuade him to get some fresh air, he got some specialist physiotherapy treatment for his back injury with the compensation he got from the Motor Insurers' Bureau (which compensates the victims of uninsured drivers). He can't read or write, so you can't give him an address to go to, you have to show him how to get there, and then he forgets the route. He can't organise himself into a journey. He can walk to the next road on a good day, but it takes him a long time to get to the park on his crutches.

The claimant is getting very upset. 'You're asking all the same questions, for fuck's sake.' (He means, of course, that the benefits officers have asked him all these questions too.) Penny calms him down. She volunteers that he can't go near the cooker no more because he burnt his hands so much. She has to remind him to take his medication, help him get up and get dressed, have a wash. The claimant: 'Sometimes I can't because my head won't let me get out of the house.' He *wants* to work but 'they' said he couldn't because of his head. Penny filled in the forms for him. He doesn't handle money. If it wasn't for Penny he'd be dead by now. He might have been sectioned (detained under the Mental Health Act). The doctors are not stupid. They're trying to find a way to get him through the day. He's scared of himself, scared to be alone, scared to be alive.

The judge thanks them for answering their questions and explains about making the decision. The claimant asks what the judge does! Then he says he's seen him on TikTok (he hasn't). He is sorry for his language. He doesn't mean it.

Not surprisingly, the appeal is allowed. It's a points-based calculation and once the claimant reaches the required number of points for needing help with such things as getting about, washing and dressing, preparing food, budgeting, planning, engaging with others, he qualifies. The tribunal tries to put the decision in writing then and there but there are printer problems so it will have to be sent in the post. It was certainly worthwhile for the claimant to come with his carers: even if they are asking all the same questions as he has been asked before, it makes a difference when an independent tribunal can see for themselves.

In the afternoon, I go across the corridor to where another tribunal of three is also hearing disability cases, but with the claimants online. Even the clerk is online. This time there is a presenting officer, also online, and the claimant has a representative, who is not in the same place as his client. This is a shame because he has the papers and the claimant does not. But the claimant, a man of South Asian heritage, is very communicative. He paints a sorry picture. He has a very severe skin condition which was controlled by drug treatment but that was stopped in March 2020 when the Covid pandemic struck because the drug was an immunosuppressant and came with other side effects. His symptoms got a lot worse and he made a claim in October 2020 which was rejected in March 2021 – so the judge stresses that they are looking at how he was during the period from summer 2020 to summer 2021. He also suffers from severe joint pains and has been diagnosed with a rare hereditary syndrome (which certainly fits all the symptoms which he is describing). Painkillers didn't help so he turned to drink and drugs. His family find it all very hard to understand and can be disrespectful although he relies quite a lot on his brothers and sisters for help – he is speaking from his sister's home. But it all boils down to what he could and couldn't do for himself during the period in question and the disability expert questions him in some detail about this. His representative has nothing to add to the written submissions he has already put in and the presenting officer is 'content for the tribunal to take a view'.

The judge thanks the appellant – he hopes that the appellant understands that they have to ask difficult personal questions, it's the nature of the benefit. They have quite a lot of evidence to discuss, but the decision will be in the post to him this evening and sent electronically to the department. Everyone is thanked and the screen goes blank. Remarkably, the department had decided that the claimant was not entitled to anything. The tribunal decides that he is entitled to the higher rate of both the care and mobility components. This is not surprising, given the evidence, but why did it have to get this far?

Repayment of over-payments

And now for something completely different. A judge is sitting alone to hear an appeal against the department's decision that the claimant has been overpaid many thousands of pounds in benefit and must pay it back by deduction from his current benefits. I am told that this is a common problem. During the lockdowns caused by the Covid pandemic in 2020, many people lost their jobs and had to claim universal credit for the first time. To get through the huge number of claims, the department at first assumed that the claims were justified without doing their usual checks beforehand. But when they did start doing the checks, they sometimes leapt in the opposite direction and assumed that the claim was unjustified and automatically started to claw the money back.

The claimant comes into the hearing room. He looks to be in his thirties or possibly forties, casually but respectably dressed. He has a bundle of papers with him. Then the department's presenting officer appears on the screen (nice touch – not there on screen until after the claimant comes in.) The judge gives the usual explanation of his role. The issues, as he sees them from the papers, are that the claimant claimed universal credit in April 2020, saying that he didn't have any housing costs. But he later informed the department that he did have housing costs and the department amended his claim to include them and paid it from the date of claim. Some time later they asked him to prove his identity and he did that, but now they are saying that he hasn't proved his housing costs from the claimed address. The judge has also spotted a procedural point which he puts to the presenting officer. There are supposed to be two decisions: the decision to revise the claimant's entitlement and the decision to require repayment. Claimants have to be told that there have been those two decisions. But the letter here simply tells him of the second, repayment, decision. It does not explain that the first decision is the reason for the second. It does not explain the reasons for the first decision or that both of them can be appealed.

The presenting officer is a middle-aged man who clearly knows his stuff. He accepts that the letter does not explain why the housing costs have been removed. He comments drily that, 'It is not the best-formulated entitlement decision I have seen.' But he has also done some digging in the electronic record. To claim housing costs, the claimant has to show that he is liable for the rent and also that he is living at the property. The claimant was asked to prove his liability for rent in 2021 and produced his tenancy agreement which was accepted. At that point he was not asked to prove that he was living there. Inquiries started up again in 2022 and it was decided that he had not proved that he was living there. But when he asked them to reconsider that decision, he did provide proof – a letter from his landlord confirming that he lived there, a letter to his GP giving the same address, and the letter from the compensation recovery unit also sent to that address. There is a tenancy agreement from 2020 to 2021 and another from 2021 to 2022. So the presenting officer is satisfied that he was living at that address throughout the period of the claim and recommends that the appeal be allowed.

The judge agrees that the appeal should be allowed on that ground (although he still thinks that there is a procedural weakness in the department's case). So the claimant is entitled to his housing costs from the date when they were stopped and is not required to pay anything back. The judge suggests that when he gets the revised decision from the department he should take it to the Citizens Advice Bureau to get the calculations checked.

The claimant is visibly relieved but says that it is 'sad that they were not listening to me'. He doesn't have a laptop so he had to go to an internet café to contact them online and he couldn't afford it. And how was he expected to live with the tiny sum left after they started clawing back the supposed overpayment? The presenting officer says he is sorry that the claimant has had these difficulties and will feed them back to colleagues.

Of course the case should never have had to go to a tribunal. There is a good reason why there have to be two decisions, and both have to be explained to the claimant, along with his right to appeal against each of them. If this claimant had been sent a letter saying that he had not proved that he was living at the address, he could easily have provided them with the evidence which he later did. But that evidence seems to have been ignored when he did send it in. I have the impression from the presenting officer of an electronic file with links which have to be clicked to get to the right place. Benefits officers are under a huge amount of pressure and never more so than during the pandemic lockdowns when so many people lost their jobs. Mistakes are bound to happen. Thank goodness, I think, we have an independent tribunal which can put things right – and fair-minded presenting officers who are willing to do the work and hold up their hands when the department has got things wrong.

Reflections

This tribunal was operating how it ought to operate – accessible, open, expert, user-friendly, and fair. It seemed to have the facilities it needed – although there clearly is a large backlog, just as there is elsewhere in the justice system, and these are claimants who cannot afford to wait for justice. But was it any different from the tribunals I visited in the 1980s? Is the tidy new system such a good thing?

It is good that tribunal judges are given the mark of respect they deserve for the difficult job they do and are part of the wider judicial family. It is probably good that they are now appointed by the independent Judicial Appointments Commission rather than by their sponsoring departments. It is not so good if all tribunals are expected to operate in the same way even if they have very different jobs to do. One size does not necessarily fit all. It is also not so good if all tribunals are encouraged to become more and more like courts. Courts operate as neutral umpires between opposing parties who are assumed to have equal power (even when they don't). In most tribunals, especially the Social Entitlement Chamber, the opposing parties do not have equal power. The job of the tribunal is to see fair play while recognising the inequality. It can only do that with a combination of expertise and empathy. Rather than making the tribunals more like courts, I would like to see our courts, especially those dealing with the everyday problems of everyday people, becoming more like tribunals. And, from what I saw in the county court and in the family court, they are.

4 Inside an Employment Tribunal

Most tribunals are there to handle disputes between an individual or an enterprise and the State – often about taxes and benefits of various sorts, and sometimes about the decisions of regulatory bodies set up by the State. But there are some disputes between private individuals or enterprises which are handled by tribunals instead of the ordinary courts. This is because Parliament has intervened in what the parties would otherwise have agreed, to give special protection to the party who is in a very much weaker bargaining position than the other.

The prime example is disputes between employers and workers. These would normally have gone to the ordinary courts like any dispute between the parties to a contract and some of them still do. But most disputes between employers and workers now go to the employment tribunals. Parliament has given workers rights which the employer might (would) not have done. The modern law began with the Contracts of Employment Act 1963, giving employees the right to a minimum period of notice and to a written statement of the terms of their contract of employment. Next came the Redundancy Payments Act 1965, giving employees the right to compensation if they were made redundant after a certain length of service. Then came the Industrial Relations Act 1971, giving employees the right not to be dismissed without a good reason. Together these are the basic employment rights, now set out in the Employment Rights Act 1996. But there are many others, such as to the minimum wage, to holiday pay, to limited working hours, and to statutory sick pay, as well as rights when businesses are transferred from one employer to another. A separate set of rights are the equality rights – rights not to be treated less favourably than other people because of such things as your sex, your race, or your disability. These began with the Equal Pay Act 1970, the Sex Discrimination Act 1975, the Race Relations Act 1976 and the Disability Discrimination Act 1996, but many other protected characteristics have been added since. All are now contained in the Equality Act 2010. There is also protection for whistle-blowers and for trade union rights. It all adds up to a complicated picture which can be politically contentious and so is liable to change.

Industrial tribunals were set up under the Industrial Training Act 1964 to hear appeals against industrial training levies imposed under that Act. But their remit was soon extended to include disputes under the Contracts of Employment Act and the Redundancy Payments Act and all the other rights which came along later. The idea was to take these cases away from the ordinary courts and give them to a specialist body which knew something about the real world of work. The courts had acquired a reputation for not being sympathetic to workers' rights because of the way in which they had dealt with workmen's compensation schemes between the two world wars. This reputation may be unfair these days, when judges are drawn from a wider range of backgrounds than they used to be. But most court judges have been in self-employed practice before going on the bench – indeed, I realised when I was in the Supreme Court that I was the only justice who had been employed rather than self-employed all my working life. It can make a difference.

Industrial tribunals had a legally qualified chairman, who was expected to know the law, and they originally had two wing members – one from the employers' organisations and one from the trade unions. They still can have two wing members but the less complicated cases are now dealt with by judges sitting alone. Tribunal chairmen became known as tribunal judges when the new system was set up in 2007. Industrial tribunals became known as employment tribunals in 1998 but their role remains the same. They are still not part of the integrated tribunal structure. Appeals go to the Employment Appeal Tribunal.

The cases can be very complicated and seem to have become more so over the years. When I was a pupil barrister in the 1960s, I well remember going along with my pupil-master to see an industrial tribunal at work – the question was whether the employee had been sacked because his role was redundant or for other reasons. It was all very informal and it did not take long for the tribunal to decide that this was not a redundancy situation. The role was still there. He'd been sacked because he was not very good at his job. Redundancy payments were the first step in compensating people for the loss of a job. In those days, most people could be sacked for no particular reason as long as they were given the required period of notice – and if they were not given that notice, the most they were entitled to was the pay that they had lost during that period. But in 1971, the next step in compensating people for the loss of a job came with the idea that a sacking could be unfair even though the employer had given the required period of notice. After a certain length of time in the job, the employee could only be sacked for a good reason and after a fair process and was entitled to compensation if his dismissal was unfair. This can involve a lot of delving into what went on. The same is true of equality cases. Working out whether a person has been treated less favourably than other people, and if so why, is not easy.

As the issues have grown more complicated, so have the procedures in the tribunals. Employment tribunals have always felt a bit more like courts than the tribunals dealing with things like welfare benefits or immigration and asylum. I well remember a tribunal chairman talking about 'going into my court'. I doubt whether anyone appearing in his tribunal felt it was any different from appearing in the local county court. But employment tribunals are meant to be more user-friendly and accessible than courts. Currently there are no fees for bringing a case and the losing party does not (usually) have to pay the other side's costs. The Government did try and bring in fees for making claims and pressing them to a hearing but (as we shall see in chapter 17) this was struck down by the Supreme Court because it denied the claimants their fundamental right to access to justice.

There is no legal aid in employment tribunals. Some employees will be able to afford a lawyer and some will have a trade union representative to put their case but many will not. The employer will usually have lawyers or experienced human resources professionals to represent them. It requires special skills to give them both a fair hearing. The judge will have to make sure that the claimant understands what is going on and what is expected of him or her. But the judge cannot appear to be favouring one side over the other and cannot put words into a person's mouth. Many judges, especially in tribunals but also in the county and family courts, are very skilled at this but it is not easy to keep everyone happy in an unhappy situation.

All of this will be well illustrated by the case I am about to see in the Central London Employment Tribunal, sitting in Victory House on Kingsway. This is an attractive modern office block, convenient for public transport, with a welcoming reception area but with functional rather than elegant or impressive hearing rooms and offices. The air conditioning is inadequate, so during the Covid restrictions everyone had to operate with the windows open to get enough ventilation and most of what they did was moved online. They are still doing the more routine work online but some cases have to be done in person including this one. It is hard to imagine how justice could have been done otherwise.

The claimant is a qualified naturopath who holds a university degree in Health Sciences. From 7 June 2010 until 9 September 2019, she was employed by a food retail business which specialises in wholesome foods. She really loved her job and took a keen interest in the science. Her work included greeting, serving, advising and assisting customers, processing transactions at the till, dealing with stock and creating attractive displays. But there were problems. Her managers thought that she was spending too much time with the customers and not enough time on other tasks. She thought that she was being true to the company's ethos of putting a high value on customer service. Things came to a head on 9 September 2019 when she resigned with immediate effect. The following month, she brought a case in the employment tribunal, alleging unfair dismissal, disability discrimination, harassment and victimisation. Her case was heard over five days in March 2022, after which the tribunal produced a written judgment running to more than sixty pages. The tribunal found that she had been unfairly dismissed, that her employer had failed to make reasonable adjustments for her disability and had treated her unfavourably because of something arising from her disability. I am observing the second hearing, to decide what her remedies should be.

The case is not thought suitable for a remote hearing because of the claimant's psychological problems with computers and screens. Even without that, I wonder whether it would be suitable. It is a complicated case. It depends a lot on the evidence given by the employer's witnesses and by the claimant. She is representing herself, with only a big suitcase full of papers for company, while the employers have a barrister and a solicitor, supported by two members of staff, to represent them. In such circumstances, would you rather be there in person to get the 'feel of the room' and press your case or would you feel safer interacting on screen? The claimant is either a very good student of employment law or has had some very good help behind the scenes, because she has a difficult case to put forward and she does it pretty well. The judge mentions that she has had some help from the Citizens Advice Bureau but she is on her own in the hearing.

The hearing room is on the ground floor. It is large and utilitarian, with none of the grandeur of a courtroom, except that the bench for the tribunal members is on a dais, higher than the rest of us. This is unlike the benefits tribunal which sits at the same level as everyone else. So does the Supreme Court. I suppose that, in between the highest court in the land and the lowliest of tribunals, there are some courts which need to emphasise their power and authority. But do employment tribunals need to do this?

This tribunal has three members – a woman employment judge and two wing members, one man and one woman. The hearing is open to the public and there are lots of seats for them but today there are only me and a student on work experience who comes in later. There were rather more people during the hearing in March. A member of the public kept approaching the claimant with unwelcome offers of help and support. This upset her so much that the tribunal decided that her contact details should be kept private. The principle of open justice means, not only that the court or tribunal should be open to the public, but also that observers should know what the tribunal knows. But that is impracticable these days, when so much of what a court or tribunal knows is contained in the documents, so there are rules about who can see what. There also have to be rules to protect the rights of others. This tribunal had to balance the principle of open justice against the claimant's right to respect for her private life and also her right to have a fair hearing in which she could represent herself properly. It's hard enough to represent yourself in a complicated case like this, when you are up against professional lawyers, without having any added aggravation.

The hearing starts later than usual, at 11.00 a.m., because the claimant's arthritic condition makes it difficult for her to get going in the morning. There is the usual fuss about whether everyone has the right papers – there are a few new ones to be added to the voluminous bundle from the previous hearing. The judge tries hard to produce a friendly and relaxed atmosphere while making sure that the claimant adds a new document to the file in the right place and with the right number. She also asks her to get something in writing to them about her financial losses by tomorrow morning but explains that she will have a chance to give evidence. Then there is a short break.

The employer has found a few things to quarrel with in the earlier judgment and has made an application for it to be reconsidered. This is a standard part of the procedure in employment tribunals, but I find it odd. When I was a judge, we gave most of our judgments straight away. They were tape-recorded but only put into writing if someone asked for a transcript. They could be revised before the order was made, but this was very rare. There is no standard procedure for reconsideration in the ordinary courts. I wonder whether this is an unnecessary complication in what is already complicated enough but the aim is to avoid the time and trouble of an appeal if the tribunal has got something wrong. The employer's barrister puts her case and the claimant reads out a carefully prepared statement in reply – she is clearly on top of the details and the arguments.

When they have finished it is time for lunch. The tribunal is going to discuss the reconsideration application and announce its decision at 3.00 p.m. The debate about remedies will begin tomorrow. Some weeks later, I am sent three judgments – the original sixty-two-page liability judgment, slightly revised as a result of the reconsideration application, but if anything strengthened in the claimant's favour; a seven-page judgment on the reconsideration application; and a thirty-page judgment on the remedies. The contrast with the first employment tribunal case I ever saw – and with the county court cases I observed – could not be greater.

So what was her case all about? She was obviously very good at some parts of her job – dealing with customers, assessing their needs and advising them what to buy. She performed outstandingly on 'Secret Shopper' assessments. But her managers felt that she spent too much time with customers and not enough time on the other parts of her job – dealing with deliveries, keeping the shelves stocked and the stockroom in order – and that her timekeeping was poor. It would not be surprising if other people working in the shop felt the same. But she argued that she was following the company policy of always putting the customer first and was reluctant to accept criticism about this (which the tribunal thought was unreasonable of her).

She suffered from a number of health problems. In particular, for about three years before May 2019 she had been suffering from chronic and debilitating pain in her back, neck, shoulder and hips. This made it very hard for her to get going in the morning and it was worse in the evenings. From 29 January 2019 to 7 May 2019, she was signed off work due to 'chronic pain'. There was no specific diagnosis but her consultant rheumatologist gave her a 'working diagnosis' of spondyloarthropathy (which he later confirmed). She was advised to avoid heavy lifting and standing for long hours.

The first question was whether this amounted to a disability (within the meaning of the Equality Act 2010) and whether her employers knew or ought to have known this when she came back to work in May 2019. It was obvious that her arthritis was having a 'substantial adverse effect upon her ability to carry out day-to-day activities' – it had kept her off work for more than three months. This was a long-term physiological condition which was likely to last for at least twelve months. So the tribunal concluded that the claimant was disabled within the meaning of the Act. They pointed out that, as laypeople, they had been able to reach this conclusion based on the same information which the employers had in May 2019 and so the employers ought to have done the same.

The claimant made three complaints of disability discrimination. First, she complained of direct discrimination – that she had been treated less favourably than other employees because of her disability. But the tribunal found that the things she complained about had nothing to do with her disability – they could have happened anyway.

Second, she complained that her employers had failed to make reasonable adjustments to their normal shift patterns. Because her pain got worse in the evenings, she had asked to be assigned to work middle shifts. Despite this, she had been scheduled to work late shifts on four days in May. If an employer's normal working practices put a disabled employee at a substantial disadvantage compared with a non-disabled employee, the employer is required to make reasonable adjustments to cater for this. The object is to level the playing field so that disabled people can operate on equal terms with other employees in the workplace. But, of course, this does involve doing things for them which the employer does not do for other employees, so it has to be reasonable to expect this. The tribunal found that the claimant had been put at a substantial disadvantage by being assigned to late shifts and there was no need to do this. So there had been a failure to make reasonable adjustments.

Third, she complained that she had lost pay because she could not complete the late shifts she had been required to work. There is a special sort of disability discrimination which happens if a disabled person is treated unfavourably because of something arising in consequence of the disability and the employer cannot show that the unfavourable treatment was justified. Here the claimant was being treated unfavourably because of something which had arisen because of her disability – her inability to complete the shifts. And the treatment could not be justified because the employer should not have rostered her for those shifts.

But that was not all. The claimant had resigned from her job, but she complained of what is called constructive unfair dismissal. This is where an employee leaves the job because the employer has committed a fundamental breach of the contract of employment. An employer must not, without a good reason, behave in a way which is likely to destroy or seriously damage the relationship of mutual trust and confidence which should exist between an employee and her employer – neither must an employee. This may happen on a single occasion – there is a case involving an angry telling-off of the bakery manager in a supermarket in front of customers and other staff. But it may also be an accumulation of incidents, which are not enough by themselves, but which taken together do destroy the relationship.

The claimant had lots of things to complain about. There were 'insensitive, unnecessary and inappropriate' jokes and telling her off in front of colleagues – capable of making a very small contribution, said the tribunal. There was the breach of the duty to make reasonable adjustments to her shifts, which was also 'capable of contributing'. There was the unjustified commencement of a formal disciplinary investigation in June, triggered by complaints made by her boss in retaliation for complaints she had made against him. Retaliatory conduct like this is likely seriously to damage the relationship of trust and confidence. Nor was it justifiable to move straight into a formal investigation without any warning or informal conversation with the claimant beforehand – again likely seriously to damage the relationship and contrary to the employer's own policy.

But the thing which most upset the claimant was her boss using the store's CCTV cameras to spy on her. The tribunal found that using its CCTV for performance or disciplinary matters was unlawful under the data protection laws – because the employees had not been told that their personal data would be used for this purpose. Not only that, it was unnecessary to do so, because there was no need to view the CCTV to investigate the sort of issues which had arisen in her case, and indeed that was not why her boss had done so. He had a personal vendetta against her. This went 'to the heart of the trust and confidence which ought to exist between employer and employee'. Not providing her with a copy of the footage when she asked for it was also capable of contributing to this. She had raised a grievance about this, but it was rejected. This was for her 'the last straw' – doing so gave the 'official seal of approval' to how the CCTV had been used.

The tribunal decided that the CCTV use was enough by itself, but when combined with all the other things which were capable of destroying trust and confidence, the position was even clearer. This was why she had resigned (her wish to avoid the formal disciplinary process was only a subsidiary element). It followed that she was constructively dismissed and this was unfair. She had also been wrongfully dismissed (in breach of her contract of employment) because she did not work, and was not paid, for the period of notice to which she was entitled.

So what was the remedy? The claimant still did not have a job nearly three years after she had left the store. There was a lot of medical evidence about the psychological problems from which she was suffering and the very limited treatment she had had for them. This evidence was heard in private, because the claimant was very distressed at being questioned about it when there were work experience students observing the hearing. The tribunal wanted her to give her best evidence. But their judgment would be published. The claimant's psychological problems included severe anxiety and depression and a phobia of cameras and the internet. This phobia made everyday life, let alone looking for a job, extremely difficult for her and she had become a recluse. She was supported by her family, who lived in another country, and did not claim benefits, because she thought that it was wrong to do so when she had family support.

There were several elements to her compensation. She was entitled to £48.56 for her loss of earnings in the shifts for which she should not have been rostered. She was awarded £1,200 for the resulting injury to her feelings (this was at the lower end of the usual range because the employer had made reasonable adjustments after that). She was entitled to the basic award for unfair dismissal, which was one week's pay for each of her nine years of service with the employers. She was also entitled to a compensatory award for what she had lost as a result of the dismissal (but not for losses which were the result of other things – such as failures in the health service). In principle, this compensation should be reduced because 'the root cause of everything which led to her constructive dismissal was her conduct' – it was unreasonable of her not to accept her employer's legitimate criticisms of her work. But it should not be reduced by more than 15 per cent because these would not in themselves have been things for which she could have been dismissed immediately. Calculating all this precisely was likely to be academic, as there is a statutory cap of fifty-two weeks' pay on the compensatory award.

I hope that both the claimant and her employers felt that they had had a fair hearing. The claimant had to contend with all the problems of representing herself in a claim where both the law and the facts were complicated. No easy task for anyone but even harder for someone with her physical and mental health problems. The employer's barrister was not intimidating but she did have to ask questions which the claimant found distressing. The judge was kind and friendly. She explained everything carefully. The tribunal did what they could to accommodate her difficulties – beginning the hearing later, having breaks, hearing some of her evidence in private. And they dealt with the evidence and issues with meticulous care.

Reflections

These cases are expensive and time-consuming for everyone. But is there any other way? Anyone who decides to make an employment tribunal claim must first notify ACAS, the Advisory, Conciliation and Arbitration Service, which will try and resolve the matter without going to the tribunal. There are also strict time limits on bringing claims. Even so, a lot of cases do find their way there. In 2023–4, the employment tribunals received 92,000 cases. But there are more new cases than disposals, so in March 2024, the backlog consisted of 450,000 outstanding cases. And roughly half the cases succeed – although it can sometimes be a struggle to get the employer to pay. Unlike courts, tribunals cannot enforce their own awards, so an application has to be made to court to do so.

Presumably we don't want to go back to the days when workers didn't have the rights which they now have – when they could be sacked for no reason. If anything, the pressure is to give working people more rather than less protection. I've tried hard to think how these complicated unfair dismissal and discrimination cases could be made simpler and easier to decide. But I haven't yet come up with an answer.

5 Inside the Family Court

It is a lovely summer day and I am off to spend it inside the Central London Family Court on High Holborn. It's a converted office block with a rather forbidding entrance but someone has tried hard to decorate the ground-floor waiting room with interesting pictures. I used to be a family judge, hearing all kinds of family cases, at first in county courts and then in the High Court, so I am curious to see how much has changed since I last did this in 1999.

Some things won't have changed. Family cases are quite different from ordinary criminal and civil cases. Criminal cases are about punishing people for what they have done in the past. Civil cases are (mostly) about compensating people for the wrongs they have suffered in the past. Family cases are about what is to happen in the future – where is everyone going to live, what are they going to live on, what will be the arrangements for the children, does anyone in the family need protection from abuse? There are no hard-and-fast rules – the court has a great deal of latitude to do what will be best for all concerned and in particular the children. This is a big task and an anxious one. It is a task carried out in what is often a very fraught situation where everyone's emotions are running high. People have strong feelings – about one another, about their children, and about what the right answers should be. What has happened in the past may or may not be relevant to what should happen in the future. Abuse of any kind, whether of an adult or a child, is usually relevant and may be crucial. The facts of child abuse cases – whether the abuse is physical or sexual – can be very gruesome. It is necessary to get over the threshold of disbelief that anyone could do such things to a child. But the minutiae of what went on in an adult relationship are not usually relevant, although the parties often think that it should be. So a family judge has to absorb all that emotion, to remain neutral and above the fray, while doing her best to empathise with the people involved, and understand where they are coming from and what their lives are like. In some cases the family judge has to be prepared to take the risks which other people – such as social workers and healthcare professionals – cannot take. I had more sleepless nights as a family judge than I ever had in any other court, no matter how momentous the decision to be made. But I probably also had more times when I felt that I might, just possibly, have done some good.

According to Leo Tolstoy, 'All happy families are alike; each unhappy family is unhappy in its own way.' I'm not sure that he is right about happy families – families come in all shapes and sizes, classes, colours and cultures. They lead very different lives. They find different ways of being happy together. But we only see the unhappy ones and he is certainly right about them – they each find their own particular way to be unhappy. That is part of the endless fascination of the work.

The problems which bring them to court fall into four broad categories. The most serious is when the local authority children's services apply to take children away from their families because of ill-treatment or neglect or the risk of it. Also serious is when an adult asks for protection from domestic violence and abuse, sometimes by removing the abuser from the family home. Then there are the cases where separating parents cannot agree between themselves about the arrangements for looking after their children now that they are living apart. And finally there are the 'money' cases where divorcing couples need to sort out what is to happen to their property and finances when they are divorced. The divorce itself is now a pure formality which can be done online. Couples can even apply jointly to be divorced and around 20 per cent are doing so. They simply have to declare that their marriage has irretrievably broken down and wait a minimum of six months.

Family court judges also come in all sorts of shapes and sizes but they too fall into four broad categories. There are the lay (non-lawyer) magistrates who sit in panels of three and mainly deal with cases about children. There are the district judges who sit alone and can deal with all kinds of case, although some of them specialise in money and sit in something called the Financial Remedies Court. There are the circuit judges who also sit alone and can deal with all kinds of case but in practice spend most of their time dealing with the more serious children's cases. And there are the High Court judges who deal with the most serious cases of all kinds, especially anything with a foreign element to it, such as international child abduction – increasingly common in these days of families across borders.

During my visits to the Central London Family Court, I am going to sit in with a senior circuit judge dealing with child care cases, a district judge dealing with mother-and-father cases, and another district judge dealing with money cases. I'll be seeing the magistrates at work when I visit the family court in York and I managed to catch a domestic abuse case when I visited the county court in Middlesbrough. So I have seen something of everything.

Child care with the circuit judge

The courtroom is modern and functional. There is a raised bench for the judge, who sits behind at least three computer screens. The clerk sits to one side of the judge, but not raised. There is a witness box with a curtain on a rail round it, in case the witness has to be screened. There is a large TV screen for remote appearances. And rows of tables and chairs facing the judge for the parties and their lawyers, if they have any. No one is wearing robes. The setting is less grand and intimidating than the huge courtroom where I used to sit in the Royal Courts of Justice but probably grand enough to project a sense of the seriousness of the proceedings and the authority of the judge. We want the parties to take things seriously. We also want them to behave themselves – not always easy when emotions are running high, especially if there is a lot at stake. But it isn't always necessary – a cosier round-the-table setting can work well with some family cases, especially if there are no lawyers.

The formal setting probably is necessary in the first case – one of the most extraordinary and mysterious that I have ever encountered. The first mystery is who these people are. In November 2021 the police and ambulance service were called to the place where a fourteen-year-old girl whom I shall call Nina was living with a woman who claims to be her mother, whom I shall call Ms Yang (not their real names): a man had forced entry into their home, assaulted the woman, and strangled Nina with an Apple cable, to the point where she almost became unconscious. He is also said to have killed their cat. Nina was also found to have burn marks on the palms of her hands. She and Ms Yang provided different explanations for these and the doctor who examined her did not think that either explanation fitted the injuries. Nina is not registered with a GP or enrolled in a school. Neither she nor Ms Yang can supply a passport to verify their identity, claiming that their landlord holds their passports.

The police believe that Nina is in fact called Jane and has a different surname from Ms Yang, also that Ms Yang has a different first name from the one she claims. The police have produced travel documents in those names. Nina and Ms Yang claim that the pictures in the documents are not their pictures. But the social workers and the police believe that they are. A girl called Jane was previously registered in schools in other areas of London. She had piano lessons from a tutor at the Royal Academy of Music. Nina claims to have had piano lessons from the same tutor, but he says he has only ever had one Chinese pupil, whom he knew as Jane.

The Home Office have reported that Jane and her mother left the country in 2019 and have not returned. Most curious of all, DNA tests have been taken which revealed that Ms Yang cannot be Nina/Jane's mother. Ms Yang disputes their reliability.

Nina/Jane has been removed from home under an interim care order and the local authority have suspended contact between Nina/Jane and Ms Yang. So what to do next?

Is Nina really Jane? The court has not yet seen the evidence which the police have seen. Is Ms Yang her mother? The local authority is prepared to fund a second DNA test. If she is not the mother, she is no longer automatically entitled to take part in the proceedings, although the court can allow her to do so. The child's guardian, an independent social worker appointed to safeguard the child's interests, thinks that she should be made a party. But if she is not the mother, she is no longer automatically entitled to public funding for her lawyers. So the child's guardian thinks that the local authority should be prepared to pay for this. If she is not the mother, the local authority does not need permission to refuse contact between her and the child. If she is, they do.

At the moment, the social workers are concerned that the observers cannot understand the conversations which Ms Yang and Nina/Jane are having. Nina/Jane presents as younger than the claimed fourteen years and she carries a teddy bear with her all the time. The local authority wants the police to scan it to see if it has a device or tracker inside.

Just before we go into court the clerk reports that the barrister representing the child's guardian has spotted that Ms Yang was taking photographs of everyone in court on her phone. The phone was seized and the photos have been deleted. Taking photographs in court is not allowed (unless there is a special dispensation). But why was she doing so anyway? Her explanation is that she wanted to be able to recognise people again but more sinister explanations are possible.

The hearing is calm and sensible. The judge hears from lawyers for the local authority, Ms Yang and the child's guardian. It is generally agreed that the case should come back to court in three weeks' time. There should be a second DNA test. Ms Yang should provide the statement which has already been ordered. The police should be ordered to provide disclosure not only about the assaults last November but also about their investigations into the other names. The piano tutor should be shown school photos of Jane, recent photos of Nina and Ms Yang, and the passport photo of the woman claiming to be Jane's mother.

The elephant in the room is the possibility of trafficking – either the child, or the woman who claims to be her mother, or both. Whatever the relationship between Nina and Ms Yang, if either or both of them have been trafficked, there is a risk of messages being passed, influence being exerted, even pressure to run away. But even if she is not a victim of trafficking, Nina has been the victim of a serious assault, she has other unexplained injuries, she is not in school, she has no identification documents or birth certificate, and there may be no one with parental responsibility for her apart from the local authority. Suspicions deepen three days later when the local authority reports that Ms Yang has refused to provide a further DNA sample, though still maintaining that she is Nina's mother. Perhaps more worrying still, Nina's teddy bear has been found to contain a phone, an Oyster card and a key. I suppose that a desperate mother who has been parted from her child might do something like this in order to stay in touch, but it also looks like planning an escape attempt. As the guardian says, this is a child in desperate need of protection.

The case is transferred to the High Court but makes very slow progress, partly because of Ms Yang's lack of cooperation. Eventually it is listed for a fact-finding hearing some fifteen months after the hearing which I observed. But it turns out that the child disappeared from her foster home over the summer and the police have discovered that she has flown to China. There was no trace of the 'mother' in this country either. So the case has come to an ignominious conclusion – not a good advertisement for the child protection services or the family justice system.

The next case is altogether more straightforward – a typical example of the problems encountered by the child care system and ending up in the family court. The father is of black African-Caribbean heritage; he regularly uses cannabis and does not intend to give up, has been through an anger-management course in the past, and has a learning disability. The mother is of white heritage, has also used cannabis regularly but says she wants to give it up. They both had troubled childhoods and spent time in the care system as teenagers. They began their relationship when the mother was sixteen and the father was eighteen. Their first child was removed and placed for adoption when they were still very young. It is said that the mother couldn't look after him. Both parents are still distressed about this.

They have since had three more children, a girl in primary school, another girl in nursery, and a baby boy. These children were not taken away. The case is in court because in November 2021, when the baby boy was a few weeks old, he was found to have a spiral fracture of his thigh bone and also to have two fractured ribs. Both parents say that the thigh fracture happened while the father was changing the baby's nappy and the mother was in another room. They deny all knowledge of the rib fractures. The older girl also had bruises and has from time to time said that her father has hit her. He denies this. There was an investigation in 2019 when she was found to have long scratches on her back, said to have been caused by a ring the father was wearing. The local authority says that the parents' heavy use of cannabis either has caused, or is likely to cause, the children significant harm and that the mother has failed to protect them from their father's violence. The children have all been in foster care since shortly after the baby was injured but they have been having good-quality contact with their parents. The parents are now living apart. The mother says that they are permanently separated and she has given up using cannabis.

The question is whether these children can be safely returned to their mother. The legal test is in two parts: first, whether the children have suffered, or are likely to suffer, significant harm because of a lack of reasonable parental care; and second, if so, what will be best for them. In order to decide this, the court has first to decide how the various injuries were caused and then to consider the relationships between the children and their parents, and the parents' parenting capacities. Ideally, this should all be done in one hearing before one judge. But sometimes it is not possible to assess the risks and explore the future of the family until the truth about what has happened is known. (I think that I tried the very first case in which this was done – a baby had suffered head injuries and his very respectable family were unwilling to accept that these were not an accident. The child psychiatrist suggested that, if I decided how the injuries had been caused, it might be possible to work with the family so that the baby could safely be returned to them. And so it turned out.)

In this case there had been a ten-day fact-finding hearing earlier in the year. The judge heard a great deal of evidence – from a specialist safeguarding nurse, the family's health visitor and GP, a social worker, two consultant paediatricians (one who treated the baby and one independent expert), a consultant paediatric radiologist, a consultant community physician, the older girl's head teacher, a psychologist who had assessed both mother and father, and of course the parents themselves. He concluded that the broken thigh was caused by the father using excessive force and twisting the baby's leg; the rib fractures were caused when the father used excessive force to pick up the baby and carry him to his mother, but neither the mother nor the father knew this at the time; the father's behaviour was at times frightening and confusing for the older girl but he had not slapped and hit her as alleged; the earlier scratching did not cause her significant harm; the mother had not failed to protect the children from the father; the parents' cannabis use had not yet caused the children significant harm but there was a real risk that it would do so in future.

Now there will have to be a hearing to decide whether the children can be returned to their mother. The mother is understandably optimistic. But in the meantime she must continue hair-strand tests for cannabis use. Contact between her and the children must be gradually built up. More reports must be prepared. And hopefully a hearing fixed before the same judge who did the fact-finding.

A huge amount of care is being taken to work out what has happened, what the risks are and what will be best for these children in the future. A great deal of expert evidence has been and will be considered. We should be proud of this. (I remember a Swiss professor who observed a care case which I was trying and was amazed that we took so much trouble over the children of the poor.) We should also be proud of the efforts made to keep this family together if at all possible. We now recognise that taking a child away from his family is the most serious thing that can happen to him, even if it is sometimes necessary. We now also recognise that the alternatives which the State has to offer are not ideal. But striking the right balance is not easy. And it all takes a long time. By the time of the final hearing these children will have been away from home for a year – almost all the baby's life. Can anything be done to speed things up? I cannot help wondering whether it was necessary to separate the hearing to decide what happened to the children from the hearing to decide what will be best for them now. I cannot help wondering whether a shortage of courts and judges compounds the problem. But sometimes taking things slowly can be a good thing – enabling the family to evolve and develop. There are no easy answers.

Mothers and fathers with the district judge

The afternoon is very different. A district judge is managing cases about the arrangements for children whose parents are separated. The parents are all appearing in person without a lawyer to represent them, so the judge engages them in an orderly conversation. These are just the sorts of cases which would work well round a table rather than in a formal courtroom. The first case is about a little girl of seven who has a mother from southern Europe and a father from South America. They are both in court. Their daughter is living with her mother but spending all day Sundays with her father, and there are also phone calls on Wednesday evenings. There is a report from the Children and Family Court Advisory and Support Service (CAFCASS) recommending that eventually she spends every other weekend with her father. The mother is content with this as long as the child has her own space – she's got her own bed and can sleep in the living room which is OK for now. But as she grows she will need her own room and access to her own clothes and toys – 'I don't want her to feel like a guest.' If only all parents could be as mature and sensible as this, I think.

But CAFCASS says that the move to staying overnight should wait until there has been a report from the local children's services – the child has told her counsellor that her father hit her on the head when she refused to pray and they also want to make checks on the people who are sharing the father's house with him. The father is upset at the allegation. Of course he didn't hit her. He does ask her to pray before going to sleep but if she says that she doesn't want to that's OK. He's living in a three-bedroomed house with his girlfriend and two other men.

The case is adjourned for eight weeks in order to get the updated information from CAFCASS and the local authority. In the meantime the arrangements are to continue as before. But the judge makes it clear that the parents can agree further contact between them without coming back to court – including overnight stays once they have the report. The father is disappointed. He is here to fight to see his daughter. The judge tells him that there is no need to fight – the mother agrees to overnight stays so they only need to come back if there's a problem.

The father wishes that the mother would be more flexible. But she wants more consistency from the father – with the timing of his Wednesday telephone calls, and dropping the child back on Sundays as it's a school day the next day. The judge points out that it is the child who needs consistency. The mother also wants to take her abroad for three weeks in the summer holidays. The judge explains that she is allowed to do this for up to four weeks but he'll make an order that if either of the parents takes the child abroad on holiday they must bring her back to this country at the end of the holiday. This is to make it easier to enforce the return if there are problems. (I wonder whether this is still true now that we have left the European Union.) If they can agree changes, that's fine. If not, they must stick to the order. But they're going to be separated parents for a long time so it's better in the long run if they can talk to one another. The mother smiles at this.

The next case is very different. The father is applying for contact with a son who is now aged eight. He also wants an order prohibiting the mother from taking the child abroad. The parents have been separated for five years and the child has had no contact with his father or his father's family for three years. The mother has made a series of allegations about the father's conduct before they separated – including financial abuse, sexual abuse and violence. There is to be a fact-finding hearing about these in a few weeks' time – although what relevance any findings about such historic allegations will have to what is now in the best interests of an eight-year-old boy remains to be seen.

Both father and mother are attending remotely – the father on screen and the mother on the telephone. The judge reminds them that although they are at home this is still a court hearing. They must mute their devices when not speaking. They must not make a recording (the court is doing that). And they must be on their own. The case is almost ready. But there is a new law which says that an alleged abuser cannot be allowed to cross-examine his alleged victim. Eventually there will be court-appointed lawyers to do this but this has not yet happened so the judge will have to question them both. They must both send in a list of the questions they want answered by the other – to the court, not to each other.

The father asks why he can't ask the questions himself. The judge explains that if the allegations are true this can be damaging for the victim so without prejudging the issue there must be one rule for everyone. He explains that the essence of cross-examination is to challenge the other person's version of events and 'put your case to her'. In the meantime the father is allowed to make indirect contact with the child through letters or messages. The mother complains that he hasn't been doing this and it's detrimental to the child's emotional well-being. The judge is sympathetic – 'indirect contact can feel like dropping love into a black hole' – but it's important that the father keeps it up.

In care cases it is necessary to decide whether the child is at risk of harm before considering how best to protect him from that risk. But in mother-and-father cases the only question is what will be best for the child. In the past we were too keen to brush allegations of domestic abuse under the carpet and assume that violence to the mother did not affect the child. Now we know that it is harmful to a child to experience violence or abuse between his parents. But I do wonder whether it is always necessary to find the facts about alleged abuse before deciding what is best for the child. Separating the two hearings adds enormously to the length of time it takes to decide a case and that too is harmful for the child. Sometimes all the factors which go to make up the best interests of a child can be looked at together.

Mother and father before the magistrates

A few weeks later I am in York to watch the final hearing of exactly the same sort of case before a bench of lay magistrates. The family court sits in some newly converted rooms in the basement of the York City magistrates' court (see chapter 6). They are not far above the river Ouse, which regularly floods. Perhaps that's why there is a black plastic floor which squeaks when anyone with rubber soles walks on it. The rooms are light and bright but very functional. There is a reception/waiting area with two consulting rooms off it. One of these is used by CAFCASS, so the mother and father may have to wait in the same room unless the other one is free. There is no lavatory in the public area so court users have to go outside and round to the front entrance of the main court if they need a comfort break. The courtroom looks a bit makeshift because there is a large gap in the wall behind the magistrates' bench with dead space behind it. The royal coat of arms (which hangs in all courtrooms) is suspended behind the central justice's chair, half on the wall and half in the gap. Why didn't they close the gap? I ask myself. It scarcely adds to the dignity of the surroundings. Otherwise it is a pleasant enough space with a good view of the river and everyone is on the level.

This case is about two children, a girl aged twelve and a boy aged nearly ten. Their father is English; their mother is of European origin but settled in England. They lived together for seven years but separated eight years ago. Until now they have made the arrangements for the children themselves without a court order. But things became less amicable after each parent found a new partner. The children currently live with their mother but spend two days with their father every other weekend and roughly half the long school holidays with him. Their homes are about nine miles apart. The father has applied for shared care – he wants a fifty–fifty split of the children's time. The mother opposes this. The first report from CAFCASS reveals that both children want to spend more time with their father: the boy would like alternate weeks with him but the girl does not want as much because of her regular out of school activities. The report recommends that the children spend alternate weekends from Friday to Monday morning with their father and also stay overnight with him on Wednesdays, together with half the school holidays, including half-terms. The father accepted this at the time but the mother did not. She felt that her concerns about the father's behaviour had not been properly listened to. So the case was adjourned for the CAFCASS officer to look into this, but her second report makes the same recommendations as the first.

On the hearing day, the three women magistrates come into court. The usher brings in the parties. The father is representing himself and comes on his own. The mother now has a solicitor with her. The CAFCASS officer is attending remotely because she has Covid. The magistrates' legal adviser suggests that it would help to clarify what the issues are. The mother's solicitor explains that she is suggesting additional contact time but not overnight. The father says that he accepted the CAFCASS report last time 'to save pain' but he would like closer to fifty–fifty – overnight Mondays and Wednesdays as well as the alternate weekends.

When she was representing herself, the mother put in a number of documents – mainly detailing her complaints against the father – which the court hadn't asked for (people often do this but it is for the court to decide what evidence it wants). The legal adviser advises the court to disregard these and the mother's solicitor does not object. The court hears from the CAFCASS officer first; each parent has a few questions, but the justices ask the most interesting ones – why pick Wednesday nights, why not fifty–fifty, and would she rule out different arrangements for each child? She explains that overnight stays on Wednesdays and Sundays will enable the father to interact with the schools – a normal part of parenting; but the girl does not want fifty–fifty and her views should be respected. The officer is also not sure that different arrangements would be beneficial as the children have been together all this time.

There is a twenty-minute break because of the long walk to the facilities. The father then puts his case very eloquently. He has always wanted fifty–fifty shared parenting responsibility. He only agreed to the CAFCASS compromise to get things sorted out that day. 'It's no fun for any of us.' Overnight stays are important so that he can take the children to school. He has also suggested some one-to-one time with each child because they are very different people – his daughter loves football and his son does not. The mother's solicitor points out that the issue is very narrow – it really boils down to whether the children stay overnight on Wednesdays and Sundays. When they have finished, the chairwoman asks the CAFCASS officer whether she has heard anything which might change her recommendations – she hasn't.

The legal adviser then tells everyone what the law is. The best interests of the children are paramount. There are a number of factors to be considered in what is known as the 'welfare checklist' – things such as the children's wishes, ages, needs, practicalities, etc. It's a mistake to think that shared care means fifty–fifty. She also explains that the mother has made allegations of domestic abuse against the father, so the court has to consider whether a fact-finding hearing is necessary, but they separated a long time ago and the children have spent regular and significant time with their father since then, so the CAFCASS officer does not think it necessary or proportionate (an interesting contrast with one of the district judge cases earlier).

We break for an early lunch. Drama as the fire alarm goes off and we all have to vacate the building. Then the magistrates retire to deliberate. The legal adviser retires with them. But my feeling is that the decision is very much their own. Then they have to draft their reasons. There is a template for doing this but it takes a good deal of time. Back in court, the chairwoman reads them out. It takes quite a long time before they get to the bottom line – reasons given by professional judges are just the same and it must be agony for the parents. They are going to make a shared care order – an order that the children are to live with both parents. They will spend alternate weekends with their father, from school on Friday until school on Monday, alternate Mondays until 8.00 p.m., and every Wednesday from school until school on Thursday morning. But the arrangements can be varied if both agree. The order is a framework so that there are no arguments. The school holidays are basically split but there is no order about exactly how this should happen. The parents are warned that this is a court order so there are consequences if it is not obeyed. The magistrates end with warm words: the children love you both and you are obviously doing a good job.

It strikes me that the magistrates are also doing a good job. The atmosphere in court is formal but friendly and relaxed. It was interesting to hear the legal adviser explain the law during the hearing – that didn't happen when I was in practice. But I think that these magistrates could have made their decision and given their reasons without the adviser's help. It would still have taken more time than a district judge would have taken, mainly because there are three of them. It also strikes me that the mother's solicitor has been a great help – she has obviously given the mother some sensible advice. Perhaps if she had had a solicitor from the outset, they wouldn't have had to come to court. It is a great mistake to think that family lawyers are there to fight cases. Mostly they are there to advise their clients of what the issues are and help to negotiate an agreed solution. It was yet another false economy to withdraw public funding from all sorts of legal help and advice in this type of case.

But these parents were lucky. They did not have far to travel. Many magistrates' courts in North Yorkshire have been closed and people often have to travel long distances to get to the court where their case is to be heard. Getting to York from my home in Richmond is not easy unless you have a car, and getting to the other courts in Harrogate or Scarborough is even harder. It also makes life difficult for the magistrates, who are also expected to travel to any of the courts in the county. Not surprisingly, recruiting magistrates has become more difficult.

Financial remedies before the district judge

And now for something completely different. As it happens, none of the parents involved in the children cases were married to one another. Unmarried couples cannot make any financial claims upon one another (all they can do is sort out who owns what and that is done in a different court). But when married couples separate or divorce all their resources, both income and capital, present and future, are put into a notional pool and shared out between them as fairly as possible (see the guidance given by the House of Lords in 'The farming family's finances' later, in chapter 13, p. 174). The watchword is equality, but priority is given to providing for the needs of both parties and their children. This can be difficult because two families cannot live as cheaply as one. And the one with more money may be anxious to keep as much of it as he (it is usually he) can. Even so, most couples can sort things out for themselves, usually with lawyers' help, and present an agreed order for the court to approve. But some cannot do this and so the court has to do it for them. This can be an expensive business. I am back in the Central London Family Court to watch a judge who specialises in these cases handle a few short appointments.

The first couple were married for twenty years before separating in May 2021 when the husband left the family home where the wife still lives. They have three teenage children, who divide their time between the parents. The wife is a part-time teacher. The husband has a number of businesses and the family enjoyed a very high standard of living during the marriage. The husband has been paying the wife £6,000 per month voluntarily but now wants to cut this down to under £3,000 because of claimed liquidity problems. The wife wants it increased to over £8,000 and has applied for an order for interim maintenance. She also wants an order that the husband meet her legal expenses. Each is represented by solicitors and a barrister, everyone appearing remotely on the large screen in court. They disagree about almost everything, including how much time their eldest child spends with each. The judge hears the arguments and retires for only a few minutes before delivering a clear and concise judgment.

She accepts that the husband's income received a short-term boost during the Covid pandemic when his business was particularly profitable. But she does not accept that the position is as simple as he suggests – there is substantial flexibility in how he draws his income and deploys the sums received. Large sums of money have passed through his hands recently. He has paid off the mortgage on the family home and bought two seaside flats, one to live in with his girlfriend and the other as an investment. He has bought a luxurious car, artwork for his home, and an expensive holiday. There are clear disparities between his disclosed income and his expenditure. He has provided no evidence of his own budget. Going through the wife's budget, and reducing some of the items, the judge concludes that she needs £6,000 per month as interim maintenance. She is satisfied that the husband can pay this in the short term. She also rejects all the husband's suggestions of how the wife might fund her legal expenses. The wife has approached two lenders and been refused, which is not surprising; a high-street bank loan is not likely; her solicitors do not work on a contingency fee basis and they need to be paid. The judge comes up with a figure to take the wife through to the next stage in the proceedings which is between the figures proposed by the husband and the wife. To give some idea of how eye-wateringly expensive these cases can be, the wife wanted over £57,000 and the husband proposed over £25,000.

The next stage in the proceedings, once all the documentation has been filed, will be a financial dispute resolution hearing (an FDR). This is an attempt to get the parties to agree and thus spare them the expense of a full trial. A judge will go through the issues with them and give an indication of how the court is likely to regard them. If they do agree, all well and good. If they don't, a different judge will actually hear the case. In fact, financial dispute resolution hearings are so popular that some couples now agree to pay an experienced barrister to conduct an FDR for them privately. The consensus among family lawyers seems to be that these are well worth the money – the evaluator has time to prepare properly, the surroundings are congenial, everyone can take their time and 90 per cent of cases end up in agreement. This has happened in both the next two cases but then circumstances changed and the judge has to give directions to get things back on track.

The last case is very different. The couple are of much more modest means. Both are in their seventies and divorced after a long marriage. The husband is still living in the former matrimonial home where he has lived for forty years. It is worth at least £1,375,000, but subject to a mortgage of around £60,000. Last year they both agreed to an order that the home be sold and the net proceeds divided 80 per cent to the wife and 20 per cent to the husband. (We don't know why but it was probably because the wife would need more to rehouse herself than would the husband, who claimed to be better off.) The husband also agreed to pay the wife maintenance of £2,500 per month and a lump sum of £200,000. Buyers were quickly found for the house but the husband has not cooperated with the estate agents, and has not signed the relevant documentation, so the buyers are becoming increasingly frustrated and the price is dropping. The husband is also in arrears with the maintenance payments.

The wife is applying for an order that the husband sign the relevant documentation, or the court do so instead, and that the husband vacate the property on completion. She also wants the maintenance arrears paid out of his share of the proceeds. She is represented by a very junior barrister. The husband is representing himself. Everyone is online. The wife's case is simple – enough is enough, there must be no more delays, it's time for action. (The judge is worried that if she only orders the husband to vacate the property on completion of the sale, the husband won't go and the wife will be liable in damages to the buyers, but she doesn't want to put ideas into the husband's head.) The husband is doing his best to appear sweetly reasonable. His business partner (who also lives in the house) is going to come into substantial funds next week. So he is offering to buy out the wife's 80 per cent share (valuing the house at £1,400,000), pay off the maintenance arrears and pay the lump sum of £200,000. He suggests an adjournment so that his business partner can verify this. The wife's counsel doesn't believe a word of it – they've heard it all before.

My guess is that the judge is in two minds – should she go ahead straight away or give the husband one last chance? In the end, she decides to adjourn the case until next week. If there is then no proof of cleared funds, she will order the sale to go ahead and the husband to vacate the property immediately (rather than on completion). And that is exactly what happened.

A good couple of illustrations of how the one with greater access to resources can make life difficult for the one with less. There are those who think that it would all be a great deal easier if we had hard-and-fast rules about who got what after divorce rather than the more flexible tailor-made approach which we currently have. Yet those hard-and-fast rules would be likely to give the one who has spent more time devoted to child care and family responsibilities less than she (it is usually she) can currently expect. And there is no guarantee that the better-off one would not continue to make life difficult if that is what he (it is usually he) wants to do. We should not forget that most people are able to work these things out for themselves (with sensible advice and help), just as they are for their children. The cases that reach the courts are not typical of the majority.

Domestic abuse

We have seen how allegations of abuse can be relevant in deciding the future of children. But sometimes the victims need the protection of the court – an order to prevent the abuser from causing more trouble for the victim. We're in a large courtroom in Middlesbrough Combined Court Centre (see chapter 2). The parties used to live together and have a three-year-old child. The mother has obtained a non-molestation order against the father, *ex parte* – that is, without notice to him. He is forbidden from using or threatening violence towards her and also from entering her home or the street where she lives. *Ex parte* orders have to come back quickly to court so that the recipient can have his say. The mother is in court but behind a screen and is represented by a solicitor. The father is in court representing himself. He doesn't accept a lot of what she has put down – he calls it 'far-fetched'. The district judge explains that some people don't oppose an order because it's prohibiting things they don't want to do anyway – they can agree to an order without accepting the truth of what's being alleged against them. He agrees that they definitely need some distance from one another. But the solicitor explains that the issues have arisen over contact with their child – there have been unsavoury texts and the police have been involved. She suggests that there should be no communication between them apart from arranging contact with the child. The father is concerned about when he can see his child. The district judge explains that that is a separate matter – either of them can apply for an order about the arrangements for their child. Today she is only concerned with matters between the two of them.

There is discussion about finding a 'middleman' who could act as a go-between in arranging contact with the child – there are relatives sitting outside court who might be willing to help. We wait while the solicitor goes out to consult them but no one is willing to help. So they are going to have to communicate through a parenting app or by text message.

The district judge explains that she has to consider all the circumstances including the need to protect the health, safety and well-being of the applicant and the child. She has read the allegations of harassment, some by messages and some face to face. She is satisfied that it is necessary to make a non-molestation order. But this is expecting nothing more than is expected of normal individuals. She begins to recite the order she will make when the father interrupts to ask, 'What about going into the road?' He's got jobs in that road. So the judge asks whether the applicant would be content with an order that he doesn't enter the property where she lives or any other property where she is. And they must not communicate for any other purpose than making arrangements for contact with the child and through text messages only. This will remain in force for a year unless varied or discharged by an order of the court – it is not something which the parties can agree between themselves. Breach of the order is a criminal offence.

All very sensible and practical, trying to take the heat out of a typically fraught situation. But I wondered why the father's mother and aunt, who were outside court, could not have come in with him. And I wondered even more why the judge could not have looked at the arrangements for the child at the same time and made a temporary order. The law allows this – orders about the arrangements for children can be made without a formal application in any family proceedings including these – but it is not the usual practice. It would have taken a little longer but it would have started the ball rolling on what was obviously the bone of contention between them. As it was, their communication about their child was severely limited and there were still no proceedings on foot to work out what arrangements would be best for the child.

A final thought

This brings me neatly to what I think is really wrong with the family justice system. At present, each of the issues which can arise when a family splits up is dealt with separately: the divorce, if they are married; the sharing out of their property and finances, if they are married; the arrangements for their children, whether or not they are married; and protection from violence or abuse, again whether or not they are married. There has to be a separate set of proceedings each time, with separate application forms, responses, attempts to get the parties to agree, separate evidence and hearings, separate fees and sometimes even separate lawyers. The proceedings can be heard together but this requires a special decision and is rarely done. But the issues are not so separate in real life. Where everyone is going to live, what they are going to live on, the arrangements for the children and protection from abuse are all intertwined. As we saw in the last case, making sensible arrangements for the father to see his son might put a stop to the harassing messages and phone calls. Why can there not be one family proceeding, with one application form, one statement setting out the family situation and explaining what the applicant wants, one response, and one attempt by the court to help them agree? And if they can't agree, the court can direct what further evidence is needed and how the matters in dispute are to be tried. In short, why can't everything which they cannot sort out for themselves be dealt with at one time and in one place by the same judge? It's an accident of history that we do things the way that we do at present and I fear that the only people who benefit from it are the lawyers. And most of those I talk to think that I am right.

6 Inside a Magistrates' Court

We've looked at the civil and family justice systems. It's time to look at the criminal justice system, from bottom to top. It's a fine summer day. Tourists are out in force in the ancient city of York. But I am not here to explore its beauties. I am here to visit the City Magistrates' Court. Over 95 per cent of the criminal cases which come to court are disposed of in the magistrates' courts either by panels of lay justices (who are unpaid volunteers) or by district judges (who used to be called stipendiary magistrates because they are lawyers who are paid). Magistrates' courts also decide whether arrested people should be held in custody or given bail. This is a high-volume business. In 2023, magistrates' courts in England and Wales received around 1.37 million cases and disposed of 1.34 million (compare this with roughly 105,000 received in the Crown Court). Magistrates' courts are used to shifting a large number of cases very quickly.

The York Magistrates' Court is housed in a grand late-Victorian building within the city walls, backing onto the river Ouse, which is prone to flood. The fine entrance is up several steep steps. But we are only allowed in one at a time. The security staff have to search our bags and there is no room inside for a queue. They are very thorough (which is no bad thing in view of what happened later in the day). They even find a nail file in my handbag which has escaped discovery at several airports recently. I happily hand it over and am given a receipt so that I can get it back when I leave.

Inside, there are two historic Victorian courtrooms, a smaller courtroom which today is being used to conduct video hearings with prisoners in their prisons, and a newly created family court suite in the basement (see chapter 5). The historic courtrooms are magnificent: they have high domed ceilings with a lantern light in the roof, freshly painted in tasteful Wedgwood blue and white (but only because the ceiling in one of them fell in last year, I am told), wooden panelling and traditional wooden courtroom furniture. The wooden dock in the middle of the room is surrounded by bulletproof glass (which makes it difficult for anyone in the dock to communicate with their lawyers, so defendants don't sit there unless they are in custody). It's all very impressive, but the majesty of the law is not helped by the clutter of computer screens and other paraphernalia, and it is really difficult to hear what anyone is saying.

Worse still, it is not at all easy for disabled people. Wheelchair users cannot get up the front steps so have to go round to a side door. Inside, there is a stairlift to get them up to the courtroom floor. But it cannot take a heavy wheelchair, so the user has to get out of the chair (if they can), go up in the lift, and wait for someone to carry the chair up the stairs. Not very dignified. And the courtrooms are on so many levels that it is hard to find a place for them.

There is a district judge sitting in York today and he is due to hear five cases which are listed for trial because the defendants have pleaded not guilty. Most defendants plead guilty: only around 21,000 cases were listed for trial in England and Wales in the first quarter of 2023. There is also a bench of three lay justices who are dealing with remands – people who have recently been arrested by the police and held in custody until the court decides whether to give them bail. And a bench of two lay justices is doing the video hearings from prisons. A fairly typical day, I am told. I decide to sit in on the district judge first.

He gets all the lawyers in front of him and goes through the list, working out the state of play on each case and giving some fairly clear indications of what he thinks should happen next. I soon begin to feel sorry for the lawyer who is appearing for the prosecution. Before 1976, most prosecutions used to be conducted by the police, who would decide what offences to charge and what offences to prosecute. In some courts, especially in the countryside, senior police officers would act as advocates. And they could be very effective, as I saw in my student days when working for the local magistrates' clerk. But it was thought that the decision to bring a prosecution should be taken independently of the police who had caught and charged the defendant. So the Crown Prosecution Service (CPS) was set up in 1976 to decide whether to prosecute and on what charges. This has the benefit of bringing a fresh and expert eye to the case, as well as a consistent policy throughout the country – set out in the Code for Crown Prosecutors. But of course it can slow things down, there can be failures in communication, and evidence can be lost. The CPS do employ some advocates who appear for them in court, but in the most serious cases they will probably instruct a barrister to present the case and in the less serious cases they may well instruct a barrister or solicitor as their agent. But agents have to act upon the instructions they are given, so big decisions – such as whether to accept a guilty plea to lesser or fewer charges – have to be referred back to the CPS. Before the CPS, the advocates could make these decisions themselves, so they found the change very frustrating. No wonder the solicitor agent for the CPS has his laptop with him and is furiously emailing from time to time.

The first case is all about a dispute between neighbours which escalated into violence. I have no idea what it was about. The defendant is facing two charges: an 'assault occasioning actual bodily harm' (ABH), when he head-butted the woman next door; and an 'assault by beating' when she retaliated and he pushed her away. The defendant has already pleaded guilty to the ABH, which is much the more serious charge. He has pleaded not guilty to the assault by beating and is due to be tried for that today. The neighbour and her family are all at court waiting to give evidence or to lend their moral support. The judge wonders why the case is being pursued: it was all part of the same incident; the outcome of the assault-by-beating charge will not affect the sentence for the ABH. The parties are given time to think about it. The prosecution won't budge and withdraw the charge. The defendant, who is represented by a very experienced magistrates' court advocate, takes the hint and changes his plea to guilty. He does so on a particular version of events which will be put into writing – the court has to sentence on the basis of that version unless the prosecution disputes it (which won't happen in this case). My guess is that his lawyer will have told him that he has nothing to lose by doing this. Insisting on a trial can only make things worse: imagine the effect if the neighbour and her teenage children who saw the incident make very good witnesses and paint a much worse picture than the basis on which he has agreed to plead guilty. And if he pleads not guilty but is found guilty he will lose the benefit of a discount from the sentence which would otherwise be imposed. Some people think the discount is an unfair incentive for innocent people to plead guilty. Others think that it is a sensible incentive for guilty people to admit it and save everyone the time and trouble of proving it. Of course it is both.

The defendant comes into court and stands in the press box (opposite to where I am sitting). He is a bearded man in his thirties or forties, very smartly dressed in a three-piece suit and tie. He is a man of good character – that is, he has no previous convictions. What on earth was going on, I wonder, to make him head-butt a neighbour? The assault-by-beating charge is put to him again and he pleads guilty. The judge explains that, because it is a neighbour dispute, he has to get a report from the probation service before passing sentence. He is not ruling anything in and he is not ruling anything out. There is the potential for a prison sentence and he should prepare himself for that. Obviously, he must cooperate with the probation service and in the meantime he must not have contact with the family next door. The case is put off for four weeks. It was to have been two weeks, but the defendant is due back from a foreign holiday the day before and is worried that he may not make it back in time (the summer of 2022 was notorious for cancelled flights and long delays at airports).

After the defendant has left, the judge calls the neighbours into court and explains what has happened. He thanks them for their attendance – it is important that people who make complaints like this do come to court, so that people who commit offences don't get away with them (and, he might have said, the court's time is not wasted). So he is grateful for the time and effort they have invested in this case. They will find out the result in due course. I notice that they come from a town south of York where there used to be a magistrates' court, so they would all have been spared the journey to York.

But that is as nothing compared with the long and difficult journeys which many witnesses and defendants face in getting to court these days. When I was a child, there was a magistrates' court in the village where we lived. Then it was closed and everyone had to go to the court in Richmond, the local market town to which all the rural villages around were connected by bus. Then Richmond was closed and everyone had to go to Northallerton, the county town, but nowhere near as accessible by bus. Then Northallerton was closed . . . There is no local justice in large parts of the county. If there is such an incident in one of the Yorkshire Dales, who is going to want to take it to court?

It seems sad that a neighbour dispute should have come to this, but the next case is even sadder. A young woman is accused of stealing spirits from Marks & Spencer in York – vodka on one occasion and two bottles of whisky on another. She is also accused of assaulting the store detective on the second occasion. Then, having been released on bail by the court, she failed to come back to court on the due date, so she is also accused of failing to surrender to bail. And then when a police officer and special constable came to arrest her, she is also accused of assaulting them – the more serious offence of assaulting an emergency worker acting in the exercise of their functions as such. When she was brought before the district judge yesterday she pleaded guilty to one of the charges and refused to plead to any of the others, so he remanded her in custody to a women's prison. The prison van is not due to arrive until later in the morning, so the case is put back.

I learn what happened next when I go into the other courtroom to watch the justices dealing with the remand cases. There is a long delay while we wait for the next prisoner to be brought up from the cells. We are told that the young woman shoplifter has assaulted four of the seven officers who are in charge of the cells, the police have been called, and no one is prepared to try to escort her into court. No doubt she will be arrested again and hauled back to prison to await another day. So I never get to see her and I wonder what she looks like – is she large and intimidating or slight but strong? It seems obvious that she has both alcohol and mental health issues but there may be no one else to deal with them apart from the police.

The same thoughts occur in the third case before the district judge: a middle-aged man who has suffered a traumatic brain injury and also has mental health problems. The neighbours complain about his loud music. He comes down to remonstrate with them and says that he has a gun upstairs: so the police are called and he is charged with using threatening or abusive words or behaviour likely to cause harassment, alarm or distress. The police don't find a gun but they do find a samurai sword displayed on his wall. This may count as the sort of offensive weapon which it is an offence to have in one's possession, even in one's own home. So they seize this and some other weapons which they also find displayed and charge him with possessing the samurai sword. There is no suggestion that he took it off the wall or used it or any other weapon to threaten his neighbours.

The district judge points out that the police have taken the weapons and he will have to apply to get them back which in practice he won't do. So wouldn't it be sensible to drop the offensive weapon charge and proceed on just the charge of threatening behaviour, to which he is willing to plead guilty? The poor prosecutor cannot agree to that without 'taking instructions'. And his witnesses are not at court. The defendant's solicitor points out that the police evidence does not say how long the blade was – it has to be more than 50 centimetres long to count for this purpose. I leave the courtroom before the outcome is known but am told that the CPS doesn't often agree to drop the charge. Before the CPS, the local police would have taken a view, perhaps informed by their sense of how much of a danger this man really was.

Even more than the shoplifter, this is a man who needs help with his mental health problems rather than punishment. In theory there are orders which the court can make to provide him with that help. But such orders can only be made if the facilities are available and they agree to take the case. I am told that there are no mental health facilities available to this court. This is poignant indeed. In 1796, the Quakers of York opened a new kind of mental hospital, the Retreat, a reaction to the cruel and inhumane treatment of people with mental disorders in those days, which pioneered what was then known as moral management. The Retreat still provides services for day patients in York, but sadly not by arrangement with the local magistrates' court.

The prosecutor does have his instructions in the next two cases. One is a domestic abuse case: a husband of Eastern European extraction is accused of assaulting his wife on two separate occasions and damaging her mobile phone on one of them. He is not accused of causing her actual bodily harm. They live at different addresses, but in the same small town. Their four children live with the wife. There is no one to look after them while she is at court, so she has brought the children with her. The prosecutor has spoken with her through an interpreter. She does not want to give evidence. He proposes to offer no evidence – i.e.

drop the charge – on the basis that the husband agrees to be subject to a restraining order. (The court has power to make a restraining order even after acquitting someone, if it considers this necessary to protect a person from harassment by the defendant.)

The husband's lawyer says that he accepts that the relationship is now over but that he wants to have as much contact with the children as possible. The present bail conditions prevent his doing so except through a third party. The judge points out that the restraining order can be tailored to meet the case. He explains to the defendant that the criminal case has been dismissed but that he is going to impose a restraining order for three years. The husband is not to go to the road where the wife and children live. He is not to have contact with them except through a third party or as directed by the family court. If he breaches the order, it will be a criminal offence punishable with up to five years' imprisonment (which is in fact more than the maximum for the offences with which he is charged). Copies will be sent to him, to his wife and to the police. There may come a time when he and his wife agree that the order is not needed any more. If so either of them can apply to discharge it. But they can't make up their own minds. He can't ignore the fact that there is a court order in force until it is discharged by the court.

The husband looks as though he understands. The judge asks the prosecutor to thank the wife for him – as she has the four children with her, he won't ask her to come into court. Some will think that this was a domestic abuser who got off lightly. Others will think that this is a sensible solution where the victim is understandably reluctant to give evidence against the father of her children and merely wants him to accept that the relationship is over. Others still may wonder why it wasn't in the family court where similar remedies are possible (see chapter 5). They will have to go to the family court to get the arrangements for the children sorted out. The family court can have problems if criminal courts set bail conditions, or make restraining orders, which are inconsistent with what they think is in the best interests of the children. So the district judge has found a neat solution.

In the last case – potentially the most serious of them all – it feels as if the CPS is in the dock rather than the defendant. He is a young man of twenty who is accused of driving while under the influence of drugs, specifically cocaine, as 124 micrograms of benzoylecgonine (a metabolite of cocaine) were found in his blood, when he was tested after driving in Richmond, my home town. He is represented by a barrister who specialises in these cases. They depend upon the expert evidence of the test result which has to be provided to the defence so that they can get their own expert to comment on it. The judge gave directions way back in February that all the evidence was to be served by 28 March. In fact it was not served until June and without the appendices and data pack to which the expert referred in reaching his conclusions. The defence expert could not prepare his report without access to all the material he needed. Despite numerous requests this was not forthcoming until three days before the case was listed for trial.

Obviously the trial cannot go ahead today, but the defence want more. The barrister argues that the rules have not been complied with, so the expert evidence cannot be admitted unless the court gives permission and it is up to the prosecution to apply for that permission, which it has not done. Not only that, there is no evidence from the healthcare professional that the defendant consented to a blood sample, again despite numerous requests.

The judge is more concerned that the directions he made in February have not been complied with and no explanation has been given as required by the rules. What on earth has been going on? he asks. What is the point of making directions if the prosecution chooses not to comply with them? If there are resource issues they can apply for more time, but that was not done. There is no good explanation why they have not done what they should have done. The poor prosecutor can only protest that it was an administrative oversight and not a choice. The judge suggests that there would be nothing unreasonable in the defence applying to exclude the whole of the prosecution case on the ground that, in all the circumstances, 'Admitting it would have such an adverse effect on the fairness of the proceedings that the court ought not to admit it.' He finds the prosecution's conduct 'quite insulting'.

The defendant is brought into court, a very young man in a blue suit with a tie. The hapless prosecutor explains that the charge is one of drug-driving, there has been a regrettable failure to serve the evidence required, and having taken instructions at a senior level in the CPS, he is offering no evidence. The judge explains that the allegation is dismissed. As the defendant has funded his legal costs himself, part of them will be paid by the taxpayer. He is free to leave. After the defendant goes, the judge comments, 'That took rather a long time.'

So none of the trials listed in his court has in fact taken place. One of the defendants has been let off because of CPS inefficiency (you may think him a very lucky young man). Three have been dealt with without a trial. And the fifth probably should be. The whole thing has been conducted calmly and courteously, but with no messing about, and all the lawyers cooperating with one another and with the court. Very far from the television image of courtroom dramas, but some very human stories and some very common problems. I am surprised that all the discussions between the judge and the advocates took place without the defendants being there. It's not surprising that the witnesses are not in court – in criminal cases the usual practice is that they wait outside until they are called to give their evidence, so that it won't be affected by what other people have said. But the defendants usually should be there, so I assume they must have agreed to what was taking place.

I round off the morning's observations with a visit to the remand court. Three justices – an elderly man in the chair and two women. The young offender in the dock has been arrested for breach of his bail conditions. He is due to appear in Harrogate Youth Court in three days' time for sentencing. The Youth Offending Team suggests that he is given bail on the same conditions as before – residence and curfew and no contact with prosecution witnesses. He understands and it is done. Then there is a long wait because of the rumpus in the cells caused by the belligerent shoplifter. But eventually another defendant arrives in the dock. He too has been arrested for breach of his bail conditions – not to have any contact with his daughter who is a prosecution witness against him. He was staying in his brother's house and his daughter came to the house knowing that her father was there. There were no threats and no violence but drink had been taken and there was a row. Should the bail conditions be extended to include a condition that he live at his address in Hull and not stay with his brother? The justices retire to discuss it (they are seated too far apart to go into a huddle on the bench) and return content to leave things as they are. The defendant leaves the dock, thanking the justices for their kind judgment.

This is where the vast majority of criminal cases end up – not in the drama of trial by jury in the Crown Court but in the workaday world of the magistrates' courts. There, solid and sensible local citizens and district judges dispense justice and, in my observation, both quickly and fairly. But they do so in a landscape of dwindling resources, of court closures which make the lives of everyone – magistrates, staff, witnesses, and defendants – much more difficult, of prosecutorial shortcomings, and of a lack of facilities to deal properly with mental health and addiction issues. There was a backlog of roughly 340,000 cases outstanding in magistrates' courts in England and Wales in the first quarter of 2023. And who knows how many cases are not brought to court at all because it is all too difficult?

7 Inside a Crown Court

Some cases are too serious to be tried in the magistrates' courts – such as murder, rape and other serious sexual offences, terrorist offences, serious violence, or high-value dishonesty. These have to be sent to the Crown Court for hearing. Other offences, such as lesser violence, fraud, burglary or theft, can be tried either in the magistrates' courts or in the Crown Court. Either the magistrates or the accused can choose. This means that anyone charged with theft can choose to be tried by a jury rather than by magistrates, no matter how trivial the amount. The reason given is that a conviction for dishonesty can wreck a person's career. But there are other offences of dishonesty, such as fare dodging, which can only be tried by the magistrates.

If an accused pleads not guilty in the Crown Court, a jury will decide whether or not he is guilty. The judge presides over the trial to see fair play, explains the law and sums up the evidence to the jury, and sentences defendants who plead or are found guilty. The Crown Court has power to impose much more severe sentences than the magistrates' courts (which are currently limited to six months' imprisonment). There is a maximum limit laid down for each offence, which can be as much as life imprisonment, but most sentences are much less than the maximum, which is reserved for the worst of the worst cases of that offence.

Before 1971, there were two types of court hearing jury trials. One was Quarter Sessions. In the counties, these were held by magistrates but usually presided over by a legally qualified chairman (astonishingly, this was not a legal requirement until the 1960s). In the boroughs, they were held by a recorder. Both chairmen and recorders were usually senior practising barristers, sitting part-time. The other was the Assizes, presided over by the High Court judges, who have been coming out from London on circuit since the reign of Henry II in the twelfth century. Quarter Sessions and Assizes were amalgamated into a single Crown Court in 1971.

There are Crown Courts in many cities and large towns. They come in all shapes and sizes and varying degrees of dilapidation. Many of them are in modern combined court centres, housing civil and family as well as criminal courts, such as the Middlesbrough Combined Court Centre (see chapter 2). Some of them are in modern buildings designed only for criminal courts, such as the utilitarian Southwark Crown Court and the architecturally adventurous but crumbling Harrow Crown Court. Some of them are in historic buildings, such as the Crown Court in Lincoln Castle or the Crown Court in Durham city, both of them purpose-built in the early nineteenth century in wonderful locations and Grade II* listed.

Today I am visiting the Inner London Crown Court, which is also a very grand building from the outside, Grade II listed, built in 1921 in the classical style, originally to house the Surrey Quarter Sessions. There are still relics of its life as a Sessions House, with separate doors labelled for the chairman and justices to go into court.

I visit the court on a fine Friday in spring. The building looks very grand as I approach from Newington Causeway, not far from Elephant and Castle. There is the usual security after the front door, but the staff are welcoming. Once through security, the entrance hall is spacious and elegant. There are four courts in the original building, all in the traditional style, with domed ceilings, wooden panelling, a very high bench facing a now glassed-in dock and red leather benches for the lawyers, a gallery for the public, a jury box to one side and a witness box to the other. It all looks very imposing until you begin to notice the telltale signs of dilapidation and water getting in where no water should be.

The resident judge is Her Honour Judge Karu, who is also the honorary Recorder of Southwark and sits at the Old Bailey from time to time. She is the first woman from the Indian subcontinent to become a circuit judge, having come here from New Delhi at the age of seventeen and built a successful career in the law. Now she is in charge of this busy London Crown Court. Today she is sentencing a defendant who has pleaded guilty to two charges of dealing in drugs, one as a wholesaler and one as a retailer. The more serious is Count 1, the charge of conspiracy to supply large quantities of cocaine: the defendant acted as a middleman, sourcing the drug for clients who wanted it. He didn't actually handle the drugs himself. The conspiracy was conducted through mobile phone messages using EncroChat – an encryption service installed on specially modified mobile phones not generally available to the public. The French police lawfully infiltrated EncroChat messages in March 2020 and that is how this conspiracy (along with many others) was discovered. Over the period in question, the defendant actually sold 14.5 kilos of cocaine and did deals to sell a further 8.5 kilos, but these transactions were not completed before his arrest.

Count 2 is possession with intent to supply. The defendant was also conducting his own retail business using a safe house. In June 2020, the police watched him enter the property with a small child. When uniformed officers approached, he slammed the door and locked it. The police broke it down and found him flushing a large quantity of cocaine down the toilet – he'd opened a plastic bag with his teeth and was covered in white powder. They also found a mobile phone (not an EncroChat phone) in the toilet bowl, which he had attempted to flush, a block of cocaine and smaller wraps of cocaine, and a knife with a scalpel blade, all consistent with retailing.

All of this was happening while the defendant was out of prison on licence. He has six previous convictions, all of them drug-related. He was released from prison in January 2020 and after his arrest in June he was recalled to prison and his licence revoked. So why has it taken until mid-2023 to bring him to trial?

Originally he planned to plead not guilty (at least to the conspiracy). The case was listed for trial three times in 2021 but did not go ahead. Lawyers in other cases were arguing that the evidence of EncroChat messages could not be put before the courts. In February 2021, the Court of Appeal (Criminal Division) ruled that it could.[1] Evidence cannot be given of messages which have been intercepted while they are being transmitted (for complicated reasons which we need not go into here). But these messages had not been intercepted at the time of transmission. They had been recovered from what was stored on the phones themselves – a hack, not an intercept. Later in 2021 the court also ruled that the possibility that the messages had been intercepted during transmission could be safely discounted.[2] The defendant changed his plea to guilty in December 2021.

There is a discount for pleading guilty and thus saving everyone the stress and expense of a trial by jury. The biggest discount is for pleading guilty at the first opportunity. So what was the effect of this defendant waiting for the Court of Appeal? The judge mildly points out that he was entitled to do this but he knew what he had done – he would still be guilty even if the prosecution couldn't prove the case. Generally the Court of Appeal has taken the view that the defendant takes his chance if he does not plead guilty at the first opportunity.

But we're now in 2023 – so why the delay since December 2021? The prosecution insist that they were ready to go. The reasons for the delay were on the defence side. The defence stresses that the defendant had a significant but not a leading role. The supplier to him was sentenced to twelve years. He made a profit of between £500 and £1,500 per kilo, nothing like what he would have got from cutting it and selling it on the streets. 'He just knows people – people who have it and people who want it.' The police didn't find any cash and he doesn't have a lavish lifestyle. There is no application to forfeit the proceeds of crime.

After prosecution and defence have finished putting their case, there is a long pause while the judge does the sums. She is largely bound by some pretty strict guidelines. She gives the defendant 25 per cent credit for his guilty plea to the lesser charge, Count 2. She gives him 17 per cent credit for his guilty plea to the conspiracy which she thinks generous – he was waiting to see how the admissibility arguments went but it was obvious what he was up to in March to June 2020. The guidelines don't strictly apply to a conspiracy charge, but she considers them nonetheless. She thinks it appropriate to treat him as having been involved in trading 20 kilos of cocaine (no evidence that it was crack cocaine). She takes the point that he was a middleman but thinks that his role was at the very top end of 'significant' or towards the bottom end of 'leading'. If he had been convicted after a trial, the sentence would have been thirteen years. With the discount for a guilty plea, it is ten years and eight months. On Count 2, she cannot sentence him to less than 2,045 days because of his record, so she does that, but to be served concurrently with his sentence on Count 1.

Within the maximum sentence laid down for each crime, there is a tariff which is meant to reflect the comparative seriousness of the offending. The purpose of the tariff is retribution or punishment. In drugs cases this usually reflects the type and quantity of drugs involved. The tariff can be adjusted for aggravating and mitigating circumstances related either to the circumstances of the offence or to the offender. All this is set out in the guidelines from the Sentencing Council. The aim is for consistency from court to court – there used to be considerable discrepancies between the courts in different places, some with a culture of harshness and some with a culture of leniency. Over the years, the tariffs have been steadily creeping up – they are now much higher than they were when I was a judge in the Crown Court let alone when I was a baby barrister. Some of this is because Parliament has intervened to set minimum sentences or otherwise hike up the punishments. But some of it is because the guidelines themselves have got harsher. There is a lot to be said for having a tariff – but where one pitches it is much more open to question. What should dealing in large quantities of drugs be worth? What should a domestic burglary where computers and other devices are taken but nothing else, and no damage done, be worth? What should a drunken 'glassing' in a pub be worth?

I have no doubt that this defendant got what he deserved according to the current guidelines. But I can't help thinking what a waste of a life. The defendant is in his thirties, good-looking and well presented, with obvious abilities that he might have put to better use. Who knows what led him into this way of life and why he couldn't give it up even after it had landed him in prison. Who knows whether a long stretch in prison will help him to turn his life around. But we do know that average reoffending rates are lower after long sentences than they are after short ones: in the first quarter of 2023 adults released from sentences of less than twelve months had a proven average reoffending rate within the first year of 56.9 per cent, compared with 19.2 per cent for those released from sentences of more than that.

Next I go into another old courtroom where His Honour Judge Silas Reid has been hoping to start a trial – the jury were sworn in yesterday but the trial of some 'Insulate Britain' supporters has run over (of which more later). He begins with a discussion with prosecuting and defending counsel. The defendant, who looks like a real hard man, is charged with assault occasioning actual bodily harm to another man and possessing a bladed article – a kitchen knife – in a private place in such a way that there is an immediate risk of serious physical harm. The defendant says that there is a voice recording on his phone in which the complainant says that it was he who got out the knife first. There is also a video recording. The defendant has not had access to his phone – the police have it – so neither counsel has watched the video. They won't be able to do that until Monday morning. They both need to do so – although rather curiously they both say that it won't change their positions. The judge suggests that at least we could have the prosecution opening speech today, but prosecuting counsel says there will be some gaps until she has seen the video. So the judge decides to have the jury in and give them all the standard preliminary directions before sending them away for the weekend and starting the trial proper on Monday morning.

The jury come into court from a separate door on the judge's side of the court. There are ten women, one of them looking very elderly but she can't be more than the maximum age of seventy-five, and two men; six are from ethnic minorities. Looking after the jury is a major part of a trial judge's job and this is no exception. Judge Reid explains that they will get copies of the charges on Monday morning but in the meantime more preparation for the trial is needed. They must not do any research into the case. They must keep an open mind. They can tell people that they are on a jury but they cannot discuss anything about it while the trial is going on, so that they can't be consciously or subconsciously influenced by other people's views. And they mustn't post on social media. If they break these instructions they could be sent to prison, but this is not a threat 'because I know you won't – we do well here in Inner London'. After the case is over, but not until then, they can research and talk about it, but they must not talk about their deliberations: 'Each must be able to give their open and honest view and this is private between you for ever.' If anyone has any concerns or questions, do raise them immediately, when they can be easily dealt with. It is more difficult if they delay. The court will sit from 10.00 or 10.30 to 1.00 and then from 2.00 to 4.00. He calls this a short day – but this is because you have to give it 100 per cent attention and this is tiring, so let us know if you need a break. The judge will be taking a note of the evidence and not looking at the witnesses. His impression of the witnesses is irrelevant, but they should be concentrating on the witnesses. There's a document about jurors' duties in the folders in front of them which they can take away. But any notes they take during the trial can't be taken away – they will be locked up while the court is not sitting.

I gave directions like these many times when I was a part-time trial judge in the Crown Court. It always struck me how hard it must be for the jurors. They didn't ask to be here and we do ask a lot of them. They are penned up in a jury box for two or two and a half hours at a time, and expected to give their full attention to what is going on in court, which may be speeches from the barristers or examination and cross-examination of witnesses. This is rarely as quick or as exciting as it is in films or on television. It is often very tedious. As I see at the Old Bailey (see chapter 8), these days it often involves the examination of lengthy schedules of phone calls and text messages. Most of us are not used to having to sit still and concentrate for such long periods of time. This jury is lucky because the trial may be relatively short and sharp, with a clear-cut issue.

It is also asking a lot to expect jurors not to talk about it with other people over the breaks – but of course that is right: the defendant is entitled to be tried by them and not by their friends and relations. That is one reason why I believe that we should not be televising the evidence given in high-profile trials. And of course jurors should not be doing their own research. There are strict rules about what evidence can be given in criminal trials, rules which are intended to protect the accused from an unfair conviction, so if jurors conduct their own research, they may discover things which they should not know.

It is only later that I look at my copy of *Private Eye* and realise that Judge Reid – who seems a mild and friendly man – has hit the headlines because of the hard line he has been taking with climate change protesters. In March he warned two Insulate Britain protesters, charged with public nuisance for glueing themselves to the road in Bishopsgate in London, that they must not rely on their concerns about fuel poverty and climate change in their defence. They defied his instructions and the jury failed to reach a verdict. Judge Reid then sentenced them to seven weeks each in prison for contempt of court – they had either tried to manipulate the jury into acquitting them even though they were guilty, or to use the trial to continue their protest, in either case setting themselves above the law and subverting the court process.

He may of course have been right that what they wanted to say was completely irrelevant to the charges they faced, although there could perhaps be a question of whether the law of public nuisance is an unjustified interference with the right to protest (these defendants were not legally represented so the point may not have been argued). It is part of the judge's job to keep the trial on track and exclude irrelevancies. But it has been the law since the seventeenth century that juries are entitled to acquit a defendant even if they are sure that he or she is guilty. It's known as jury equity – a safety valve if the jury feel that the law is unjust. So during the Insulate Britain trial, a group of environmental activists staged a demonstration outside the Inner London Crown Court, holding up placards telling members of the jury, 'Jurors have an absolute right to acquit a defendant according to their conscience.' Judge Reid referred them to an Old Bailey judge who referred them to the Attorney General to decide whether they should be prosecuted for contempt of court or attempting to pervert the course of justice. The Attorney General did prosecute but a High Court judge threw the case out – this was not an actionable contempt, and prosecution was disproportionate in a democratic society. The Attorney General's office contemplated but eventually – in April 2024 – abandoned an appeal. The centuries-old safety valve of jury equity survives, along with the right to remind jurors about it.

I do wish that I had been there to see the previous days' dramas. The defendants were convicted despite the demonstration outside. But I am sure that today's proceedings are a more typical picture of life in the Inner London Crown Court. But why could neither the prosecution nor the defence have got hold of the mobile phone evidence earlier?

In the afternoon I go through to what's known as the 'chocolate box', a modern building built onto the old one in the 1950s, which houses six courts. It was meant to be temporary, but it is still there and something of an eyesore. This courtroom is very different from the elegant courts in the old building. The floor is flat, with only a low dais for the judge's bench and the jury box. The ceiling is low. The walls seem to be painted breeze blocks. There are rows of tables and chairs and screens everywhere. The furniture does not look comfortable. There are two very young men in the glass-fronted dock at the back of the court.

Her Honour Judge Baraitser is sentencing them for attempted aggravated burglary. The incident was a serious one. A group of youths wanted to get at another youth who was at home. No doubt there was some vendetta. There was clearly a threat of serious violence. They tried to break down his front door by ramming it with an electric scooter, stabbing it with a knife, and kicking it. Fortunately for their intended victim, they did not succeed.

One of the defendants was only just seventeen at the time (he is now eighteen). He had no previous convictions. His role in the attack was relatively minor – he had just kicked the door. The prosecution accepts that there was a high degree of peer pressure and exploitation – the judge points out that it is agreed that he was coerced into joining in. He has a good school record, the support of his family and the prospect of an apprenticeship. There is a very thorough Youth Offending report from a probation officer which recommends a Youth Rehabilitation Order. The judge explains that the notional sentence is reduced from three years to eighteen months because he was a child at the time. He was in custody on remand for five months. A return to adult custody is unlikely to improve his prospects. So she decides that she will follow the recommendation in the report and impose a Youth Rehabilitation Order for twelve months. This will include a curfew at his mother's address from 7.00 p.m. to 7.00 a.m. for six months; exclusion from the SE11 postcode; a ban on contact with the other defendant; and weekly attendance with his supervisor. His mother is in tears at the back of the court. The probation officer is visibly delighted as he leaves the dock.

The other defendant does not fare so well. He has been referred from two other Crown Courts where he was awaiting sentence for two sets of drug-related offences, the second committed while on bail for the first. He already has a suspended sentence for possession of a knife. He took a leading role in the attempted aggravated burglary. He borrowed the electric scooter and was the first to attack the door with it. The only mitigation is his age and immaturity. Totting it all up, the judge imposes a total of sixty-six months (five and a half years) in a young offenders' institution. The more serious drug-related offences deserve a range between twenty-four and thirty-two months, the less serious deserve twenty months concurrent with that, the attempted aggravated burglary deserves between thirty-six and forty-three months, consecutive to the drug-related offences; and the suspended sentence of six months has to be activated. So the judge has actually picked the lowest figures that she could, given the guidelines.

I reflect that sentencing is now a much more exact science than it was when I was in practice as a barrister fifty years ago and even when I was a part-time Crown Court judge some thirty years ago. The guidelines have become more detailed and specific, and the overall length of sentences has risen sharply. This is certainly what many politicians and much of the media want. It may or may not be what the public want. Opinion polls say that more than half the public think that sentences are too lenient. But when presented with real scenarios, they impose lesser sentences than the courts now do.

The crucial test is how these two young men – similar in some ways but very different in others – will turn out. Overall, juvenile offenders have a higher reoffending rate (within the first year) than adults – 33.12 per cent and 26.2 per cent respectively in the first quarter of 2023. But it differs sharply according to the sentence imposed – 21.32 per cent after a reprimand, warning or caution; 31.9 per cent after a community penalty of some sort; and a whopping 62.5 per cent after a juvenile offender is released from custody. But, as a judge, you rarely find out what happens to the people who have appeared in front of you.

It has been a very instructive day in a typical inner-city Crown Court. Now it is time to go right to the top and see what life is like in the Central Criminal Court, otherwise known as the Old Bailey.

8 Inside the Old Bailey

The monarch of all the Crown Courts is the Central Criminal Court in Old Bailey, just around the corner from St Paul's Cathedral. There has been a court on this site for centuries, but the present main building dates back to 1902. It is very grand, with a fine dome crowned by the golden statue of Justice with her sword and scales. Adjoining it is a modern wing, opened in 1972, built on the site of the old Newgate Prison. The general public don't get to see most of the building, except on guided tours or special occasions. The public galleries are just that: each looking down into each courtroom, rather like the gallery in a small theatre. The public have their own little entrance down a side passage and are kept completely separate from the working parts of the building. No doubt there are good security reasons for this, but it does mean that there is a great deal of empty space.

The old wing has four traditional courtrooms leading off the great hall on the first floor. The great hall is magnificent, richly decorated with paintings and classical statues. There is also a large statue of Elizabeth Fry, who campaigned for prison reform in the early nineteenth century: I wonder what she would think of the state of the criminal justice system today when the prisons are overflowing and can do very little to help their inmates to avoid reoffending when they are released. There is a series of texts running round the room where the walls join the ceiling: 'The Law of the Wise is the Fountain of Life'; 'The Welfare of the People is the Supreme Law'; 'Right lives by Law and Law subsists by Power'; 'Poise the Cause in Justice's Equal Scales'; 'Moses gave unto the People the Laws of God'; and 'London shall have all its ancient Rights'. How many of these would today's politicians subscribe to? The last is but one of the many reminders in the building of the close connection between the Old Bailey and the City of London.

The new wing has four modern courts on each of the ground, first and third floors, with spacious waiting halls outside. The only people allowed there and in the great hall are the people involved in the cases being heard: the jurors, lawyers, defendants who are on bail, witnesses, police officers and the press (and privileged visitors like me). There is also a spacious and comfortable witness area on the second floor. Giving evidence must be a nerve-racking experience for anyone who is not a professional witness (and perhaps even for some of them). So here they can wait and be supported by volunteers. There are separate sitting rooms for the prosecution and defence witnesses. There's a playroom for children. There are also little rooms where children and other vulnerable witnesses can give their evidence by video-link with the courtrooms – although these days I'm told that most prefer either to be in court, with the witness box screened from the dock, or to give their evidence remotely from another location. All in all, it is most impressive. There is certainly nothing like it in the York Magistrates' Court or the Inner London Crown Court (where a charity-funded family room had to be closed because of a leaking roof).

The ISIS terrorist

The Old Bailey handles the most serious of cases, mostly homicide and terrorist offences. Whether you're in the public galleries or in the working areas, there is plenty of interest going on. I potter between four courts, one old and three new. Three of them have interesting trials going on. But first, I go and listen to some legal argument being heard by the Recorder of London, His Honour Judge Lucraft KC. He is the Resident Judge in charge of the Old Bailey (and ex officio an alderman of the City of London), although High Court judges come and sit here too. The defendant, a British citizen, is accused of fighting for ISIS in Syria. He was originally thought to be one of the notorious 'Beatles', so called because of their English accents. He has been tried, prosecuted and convicted, and has served a sentence for being a member of a banned organisation in Turkey. The Turkish authorities have deported him to this country and he is now being prosecuted here.

I am especially interested in this, because when I was in the Supreme Court we heard a case about Shafee El Sheikh,[1] who definitely was one of the 'Beatles'. The UK Government was proposing to send the evidence against him to the United States authorities so that he could be prosecuted there. But the Government was not proposing to insist on the usual assurances from the US that the death penalty would not be imposed or carried out. The Trump Government really wanted the UK to prosecute him here, but our prosecuting authorities did not think that there was enough evidence to do so. They were also afraid that a prosecution would be seen as an abuse of process if he was brought to the UK without going through the usual extradition procedures. The Trump Government was outraged at the idea that we would not prosecute him here but were seeking to control what they did with him in the United States. Shafee El Sheikh's mother challenged the UK Government's decision to send the evidence without the usual assurances. She argued that it was unlawful in this country to do anything to facilitate a trial that might result in the death penalty. The majority of the Supreme Court did not accept that argument, but we all agreed that the Government had not even thought about the Data Protection Act, which it should have done. The Act prohibits the transfer of personal data (which this was) if the 'fundamental rights and freedoms of the data subject override the public interest in the transfer'. There is no more fundamental right than the right to life, no matter how heinous the crimes committed. We don't know what the Government made of our judgment, but we do know that it sought the usual assurances; the information was supplied; Shafee El Sheikh was tried and convicted in the United States; and the death penalty was not imposed.

Back to Court 6 in the Old Bailey. No question of the death penalty. But the defendant's barrister is arguing that it would be an abuse of process to prosecute him here. Part of the argument is similar to that which may have troubled the prosecutors in Shafee El Sheikh's case. The UK did not ask Turkey to extradite him, which is the normal way of getting people from foreign countries who are wanted for trial in this country. Instead they relied upon the Turkish authorities' decision to deport him after he had finished his sentence there. It is said that the UK authorities were so keen to get him here that they connived in a deportation which he was given no opportunity to challenge in Turkey. Another part of the argument is that because he has already been prosecuted, tried and convicted in Turkey for terrorism-related offences and has served his sentence there, he should not be punished twice for essentially the same conduct. So the Recorder is hearing argument about exactly what he was prosecuted for in Turkey. Are these quibbles to prevent a dangerous terrorist receiving his just deserts? Or are they fundamental to the whole notion of justice? Which, as Eleanor Roosevelt said, cannot be for one side alone but must be for both. No one should be punished twice for the same conduct.

We'll have to wait for the Recorder's ruling, so I go off to see what is happening in another court. I learn later that the Recorder has rejected both the abuse arguments. It is perfectly normal practice to deport foreign nationals back to their home country once they have served their sentence and it had not been shown that British officials had connived in depriving him of his rights to challenge this. He had been prosecuted in Turkey for membership of a banned organisation, ISIS. He is being prosecuted here for possessing a firearm for purposes connected with terrorism, for funding terrorism, and for arranging for money to be made available for terrorism – a friend of his wife's was caught carrying a large sum of money out of the country which is alleged to be destined for terrorist purposes. As expected, when his attempts to appeal the Recorder's ruling failed, he pleaded guilty.

The teenage nerd

Meanwhile, back to Court 1 in the Old Bailey. This is one of the traditional courtrooms off the great hall, the historic courtroom where famous murderers like Dr Crippen were tried and *Lady Chatterley's Lover* by D. H. Lawrence was acquitted of obscenity. It is a grander version of the traditional courtrooms in York City Magistrates' Court. Oddly, however, there is a huge wooden armchair in the middle of the judges' bench; it is empty (the judge is sitting slightly to one side), waiting for the Lord Mayor of London if he chooses to come and sit in the court. The Lord Mayor and aldermen are all entitled to do so if they wish, although they will play no part in the case. The sheriffs actually live in the building during their year of office and entertain the judges and guests to lunch.

Today a senior circuit judge, His Honour Judge Leonard KC, is presiding over the trial of a young man called Mohammed Saleem. He is accused of eight counts of possessing recorded information likely to be useful to a person preparing or committing an act of terrorism. The prosecution case is that the police found documents which had been downloaded onto two smartphones and a laptop while he was still a schoolboy. The documents contained information about, for example, roadside Improvised Explosive Devices, microwave oven bombs, Molotov cocktails, nail bombs and ISIS tactics. It is enough that he had this material without a reasonable excuse: the prosecution does not have to show that he was a terrorist or that he ever intended to use it for terrorist purposes.

Both the prosecution and the defence barristers are senior women of south Asian heritage. The defence barrister is the first woman KC practising in criminal law to wear a hijab. She is in the middle of taking her client through his evidence when I creep in as quietly as I can. I am sitting behind the jury – eight women, mostly young, one wearing a hijab, and four men, a good ethnic mix – so I share their view of the barristers and of the defendant in the witness box. The trial has already been going on for more than a week.

The defendant is a slight young man with a dark beard which he keeps plucking. Well-spoken and studious. Since downloading the documents in question he has passed three A levels and gone on to university to study computer science. He accepts that he knew the nature of the documents referred to in three of the charges: 'The Successful Pressure Cooker Bomb', 'Procedures to Make Explosives', and 'How to Become an Assassin'. But he says that he had a reasonable excuse for having them, because he was carrying out research into Islamic history and theology. But in relation to the other five charges, he says that he bulk-downloaded the documents but did not take them in or understand what they were about. At the time he was suffering from an undiagnosed autistic spectrum condition. There is conflicting medical evidence about whether this is likely to have led to the bulk-downloading.

So a lot depends upon his mindset at the time when he downloaded the documents. Both the prosecution and the defence have put in long schedules of text conversations. His barrister is taking him through one of these and asking him to explain them. He's exchanging messages with a school friend (whom he calls his dumbest friend) about his future plans. He's studying for his A levels (in maths, physics and chemistry), planning to do a degree, a master's and then a PhD, then move to the Middle East and get an Islamic qualification. 'Then after a bit I'm gonna go jihad.' He explains to the court that he wasn't seriously thinking of going to the Middle East. Jihad simply means struggle. He was considering humanitarian assistance. There are people starving in refugee camps. He draws a distinction between legitimate resistance and extremist groups who kill innocent people. He dissociates himself from the latter. But he also says that there is no better way to die than serving the oppressed.

I later learn that the jury has convicted him of the three counts where he admitted knowing what he was downloading. The jurors must have concluded that they were not sure that he knew what was involved in the bulk-downloaded material, perhaps because of his autistic spectrum condition. But they must also have concluded that he did not have a reasonable excuse for possessing the offending material. It's a difficult sentencing exercise for the judge: the jihadist mindset went on for a long time, because the first offence was when he was sixteen and the other two when he was eighteen; in court he was still defending suicide bombing in an extreme case; but he is a highly intelligent young man of previously good character who has a lot to offer. In effect the judge sentences him to eighteen months' imprisonment 'to reflect the overall criminality'. Here is a young man who committed these offences while a teenager and has since led a constructive life: there is an obvious risk that he will be further radicalised in prison. But we also know how important it is to nip any terrorist sympathies in the bud as soon as possible.

The organ traffickers

There is an even more fascinating case in Court 5, one of the modern courts. Apparently it is the first of its kind. Mr Justice Johnson is trying a case of conspiracy 'to arrange or facilitate travel for the purpose of exploitation', otherwise known as trafficking. The exploitation in question is the harvesting of an organ for transplantation for reward. This is illegal, irrespective of whether the donor of the organ consents. The alleged traffickers are Ike Ekweremadu, a prominent Nigerian politician, his wife Beatrice, his daughter Sonia, and a Nigerian doctor, Obinna Obeta. Sonia has a serious kidney condition and needs a transplant if she is to have a chance of leading an ordinary life. The defendants are alleged to have arranged for a young Nigerian man, whom the judge calls 'C', a trader in telephone parts from a wheelbarrow on the streets of Lagos, to travel to this country with the promise of money and the opportunity to work here, in exchange for donating his kidney to Sonia. He was provided with a passport and a visa to come here for medical treatment. The Ekweremadus arranged with a surgeon and a hospital for him to donate a kidney, falsely claiming that he was a cousin on Mrs Ekweremadu's side. Dr Obeta is alleged to have made all the arrangements, including finding the young man, arranging the necessary medical tests, getting him to sign an affidavit falsely stating that Sonia is his cousin, getting him a visa, and arranging for payment. There is an email referring to a 1 million Nigerian naira 'agent fee' and a 2.5 million 'donor fee'. Mr Ekweremadu paid this sum to Dr Obeta, who did not pass it on to C. But the operation did not take place – the surgeons believed that C was Sonia's cousin but did not think that he was a suitable donor and refused to go ahead. He returned to Dr Obeta's flat but ran away some time later and eventually found his way to a police station, claiming that he was a child who had been badly treated (because of well-meaning advice that he was more likely to get help that way). But his passport said that he was twenty-one. The Ekweremadu parents were arrested at Heathrow, apparently having made arrangements for another donor in Turkey. So the issue is this: did the defendants agree among themselves to bring the young man here to donate his kidney for reward – money or work – or did he come here agreeing to donate his kidney altruistically to a young woman in need who, although she is not a relative, does come from the same Nigerian tribe as he does? If there was a conspiracy, how many of the defendants were parties to it? The trial has already been going on for some weeks when I arrive to observe it.

The modern courtrooms are not as grand as the old ones, but they have much the same feel of seriousness and authority. They have blonde wooden panelling and furniture. The lawyers' benches are facing the judge rather than to one side. There is a space in the well of the court on the side opposite the jury box where the press and people such as the complainants' family, police officers and visitors like me can sit. Dr Obeta is giving evidence. He is being asked about text messages and phone calls about the money. Once again, the members of the jury are poring over long schedules. Once again, they are ethnically mixed, with eight women, mostly young, and four men. They all seem pretty engaged, as well they might. Even though they may not have expected to have to serve in such a long trial, the evidence is absorbing. A week or two later, the press reports that the Ekweremadu parents and Dr Obeta have been convicted, but Sonia has been acquitted.

I later learn that Dr Obeta has been sentenced to ten years' imprisonment; Mr Ekweremadu to nine years and eight months' imprisonment; and Mrs Ekweremadu to four years and six months' imprisonment. The judge is following the sentencing guidelines for trafficking offences. C would have suffered serious harm had the transplant gone ahead as they intended. Even without that, there has been a 'substantial and long-term adverse impact on his daily life' because he is afraid to go back to Nigeria. The judge was thinking of making a substantial compensation order but C has rejected this – he does not want anything more to do with the bad people. The doctor and the father were both highly culpable but there was some mitigation in the father's case. The mother was much less culpable and Sonia would suffer from losing her care.

The child abusers

I move on to Court 10, another modern courtroom. Here Mr Justice Sweeting is trying a murder. The victim is a baby called Jacob, nearly sixteen months old. His mother called an ambulance around 6.00 a.m. but when it got there very soon afterwards the baby was not breathing and could not be revived. He was in a shocking state: his head was badly swollen and his eyes were swollen shut. He had suffered traumatic head injuries on three separate occasions and numerous other injuries of a non-accidental nature. He had also suffered a tear to his penis and a stabbing injury to his scrotum. A photograph showed a bright and cheerful toddler on 12 August 2019. On 27 August 2019 he was dead. The mother's boyfriend is accused of murder and wounding the penis and scrotum with intent to cause grievous bodily harm. The mother is accused of allowing the death of a child – that is, that she failed to take reasonable steps to protect the child from the serious risk of serious physical harm being caused to the child by the unlawful act of her boyfriend, a risk of which she knew or ought to have known. The mother is also accused of failing to seek medical help for the child when she should have done; she pleaded guilty to this at the end of her evidence.

The boyfriend is saying that he is a responsible person and that the mother killed the child. The mother is saying that the boyfriend did it and she couldn't reasonably be expected to stand up to him and protect the child or seek medical help for her son because she was scared stiff of the boyfriend: he had subjected her to what is now called coercive control.

The boyfriend is in the middle of giving evidence. The mother's barrister has asked for permission to cross-examine him about his bad character. So the judge has to give a legal ruling before the jury comes back into court. (This sort of thing happens quite frequently in criminal trials because the rules of evidence are so complicated; the jurors must often wonder what on earth is going on.) The general rule is that defendants cannot be asked about their previous convictions or other evidence of bad character. It is thought that juries will be prejudiced by this and convict a defendant simply because he is a bad person rather than because he has been proved to have committed this particular crime (after all, the police have been known to round up the 'usual suspects'). But there are now several exceptions. One is where the evidence 'has a substantial probative value in relation to an important matter in issue between the defendant and a co-defendant'. Evidence of this man's propensity to use violence against women might help the mother's case that she was scared of him.

Way back in 2005, when the defendant was fifteen, he was given a police caution for threats to kill his own mother. He admitted that the police were called when he had been swinging a hammer about, hitting doors and walls and the locks on the freezer (because he wanted some food), putting a knife with an eight-inch blade to his mother's neck, demanding money, and getting out a Stanley knife, threatening to kill his mother. He admitted then that he had anger management problems. Then again in 2008 he agreed in a police interview that he had argued with another girlfriend, grabbed her by the arm and pushed her against the wall to stop her shouting. And finally in 2013 there was evidence from a former partner that he had tried to strangle her. The judge decides that the questions can be asked.

The jury comes back into court and the defendant goes back into the witness box. The mother's barrister cross-examines him. She explores how he and the mother got together; whether he was still in a relationship with another woman, Julie, the mother of his two children, at the time. He admits to trying to have his cake and eat it. They also go into his expensive use of large amounts of cannabis and cocaine, which he admits, and how he funds it. He claims to have had cash savings from building work despite having no job at the time. He was using cocaine because he was sad at not seeing his kids. It stopped him from crying his eyes out every night. It gave him half an hour's respite from depression but forty-five minutes later he'd get depressed again. He agrees that he was up all night contacting Julie. He didn't realise how bad the messaging was until he saw the schedule (so yet again a schedule of phone calls and text message features heavily – he was sending her dozens of messages every day). He insists that he isn't mean. He's a nice person.

The mother's barrister puts it to him that he abused the mother, he raped her, he terrified her into not leaving with her children when a friend wanted her to, he got hold of the PIN to her phone, he spied on her and blacklisted her male friends, he picked on women in a domestic environment, he was a bully, he was violent and aggressive when he didn't get his own way. All of this he strenuously denies. Then she asks him about the incident in 2005 when he swung a hammer about, hitting doors, walls and the freezer, put an eight-inch knife to his mother's neck and threatened her with a Stanley knife. All of this he admits. He doesn't remember threatening to kill her. But he wanted to frighten her. She was looking after his money for him but wouldn't let him have it when he wanted it. He agrees that when he was a kid he was not a nice person. But he grew up and changed in his late teens (he is now in his thirties).

So the barrister points out that he hadn't changed in 2008, when he admitted assaulting his then girlfriend. The police were called by her mother who heard them arguing. The girlfriend had bruises on both arms. She made a complaint but withdrew it. He agrees that they'd been arguing a lot since she had had a miscarriage. She'd been drinking a lot while she was pregnant and had lost the baby. He was upset because he wanted to be a dad. She was angry and hysterical. He told the police that she didn't raise a hand to him because he didn't want to get her into trouble. But she would hit him when she got angry, so he grabbed her by the arms and pushed her against the wall 'to stop her hitting me'. He was willing to be a man and take the blame. He took an anger management course when he was a teenager and it helped.

The mother's barrister puts it to him that it must have worn off when he tried to strangle Julie, his long-term girlfriend, in 2013. He denies that he ever tried to do so. He denies being jealous of her youngest son – he was a responsible loving parent to his own kids and to his stepsons.

This jury too is eight women and four men, mostly under forty, with a good ethnic mix. It is hard to tell what they are making of all of this. Are they shocked by the lifestyle, the drugs, the two-timing, the violence? Or are they taking it in their stride?

We get to the end of the court day. They'll be starting a bit later tomorrow because one juror has an appointment. The jury leaves – walking past the witness box where the defendant is still sitting. The defendant goes back into the dock – he is in custody. The mother leaves it – she is on bail. The mother's barrister still has some cross-examination left for tomorrow. Then it will be the prosecution's turn to cross-examine him. The mother intends to give evidence, so then she will be cross-examined. It's not looking as though the trial will be over next week.

I later learn that both defendants have been convicted of both charges against them. In the light of the medical evidence, this is not surprising. Whoever caused those injuries must have meant to cause really serious harm to the child. And because of the serious injuries which he had suffered before the fatal ones, for which no medical help had been sought, the mother must have been aware of the risk which her new boyfriend posed to her child. And she could so easily have avoided this by leaving when her friend urged her to. I suppose that any coercive control to which she might have been subject could explain the delay in seeking medical help for the fatal injury, but it couldn't excuse her covering up of the earlier injuries or failing to leave when she had the chance.

But I also learn that the judge does not accept that she was subject to any degree of coercive control. Her evidence and the exchanges of messages between them showed a quite different relationship, one which she prioritised ahead of any concern for the child. He sentences her to ten years' imprisonment for the main offence, while recognising that her ultimate punishment is learning to come to terms with her role in Jacob's death. She has also lost his older brother, who has been removed and adopted. I reflect that we heard many similar cases in the Family Division of the High Court, where the evidence was just as awful, and often had to take decisions about how to protect the children even if the criminal process had not yet run its course.

The boyfriend is sentenced to life imprisonment, as all murderers must be. The judge must set a minimum period of imprisonment before he can even be considered for parole – thirty-two years in this case. This was a particularly serious offence because it involved a course of conduct of deliberate cruelty of a sadistic nature, aggravated because Jacob was so young and vulnerable, along with the defendant's previous offending and his attempts to pin the blame on the mother. It may come as a surprise that the offence of murder does not require an intent to kill – it is enough that the person who causes death intended either to kill or to cause really serious bodily harm. The judge accepts that in this case the intention was to cause serious bodily harm rather than to kill – but the distinction couldn't count for much in this case. You may think that cases like this are the reason why the prosecution does not always have to prove an intent to kill.

Reflections

So ends my day in the grandest criminal court in the country. But what do I make of it all? My first thought is that enormous trouble is being taken. Long gone are the days before the twentieth century when the judges could try many cases in one day, they were not expected to be impartial, the defendants could not give evidence in their own defence and only had legal representation if they could afford it, and jurors were not encouraged to take much time in their deliberations. These days, serious cases like these can take weeks. The judges are not supposed to be part of the prosecution team. Defendants have lawyers to represent them and can give evidence in their own defence if they want – although, as the child abuse case showed, there are risks in doing so. Jurors are given a great deal of help – the judge's directions on the law will usually be written down for them, along with a route to verdict, a sort of map of how to go about making their decisions. This is surely the least we can do when we expect such a lot of them.

My next thought is how much the nature of the evidence has changed since the advent of mobile phones and other digital devices. In each of the trials I saw, evidence of phone traffic and emails and text messages played a large part in the prosecution case (although, as we know, it can also play a part in the defence case). Going through the schedules took a lot of time but again it gave the jurors something solid to go on.

This leads on to the importance of good legal representation, both for the prosecution and the defence. Some of the present backlog in Crown Court cases is because the barristers doing criminal cases went on strike. They were not earning enough to make ends meet. Barristers are self-employed sole practitioners. They have to meet all their expenses – chambers, clerks, travel, insurance, pensions – out of their brief fees. The problem may have been eased but many barristers have stopped doing criminal work because it just doesn't pay enough. And they are not being replaced by young people coming to the Bar – many of whom may have started out wanting to do criminal work but found themselves having to concentrate on more lucrative areas of practice, not least because they have student loans to repay. It is easy to scoff at supposedly fat-cat lawyers – but this work is vital if we want to live in a society where only the guilty are punished for what they have done. We are only too well aware that miscarriages of justice can take place – for all sorts of reasons – but we must strive for a system which does its best to avoid these. Fair judges, responsible prosecutors and competent defence counsel are essential to this.

But some things have changed for the better in recent years. On the day of my visit in 2023 there were fifteen full-time judges sitting permanently at the Old Bailey. Eight of those judges were women. This is a far cry from the days, not so long ago, when there was only one woman judge at the Old Bailey – the first was Nina Lowry QC, from 1976 to 1995, the second was Ann Goddard QC, from 1997 to 2008, and the third was Wendy Joseph KC, from 2012 to 2022. Wendy Joseph was told by the then Recorder of London that she should 'fit in' with the men. But after her appointment many more women arrived and no one would now dream of telling them to fit in. They are just as much part of the furniture as the men.

My final thought, though, is that I can't help agreeing with the judge who said, 'it's the best show in town and all for free.'

Part Two

RIGHTS ARE FOR EVERYONE

Introduction

In Part One we saw how, every day, up and down the country, courts and tribunals are deciding on people's rights and obligations. Now we need to turn to what the law says about some of those rights and obligations. We can see how the law is tailored to the particular situation of a variety of people in a variety of settings. This is especially true of people who, for one reason or another, have typically been marginalised or disadvantaged in the law. We can see how, bit by bit, the law has recognised this and tried to deal with it. But it's not always easy. And it throws up some difficult questions which you might find it interesting to try and solve. What rights do children have in their schooling? What rights do people with disabilities have when navigating a world which other people may find easier? What rights do LGBTQ+ people have to live the lives which they wish to live? What rights do workers have in the workplace where bosses are so powerful? What rights do women have in a world which was originally designed by and for men? What rights do patients, ill or injured, have when they are at their most vulnerable and powerless?

This isn't a textbook. I'm not trying to tell you all the law on these complicated subjects. I've picked out a few real cases to illustrate the sort of problems the law has to grapple with. I've told the story and then asked you, the reader, what you think the answer should be, before telling you what the court said the answer was. You won't always agree – I certainly don't in a few cases – but I hope you'll get a picture of how the law works, how the law can indeed be on our side.

9 Skoolkids Have Rights

Adults are used to thinking about what will be best for their own children. Courts are used to thinking about what will be best for the children whose parents can't agree. We tend to assume that the adults know best. We don't tend to think that sometimes children know better than we do what will be best for them. We don't tend to think of children as human beings who have rights just like the rest of us – rights to be treated fairly, rights to be listened to, and rights to have their views taken seriously. Nowhere is this more important than in school, where most children spend most of their waking time, where the whole idea is to bring out the best in each individual child, so that each can grow up to be the best they can be. So here are a few real-life stories to illustrate how even school children can have rights. (Names have been changed to protect the children's identity, except where this is already public knowledge.)

The boy who was excluded from school

Mr Smith was head teacher of Downtown High School, a mixed comprehensive school in a provincial town. He was having a hard day. He tried to be approachable to all the pupils and staff in his school but sometimes they brought him problems that he'd rather not have. That day in February, two of the girls in the school, whom I'm calling Anna and Jane, came to see him. Anna was very upset. She told Mr Smith that she was terrified of an older boy who was then in his GCSE year, whom I'm calling Jason. She described all sorts of bullying behaviour, both in and out of school. But she didn't want to make a formal complaint and she didn't want Mr Smith to tell Jason that she had spoken to him about it. Mr Smith assured them that he would help her in any way he could. Later that day, Jane came back and told him that Anna was very, very distressed and thinking of ending it all because of what was described as 'subtle and silent covert intimidation'. By now, Mr Smith was seriously concerned. He spoke to Anna's mother, who was also troubled about the risk that Anna would commit suicide and said that Jason was to blame. So he arranged for Anna and her friends to have a classroom to use during breaks and at lunchtime.

Meanwhile, the school had learned that allegations had also been made that Jason was committing serious crimes outside school. They convened a meeting with representatives from the school, social services, the local authority's child protection officer and the police. It was decided that Jason would be suspended from school for five days, not because he was guilty of the crimes or the intimidating behaviour alleged, but 'as a precautionary measure'. No one asked Jason for his side of the story. No one explained to him and his family what the allegations against him were or who had made them. No one gave them a reason for his suspension except that it was based on unspecified information presented at the meeting. After this the school made no further inquiries. They were apparently waiting for the results of an assessment, which social services were meant to be carrying out, of the allegations made by Anna and any impact on her emotions, but this does not seem to have happened. Hearing nothing about this, the school extended Jason's suspension for a total of five weeks. They set him work to do at home but he does not seem to have done this. After the five weeks, a home tutor was arranged for eight hours a week for him and he did engage with this. For the next six weeks he was marked as being 'educated off site'. After that, he was recorded as being on study leave before his GCSEs. So he was effectively away from school from February for the rest of the school year, although he was allowed to return in June to take his GCSEs in a room by himself. History does not relate how well he did or what effect his prolonged absence from school had had upon his studies.

Soon after he was suspended, Jason took the school to court, complaining that his suspension was unlawful. If the case had been decided quickly, the court might have ordered the school to let him come back, but that did not happen. It took another three years for the case to be finally resolved.

What do you think?

1. At the time, the rules did not allow schools to suspend a pupil 'as a precautionary measure' but only for proven ill-discipline. They also required the school to give the pupil an opportunity of defending himself and the parents an accurate explanation of the reasons for the pupil's suspension. None of this happened. So do you think that Jason should have had a remedy – to put him back in school or to be compensated for what he had lost?
2. But wait – the school was in an impossible position – should the rules have allowed them to take precautionary measures?
3. But that wouldn't solve the problem of Anna's understandable reluctance to have Jason told about her fears. Yet knowing the case against you is the basic right of anyone threatened with sanctions like this. Is there any way in which Mr Smith could have protected the rights of both Jason and Anna?

What did the court think?

The case came from Northern Ireland.[1] The Supreme Court of the United Kingdom held unanimously that Jason's suspension was unlawful. But they didn't give him any remedy. By the time the case got to them, it was too late to order the school to take him back. And there is no general right to compensation for unlawful acts by public authorities. There can be compensation for breach of the Convention rights – that is, the rights contained in the European Convention on Human Rights which have been translated into rights contained in UK law by the Human Rights Act 1998. But although article 2 of the First Protocol to the Convention says that 'No person shall be denied the right to education', this only means the right to whatever education the State provides in the circumstances. Jason had been provided with what Northern Ireland did for excluded pupils. So no compensation.

My comment was this:

'Where adults are in control of children's lives they have a moral duty to be fair and sometimes this is also a legal duty. If children are faced with a world which is arbitrary and unfair they may see little point in obeying the rules or being just and fair in their own dealings with others when they grow up.'

So we had to empathise with Jason, aged fifteen, coming up to his GCSEs, effectively excluded from school for the three months before his exams, not told the real reason for this or given an opportunity to defend himself.

'But we should not forget the complainant either . . . What lessons has she learned? It is good that the school was prepared to take her seriously and give her support. It is not good that an anonymous report of complaints which could not be disclosed was seen to lead to sanctions against the alleged perpetrator . . . In the words of Eleanor Roosevelt on the screen at the end of our courtroom, "Justice cannot be for one side alone but must be for both." '

School rules can apply to parents as well as children, as the next case shows.

The girl who was taken out of school

Mary was excited. She was only six, rising seven, and she was going on holiday for a second time this term! Her father was going to take her away for seven days in April. Her parents were living apart and Mary was spending roughly half her time with each of them. It looked as if they were in a competition to give her treats. Back in February her mother had taken her on holiday for five days. Her mother had booked the February holiday soon after Mary's father had told her that he wanted to take Mary on holiday in April. Her father booked the April holiday on the same day. Neither of them had the other parent's permission to take Mary on holiday. Neither of them had the school's permission to take Mary out of school during term time.

A parent is guilty of a criminal offence 'if a child of compulsory school age who is a registered pupil at a school fails to attend regularly at the school'. There are a few excuses, such as sickness or the school's permission, but a family holiday is not one of them. Apart from these two holidays, Mary's attendance record was good, around 90 per cent The local authority can issue a parent with a fixed penalty notice, which means that the parent will not be taken to court if he or she pays a fixed sum by the stipulated deadline. After the February holiday, the local authority issued Mary's mother with a fixed penalty notice, requiring her to pay a penalty of £60 for taking an unauthorised holiday during term time. They did not issue a notice to the father at that time, because he had not agreed to the February holiday. Her mother paid the penalty. After the April holiday, the local authority issued the father with a fixed penalty notice in the same terms, warning him that if he didn't pay by a particular date the penalty would go up to £120, and if he didn't pay that he would be taken to court. They did not issue another notice to the mother, because she had not agreed to the April holiday. The father refused to pay. So the local authority prosecuted him in the local magistrates' court. The magistrates found that he had 'no case to answer' and the local authority appealed.

What do you think?

1. The case turns on what is meant by 'regularly'. Is it: (a) 'at regular intervals', as in 'every Sunday'; (b) 'often enough', as in say 90 per cent of the days required; or (c) 'as required by the school rules'?
2. Going away on holiday during term time is usually much cheaper than taking a family holiday during the school holidays: would you think a fixed penalty of £60 a small price to pay for getting a cheaper holiday?
3. Does that mean that the law should be changed to allow it or that the penalty should be higher?

What did the court think?

The Supreme Court of the United Kingdom held that 'regularly' meant 'in accordance with the rules'.[2] So Mary's father had a case to answer. Unless he could show an excuse, which was unlikely, the penalty notice had been properly issued and he would have to pay. 'Regularly' couldn't possibly mean, for example, 'every Monday' because school attendance was meant to be compulsory. Nor could it mean 'often enough', because no one would be sure what that meant. I gave the court's judgment, with which the other four justices agreed, finding ten reasons for this, but the most important were nine and ten:

'It is not just that there is a clear statistical link between school attendance and educational achievement. It is more the disruptive effect of unauthorised absences. They disrupt the education of the individual child. Work missed has to be made up, requiring extra work by the teacher who has already covered and marked this subject matter with other pupils. Having to make up for one pupil's absence may also disrupt the work of other pupils. Group learning will be diminished by the absence of individual members of the group. Most of all, if one pupil can be taken out whenever it suits the parent, then so can others. Different pupils may be taken out at different times, thus increasing the disruptive effect exponentially.'

Finally, taking children out of school in blatant disregard of the school rules 'is not an approach to rule-keeping which any educational system can be expected to find acceptable. It is a slap in the face to those obedient parents who do keep the rules, whatever the cost or inconvenience to themselves.'

You may begin to see a theme here: there is more to education than learning facts and skills – there are values involved too. However, parents are allowed to educate their children out of school as long as they provide the child with 'efficient education suitable to his age, ability, aptitude and any special educational needs he may have'. But who checks on what they are doing? There has recently been the terrible case of Sara Sharif, taken out of school to be home-schooled when her school began to suspect that she was being abused at home, as indeed she was, so badly that she was eventually killed and her father and stepmother convicted of murder.

School uniform

Mrs Yasmin Bevan was head teacher of Denbigh High School, a secondary school for boys and girls aged eleven to sixteen in Luton. It was mixed in more ways than one, with twenty-one different ethnic groups and ten different religious groupings amongst its pupils. Nearly four-fifths of the pupils were Muslim, Muslims were well represented on the governing body, and Mrs Bevan herself was from a Bengali Muslim family. The school had performed very well under her leadership. She believed that school uniform played a part in this, promoting a positive sense of community identity. It also ensured that pupils did not feel disadvantaged because they could not afford the latest designer clothes and made them less vulnerable to being teased because of the clothes they were wearing. All pupils had to wear a V-neck jumper (bought from the school), a school tie, a white shirt and black shoes. Girls could choose between wearing a navy-blue skirt, trousers or shalwar kameez, all in the regulation design. If they wanted to, they could also wear a lightweight navy-blue hijab, or Islamic headscarf. These rules had been carefully thought through in consultation with parents, pupils, staff and the imams of local mosques. It was also carefully explained to parents and pupils before they entered the school.

On 2 September 2002, the day when the school returned from its summer holidays, Mr Moore, the deputy head, had a difficult encounter. Shabina Begum was a pupil of Bangladeshi Muslim heritage, whose parents were both dead. She had been at the school for two years, wearing the shalwar kameez without complaint, but she was now aged nearly fourteen. She had turned up at school with her older brother and another young man, wearing a jilbab – a long, loose, black garment which conceals the shape of the female body, arms and legs. They asked to see the head teacher, but she was not available, so they saw her deputy. They demanded that Shabina be allowed to wear the jilbab and threatened legal proceedings if she was not. Mr Moore told her to go home and change into the school uniform and return properly dressed. Despite the school's efforts to persuade her, she never did so. In her view, at her age, this was what her religion required of her. Her brother did say that he would not allow her to go to school if she could not wear the jilbab, but it was accepted that her views were sincerely held. She had an older sister at the school, who had always worn the shalwar kameez and continued to do so after reaching the age of fourteen.

The school took independent advice from a variety of sources and was reassured that the school uniform did not offend against the Islamic dress code. The Muslim Council of Britain made a statement that there was no recommended style of dress for women; modesty must be observed at all times; trousers with long tops or shirts for school wear were 'absolutely fine'. So the school maintained its stance. There were two local schools where Shabina would have been allowed to wear her jilbab and there was also an all-girls' school where the problem would not have arisen. But for some reason, these possibilities were not taken up while Shabina was still insisting on her right to attend Denbigh High School wearing a jilbab. It was not until some two years later, after Shabina had taken the school to court, that she was admitted to a school where she was allowed to wear her jilbab.

Shabina brought legal proceedings against the school, complaining that it had interfered with her right to manifest her religion under article 9 of the European Convention on Human Rights and had also denied her right to an education under article 2 of the First Protocol to the Convention. This prompted a number of Muslim girls at the school to tell Mrs Bevan that they did not want to wear the jilbab and were afraid of being pressurised into wearing it if the school allowed this. Some of them did not want to be associated with what they saw as an extremist group. Mrs Bevan and Mr Moore, and some parents, were worried that this would lead to distinctions between Muslim girls according to the perceived strictness of their views, which would be contrary to the sense of communal identity which the school tried to promote.

What do you think?

1. Did the school interfere with Shabina's right to 'manifest her religion', given that there were other schools to which she could have gone?
2. If they did, was the interference justified 'for the protection of the rights and freedoms of others', specifically the other girls in the school who did not want to wear a jilbab?
3. Do you think that school uniform is a good thing, fostering community and protecting against disadvantage, or a bad thing, preventing young people from wearing what they feel most comfortable in and can afford?
4. Would your views of this case be the same without the religious dimension, if, for example, Shabina had wanted to go to school in frayed jeans, which were also not allowed?

What did the court think?

The case went all the way to the Appellate Committee of the House of Lords, the highest court in the UK before the Supreme Court took over in 2009.[3] Three out of the five Law Lords held that this was not an interference with Shabina's right to manifest her religion, because she had chosen to go to the school knowing what the dress code was and she would have had no difficulty in going to another school where she could have worn a jilbab. Two out of the five Law Lords thought that it was an interference – the possibility of going elsewhere is not always an answer. But all five of the Law Lords held that the interference was justified to protect the rights and freedoms of the other pupils who did not wish to wear the jilbab. Nor had Shabina's right to education been infringed, as it was her decision not to attend Denbigh High School and there were other schools which she could have attended.

The case was all about Shabina's freedom of choice. But how free were her choices? She was not an adult when the proceedings were brought, so they were brought in her name by her older brother as litigation friend, the same brother who had taken her to school on 2 September 2002 and insisted that she be allowed to wear the jilbab. Yet she was represented in court by Cherie Booth QC and Carolyn Hamilton, Director of the Children's Legal Centre, who thought that it was her choice to bring the proceedings. But was it her choice to insist on wearing the jilbab? Who knows? As I pointed, we can readily assume that an adult woman who wishes to wear Islamic dress in this country has made a free choice – there are many reasons why she might wish to do so – 'as a mark of her defiant political identity and also as a way of regaining control over her body':

'But schools are different. Their task is to educate the young from all the many and diverse families and communities in this country . . . Their task is to help all their pupils achieve their full potential. This includes growing up to play whatever part they choose in the society in which they are living. The school's task is also to promote the ability of people of diverse races, religions and cultures to live together in harmony . . . Like it or not, this is a society committed, in principle and in law, to equal freedom for men and women to choose how they will lead their lives within the law. Young girls from ethnic, cultural or religious minorities growing up here face particularly difficult choices: how far to adopt or to distance themselves from the dominant culture. A good school will enable and support them. This particular school is a good school.'

You could say that Shabina Begum's case was about her freedom of choice. But you could also say that it was about how far people from religious minorities should be expected to conform to majority views. And what if what used to be a majority view has now become a minority one?

Corporal punishment in schools

Until 1987, schoolteachers had the right to inflict corporal punishment upon their pupils. Many schools did so and some even authorised the older pupils to punish the younger ones. These punishments were supposed to be only 'reasonable chastisement' but views of what was reasonable varied greatly – over time and from place to place. Again, many schools believed that this was an effective way to get their pupils to do as they were told, although there were also many schools where such punishments were never, or hardly ever, used. Again, some of the schools which used corporal punishment had religious reasons for doing so. But in 1987, corporal punishment was banned in all State schools, and for all State-funded pupils in independent schools. Then in 1998 the ban was extended to all schools, including independent schools which took no money from the State.

Janet and John were pupils at a small independent school run by devout Christians, who believed that Christian education involved strict observance of the Bible. 'As part of our beliefs we believe it is an integral part of the teaching and education of children both by their parents, and by teachers, that physical discipline should be administered if and when appropriate.' This was not the sort of savage beating described in *Tom Brown's School Days* in the nineteenth century or more recent films depicting school life in the twentieth century, such as *If* and *Kes*. In this school, corporal punishment for boys meant 'administering a thin, broad flat "paddle" to both buttocks simultaneously in a firm, controlled manner'. Girls might be strapped on the hand by a female teacher (how many times is not made clear). The child would then be comforted by a member of staff, encouraged to pray, and given time to compose himself or herself before returning to class. In practice, the schools said, it was hardly ever necessary: the possibility was deterrent enough.

Let's imagine that John and Janet were relieved that the new law meant that it would never happen to them. But then they learned that their parents and teachers were taking the Government to court, complaining that the law interfered with the adults' 'freedom to manifest their religion or belief, in worship, teaching, practice and observance', protected by article 9 of the European Convention on Human Rights. Janet and John wondered whether there would be anybody at court to speak up for the children and their rights.

What do you think?

1. Is inflicting corporal punishment in school, or sending your child to a school which does this, a 'manifestation' of the sort of religious beliefs described above?
2. Does prohibiting schools from doing this 'interfere' in the parents' rights if the parents can still do it themselves?
3. Is the ban justified for the protection of the rights and freedoms of the children? Everyone has the right not to be hit. Should this include children?
4. There is still an exception for parents in England, who can impose 'reasonable chastisement' on their children, provided that this does not cause them actual bodily harm. Should this exception be abolished?

What did the court think?

The House of Lords held that it was not for the courts to decide whether the parents' and teachers' beliefs were consistent with biblical teaching: so the trial judge had been wrong critically to examine the theology.[4] The courts had only to decide whether their religious beliefs were genuinely held. The beliefs in question were genuinely held and prohibiting corporal punishment did interfere with the parents' and teachers' rights to manifest those beliefs. However, the interference was justified for the protection of the rights and freedoms of children; it had the legitimate aim of promoting the welfare of children by protecting them from the deliberate infliction of physical violence on them; the adverse effect upon the parents' manifestation of their beliefs was not disproportionate.

But I pointed out the curiosity:

'... This is, and has always been, a case about children, their rights and the rights of their parents and teachers. Yet there has been no one here or in the courts below to speak on behalf of the children ... The battle has been fought on ground selected by the adults ... This has clouded and over-complicated what should have been a simple issue ...

'The practice of corporal punishment involves what would otherwise be an assault upon another person. The essential question, therefore, has always been whether the legislation achieves a fair balance between the rights and freedoms of the parents and teachers and the rights, freedoms and interests, not only of their children, but also of any other children who might be affected by the persistence of corporal punishment in some schools.'

I went on to quote the 'array of international and professional support' for a ban on institutional corporal punishment (which no one else had mentioned) and concluded that 'If a child has a right to be brought up without institutional violence, as he does, that right should be respected whether or not his parents and teachers believe otherwise.'

Lessons learnt?

We have been looking at cases dealing with school rules and discipline. We have learned that children are entitled to be treated with basic fairness. We have learned that they and their parents are obliged to comply with the school rules on attendance. We have learned that school rules on such things as uniform have to balance the beliefs and wishes of individual children (or their families) against the best interests of the school community as a whole. We have learned that children have the same right as other people not to be subjected to institutional violence. All of this shows that children are people, with many of the same basic rights that other people have.

But it also shows that children are entitled to more than that. They cannot be left to fend entirely for themselves. They have to be provided with their basic needs – not only for food, shelter and nurture, but also with an education which will give them the tools for adult life. Exactly how much should be provided by the State and how much left to the family is a political question which the courts cannot answer. But once the political question has been answered, the courts can, and should, see that children get what they are entitled to and that their voices are heard.

10 Disabled People Have Rights

We have had laws prohibiting discrimination on grounds of race and sex since the 1970s. The object is to stop people and enterprises – providers of jobs, housing, goods and services – treating some individuals less well than they would treat others because of their sex or race: in other words, to make them treat everyone equally unless there is a very good reason for treating them differently. Women should be treated the same as men, men the same as women, white people the same as people of colour, people of colour the same as white people.

We have also had laws prohibiting discrimination on grounds of disability since the 1990s. They too prevent providers from treating people with disabilities less well than they would treat non-disabled people unless there is a very good reason. But they go further than that. We used to hear a lot about levelling up – which seems to mean giving the less advantaged parts of the country a helping hand to bring them up to the level of the more advantaged parts of the country. No easy task. But people with disabilities sometimes need a helping hand to bring them up to where the people without those disabilities are, creating a level playing field so that they have the same chance to flourish in life as everyone else has. So sometimes the providers of jobs, housing, goods and services have to make reasonable adjustments to cater for the needs of people with disabilities; in other words, to treat them differently from people without disabilities. Working out when and how to do this is also no easy task, as three of these stories show.

Quite apart from the law against discrimination, now contained in the Equality Act 2010, we also have the Human Rights Act 1998. This protects the fundamental rights which everyone ought to have, such as freedom from torture or inhuman or degrading treatment or punishment, from invasion by the State. And the State must not discriminate between people in the enjoyment of those rights for a variety of reasons, including sex, race and disability. So two of these stories illustrate how the Human Rights Act can help people with disabilities.

Wheelchairs versus buggies

Doug Paulley was a wheelchair user. He lived in Wetherby, a historic town in West Yorkshire, north-east of Leeds. On 24 February 2012, he was going to travel to Stalybridge, a town on the other side of the Pennines, to have lunch with his parents. The journey required meticulous planning. First, he would catch the 9.40 a.m. bus from Wetherby to Leeds. Then he would catch a train from Leeds to Stalybridge. But when he arrived at the bus station in Wetherby, he was unable to board the bus. The bus was equipped for wheelchairs. It had a lowering platform and a ramp. It had a space where the wheelchair could go, with a sign which read, 'Please give up this space if needed for a wheelchair user.' But the space was occupied by a woman with a sleeping child in a pushchair. The bus driver asked the woman to fold down her pushchair and move out of the space. She refused, saying that her pushchair did not fold down. Mr Paulley then asked whether he could fold down his wheelchair and use an ordinary seat on the bus. The driver refused, saying that there was no safe way of securing the wheelchair. He made no attempt to persuade the woman to move. He did not suggest that the law required her to do so. So Mr Paulley could not get on the bus. He had to wait for the next one. This meant that he missed his train in Leeds. He arrived in Stalybridge an hour later than planned.

The driver was following the bus company's policy. At the time, this said that 'other passengers are asked to give up the space for wheelchairs' but also that 'wheelchairs do not have priority over buggies . . . Unfortunately, if a fellow passenger refuses to move you will need to wait for the next bus.' The company had adopted this policy to be 'user-friendly', because they had been told that passengers thought that they were putting up too many peremptory notices on buses. But their Bus Projects Manager gave evidence that 'there was no reason why the signs which were in the form of a request could not be worded differently so as to make it clear to all passengers that wheelchair users not only had such priority but that such priority would be enforced'.

There are detailed regulations which require the providers of public transport to provide access to wheelchair spaces in public service vehicles. There are also regulations requiring bus drivers and conductors to allow a wheelchair user to board if there is a wheelchair space which is not occupied (a) by another wheelchair user, or (b) by passengers and/or luggage which cannot reasonably be moved to another part of the bus. Passengers are prohibited from putting at risk, or unreasonably impeding, or causing discomfort to, other passengers, and can be removed from the bus if they do. A driver or passenger who breaks these regulations is guilty of a crime. Finally, and most important, bus companies are guilty of discrimination if they fail to make reasonable adjustments to cater for people with disabilities. They fail to make reasonable adjustments if they have a 'provision, criterion or practice' which puts disabled people at a substantial disadvantage in comparison with people who are not disabled and don't take reasonable steps to avoid that disadvantage.

So Mr Paulley took the bus company to court for discriminating against him as a disabled person by failing to make reasonable adjustments for him.

What do you think?

1. Should the bus company have changed its policy?
2. If so, what should it have said?
3. What should the bus driver have done?

What did the court think?

The county court judge found that the bus company had failed in its duty to make reasonable adjustments for Mr Paulley and awarded him damages. The Court of Appeal overturned that decision, but the Supreme Court allowed his appeal.[1] You may think it strange – absurd even – that a dispute which meant that Mr Paulley was an hour late for lunch in Stalybridge should end up in the Supreme Court. But there was a serious point of principle involved. Imagine how difficult it is to get about and lead an ordinary life if you cannot walk. Every outing, to the shops, to work, to social events, requires careful planning to make sure that it will be possible. You need to know whether the pavements will be navigable, whether there will be ramps to get into the buildings, whether the trains and buses will be accessible. The bus company not only had a legal duty to provide an accessible wheelchair space, it also had a duty to make reasonable adjustments to cater for Mr Paulley's disability. In this case it could and should have done more to ensure that the wheelchair space was available for him. So he won the case. The principle was established that providers of public transport must not only have spaces available for wheelchairs but also do all they can reasonably be expected to do to enable wheelchair users to use them.

The court made clear the point of principle, but it did not restore the county court judge's award of damages: it had not been proved whether it was the company's failure to try harder or the woman's intransigence which caused the loss. This was a majority decision with which I strongly disagreed – the driver was entitled to insist that the woman got off the bus if she wasn't prepared to move. You may, of course, think that the law should also require reasonable adjustments to be made to cater for children in buggies but at present it does not do so.

The road sweeper who could no longer sweep

Mrs Susan Archibald was employed by Fife Council in Scotland as a road sweeper. This was on Industrial Grade 1. After she had been in the job for nearly two years, disaster struck. A very rare complication following a spinal anaesthetic for a minor surgical procedure led to severe pain over her heels. She was no longer able to walk and sweep. At first she was confined to a wheelchair and later had to use sticks to enable her to get about. She would not be able to carry out the job of road sweeper for the foreseeable future. She could, however, take sedentary work and was keen to do so. The council arranged for her to do a number of computer and administration courses to equip her with the appropriate skills. She was assessed as being 'more than capable of carrying out work in an office environment'. So she applied for more than a hundred posts with the council. These were all on the APT&C (Administrative, Professional, Technical & Clerical) scale rather than on the industrial scale, although the basic salary on the lowest APT&C grade was only marginally higher than that on Industrial Grade 1.

According to the council's usual redeployment policy, people seeking redeployment at a higher grade had to undergo competitive interviews. Mrs Archibald failed them all. She felt that this was because they were still seeing her as a street sweeper – someone coming from an industrial background who was having to compete with people coming from a staff background. Eventually, as she was still unable to work as a street sweeper and had not been offered any other job, she was dismissed. She complained to an employment tribunal that the council had not made reasonable adjustments for her disability. She should not have been required to go through competitive interviews if she could show that she was qualified and suitable for the vacancy in question.

If any arrangements made by an employer place a particular disabled person at a substantial disadvantage compared with people who are not disabled, the employer has to take reasonable steps to prevent the arrangements having that effect. Among the examples given of steps an employer might take is transferring the employee to fill an existing vacancy.

What do you think?

1. Should Mrs Archibald be compared with other street sweepers? If so, there was nothing the council could do to enable her to keep her job.
2. Or should Mrs Archibald be compared with other people working for the council? If so, what steps might it be reasonable for the council to take?
3. In particular, is it reasonable to expect them to waive their usual requirement of competitive interviews in circumstances like these?

What did the court think?

This story has a happy ending. The House of Lords, then the highest court in the United Kingdom, held that there was still a duty to make reasonable adjustments, even if a person became so disabled that she could never do the job for which she had been employed.[2] She could be transferred to a job which she was able to do if it was reasonable to do so. It might be reasonable to expect the council to waive its competitive interview policy for transfer to a higher grade in order to meet the needs of a well-qualified and well-motivated employee who had become disabled. The case was sent back to the employment tribunal for them to consider whether this was reasonable. Mrs Archibald succeeded in her claim and since then has gone from strength to strength as a disability rights campaigner and advocate.

The difficult tenant

Jonathan Ackerman-Livingstone was a highly intelligent and gifted man who suffered from chronic and severe mental ill health as a result of sustained physical and emotional abuse by his parents when he was a child and the failure of the system to protect him properly from it. A chartered psychologist described him as 'very vulnerable' and 'desperately in need of intensive therapy to help overcome the traumas' which he had suffered. The psychologist later commented that 'we are not dealing here with a man who thinks and behaves in a reasonable and socially acceptable way but with someone who is profoundly mentally ill and who needs help'.

He became homeless in 2010 and his local council arranged for him to take a tenancy from a housing association of a one-bedroom flat in a small block of flats in Glastonbury. This was meant as a temporary measure, until a more permanent home could be found. Over the next nine months, various attempts were made. No fewer than eleven properties were considered. One of the difficulties was that several of the properties which became available were in Wells, to which he objected because he associated it with his childhood abuse, and in this he was supported by his community psychiatric nurse. Another property was too far away from his GP. Eventually, he was made a final offer of a property in Street. Street also had associations with his childhood abuse and he declined the offer.

The local council considered that they had done all they could and terminated his temporary accommodation. The housing association served him with notice to quit and brought proceedings to evict him.

Mr Ackerman-Livingstone then made a fresh homelessness application and the local council, having reviewed matters, agreed that the previous offers had not been suitable, so they accepted that he was not intentionally homeless. The eviction proceedings were paused. But then they made an offer of permanent accommodation in the very same street where he was living in Glastonbury and Mr Ackerman-Livingstone turned that down too. The eviction proceedings were restarted. The chartered psychologist commented that, 'It is impossible to say definitively that [his] inaction and/or failure was *wholly* attributable to his condition, but I would say that his condition appears likely to have played a major part in this inaction and/or failure.' His mental disability was such that he could not make a decision.

In addition to the duty to make reasonable adjustments, there is a special sort of disability discrimination (in the Equality Act 2010). If a landlord (or other provider) treats a disabled person unfavourably 'because of something arising in consequence of his disability', the landlord (or other provider) has to show that 'the treatment is a proportionate means of achieving a legitimate aim'. In other words, a landlord may sometimes have to treat a disabled person more favourably than he would treat a person who was not disabled. A fair balance has to be struck between the landlord's need to achieve its objectives and the impact upon the disabled person.

What do you think?

1. Do you think that the housing association was evicting Mr Ackerman-Livingstone 'because of something arising in consequence of his disability' (note, not 'because of his disability')?
2. If so, which would weigh more heavily with you: the housing association's need to regain the property or the effect upon Mr Ackerman-Livingstone of making him homeless?

What did the court think?

The county court judge had thought the case so easy that he had granted the eviction order without listening to the arguments. The

Supreme Court held that he should not have done so.³ The landlord had to show either (a) that the eviction was not because of something arising in consequence of Mr Ackerman-Livingstone's disability, or (b) that if it was for that reason, eviction was nevertheless a proportionate means of achieving a legitimate aim. It could not be taken for granted that vindicating the landlord's property rights and enabling the local authority to fulfil its housing obligations would outweigh the tenant's right to have due allowances made for his disability. So that argument should have been had.

However, there was now no point, and it would be no kindness to Mr Ackerman-Livingstone to send the case back to the county court. Aster Communities only had a lease of the property and the freehold owner had ended the lease because it wanted to sell the property. In the circumstances, evicting Mr Ackerman-Livingstone was inevitable. (It is not clear whether the property he had been offered in the same street was still available, but let's hope that it was.)

The bedroom tax

In 2012, as part of its austerity measures, the Government made new regulations reducing the amount of housing benefit payable to tenants of social housing if they had more bedrooms than the regulations said they needed. The Government called this the 'removal of the spare room subsidy' but most people called it the bedroom tax. If a household had one bedroom too many, the benefit was reduced by 14 per cent. If they had two or more bedrooms too many, it was reduced by 25 per cent.

Mr and Mrs Carmichael lived in a two-bedroom flat. Mrs Carmichael had spina bifida and hydrocephalus and was doubly incontinent. She needed a special bed with an electronic mattress because she was unable to bear weight and had recurring pressure sores. She also needed to have a wheelchair by the bed. She could not share a bed with her husband and there wasn't space for them to have two beds in the same room. The regulations said that married couples must share a room, so they had one bedroom too many.

Mrs Rutherford lived in a three-bedroom house with her husband and her teenage grandson, Warren. Warren suffered from profound mental and physical disabilities and she had looked after him since he was a few months old. The house had been adapted to suit their needs. Respite care was provided by carers who stayed overnight for two nights each week. They needed a bedroom. Without their help, Mr and Mrs Rutherford would not be able to cope and Warren would have to go into a care home. The regulations said that the household only needed two bedrooms.

James Daly lived in a two-bedroom property. His son Rian was severely disabled, used a wheelchair and had other health problems including incontinence. Rian's parents were separated and they shared his care. Rian stayed with his father every weekend, for at least one day during the week and for part of the school holidays. The regulations said that Mr Daly only needed one bedroom.

Housing benefit counts as a possession for the purpose of article 1 of the First Protocol to the European Convention on Human Rights, which says that no one shall be deprived of his possessions except in the public interest. Article 14 of the Convention says that the enjoyment of this right, and all the rights in the Convention, must be secured without discrimination on a list of grounds which includes disability. Discrimination means treating people differently when they should be treated the same or treating people the same when they should be treated differently. All these people complained that, because of their disabilities, they should have been treated differently from other households.

What do you think?

1. Do you think that Mr and Mrs Carmichael should have been allowed two bedrooms? (By the way, although two children under ten, and two children of the same sex under sixteen, were normally expected to share a room, an exception was made if, because one of the children was disabled, they could not do so.)
2. Do you think that Mr and Mrs Rutherford should have been allowed three bedrooms? (By the way, an exception was made if a disabled adult required overnight carers.)
3. Do you think that Mr Daly should have been allowed two bedrooms?

4. As well as housing benefit, there are discretionary housing payments which local authorities can make to people whose housing benefit is not sufficient for their needs. The local authority can decide whether or not to make such payments and only has a fixed pot of money from which to make them. Does this affect any of your answers?

What did the court think?

Discrimination in the enjoyment of a Convention right means a difference in treatment (or a lack of difference in treatment) which is not justified as a 'proportionate means of achieving a legitimate aim'. Where entitlement to State benefits is involved, the Supreme Court had held in an earlier case that a difference in treatment (or a lack of difference in treatment) would be justified unless it was 'manifestly without reasonable foundation'.[4] This is a tough test and the Supreme Court applied it to these and some other bedroom tax cases.[5] The court held that the test was satisfied if there was a 'transparent medical need' for another bedroom. So Mr and Mrs Carmichael won because Mrs Carmichael's disability meant that they could not share a bedroom. And Mr and Mrs Rutherford won because their grandson needed an overnight carer. But the regulations couldn't cater for every situation and where there was no such 'transparent medical need', it was reasonable for the need to be assessed on a case-by-case basis under the discretionary housing payments scheme. So Mr Daly lost.

But do you think that Mr Daly should also have won? It is often in the best interests of a disabled child (or indeed any child) that his parents share the responsibility of looking after him. This gives each of them a break and enables the child to feel loved and wanted by both his parents. Is it manifestly without reasonable foundation to fail to recognise this?

The thalidomide prisoner

The disabilities are escalating in their severity. Now we get to the worst. Ms Price was a thalidomide victim. Thalidomide is a drug which was originally developed as a tranquilliser. It was prescribed to pregnant women who suffered from pregnancy ('morning') sickness. But it turned out that the drug caused serious birth defects in babies born to mothers who had taken it. In particular, they might have no, or only very short, arms and legs. Ms Price had no proper arms or legs and also suffered from kidney problems. She was also a very strong character. In the afternoon of 20 January 1995, she appeared before Lincoln county court for non-payment of a debt. As a general rule, people cannot be sent to prison for non-payment of a debt – it is not a crime. But they can be required to appear before a judge to answer questions about their financial circumstances so that the judge can decide how they should be ordered to pay. Ms Price appeared before the judge but refused to answer questions. Failing to obey court orders is contempt of court, a crime for which a person can be sent to prison, although usually only for a short time in circumstances such as these. The judge sent her to prison for seven days and the remission rules meant that she would only have to serve three and a half days. The judge did not make any inquiries about where she would be sent or whether that place would be capable of coping with her complex needs.

It was too late to take her to the prison in Wakefield and so she spent the night in the cells at Lincoln police station. She was refused permission to take the battery charger for her wheelchair with her. There was a wooden bed and mattress in her cell, but she felt she could not use it because it would be too hard, so she stayed in her wheelchair. She kept complaining of the cold and a headache and asked to see a doctor. She told the doctor that at home she slept sitting up on a sofa. The doctor noted that she needed a very warm room – which this was not – because she was unable to move around. But she refused offers of food and a hot drink.

The next day she was transferred to a women's prison in Wakefield where she was admitted to the healthcare centre. This was better than the police cell, but there were still problems – with reaching the bed and the toilet, with hygiene and fluid intake, and with mobility if the battery of her wheelchair ran down. In particular, the nurse on night duty had to seek the help of two male officers to get her on and off the toilet. The prison governor authorised staff to try and find a hospital to take her, but this could not be done. Before she was released, she needed catheterisation because lack of fluid intake and the problems of getting to the toilet had caused urine retention.

After her release she was advised that it would be difficult to prove a claim against the Home Office (which was then responsible for prisons) and that, even if she did, the damages were unlikely to be more than £3,000, so her legal aid was withdrawn. She then brought a claim against the United Kingdom in the European Court of Human Rights in Strasbourg. She claimed that sending her to prison, and her treatment while she was detained, had violated her rights under article 3 of the European Convention on Human Rights. This says that 'No one shall be subjected to torture or to inhuman or degrading treatment or punishment.'

What do you think?

1. Was her punishment inhuman or degrading?
2. What else might the judge, the police or the prison have done?
3. Was it all her own fault? Does that matter?

What did the court think?

The European Court of Human Rights held that Ms Price had been subjected to inhuman or degrading treatment, sufficiently severe to meet the high threshold for a finding that article 3 of the Convention had been breached.[6] The court accepted that there was no evidence of an intention to humiliate or debase her. But it considered that detaining a disabled person in conditions where she was dangerously cold, risked developing sores because her bed was too hard or unreachable, was unable to go to the toilet or keep clean without the greatest of difficulty (including the need for male prison officers to lift her on and off the toilet), constituted degrading treatment. The British judge on the court added that in his view the primary responsibility lay not with the police and prison authorities but with the judge who sentenced her to an immediate period of imprisonment without ensuring that there were adequate facilities available to meet her special needs. She was awarded £4,500 damages.

Lessons learnt?

Let's hope that the first lesson we have learned is that the Human Rights Act 1998 is a very good thing. Ms Price could not seek a remedy in the UK courts for the degrading treatment she had suffered at the hands of the British State because it all took place before the Act was passed. So she had to go to the European Court of Human Rights in Strasbourg. The object of the Act was to 'bring rights home' and spare people like her the trouble, the expense and the delay involved in going to Strasbourg. It meant that Mr and Mrs Carmichael and Mr and Mrs Rutherford could challenge the regulations which deprived them of the accommodation they needed to look after their seriously disabled family members in the UK courts.

We have also learned that it is not always right to treat everyone alike. Some people may need to be treated differently from others because of their disability. But the object of treating them differently is to level the playing field – to enable them to play the same part in society as people without disabilities. So Mrs Archibald could get a job which she was able to do and Mr Paulley could get about the country to see his parents.

But working out how far it is necessary to go to level the playing field is not easy, as all these cases show – and perhaps none more clearly than Mr Ackerman-Livingstone who must have tried everyone's patience sorely. But the judge should have given his case a hearing. That's always a lesson.

11   LGBTQ+ People Have Rights

How quickly things can change! Until 1967, most of the things which gay men enjoyed doing with one another were criminal, as was soliciting another person for that purpose. Policemen used to lurk in public toilets to catch men out. Lives were ruined. Even after homosexual acts between two people aged twenty-one or over in private were legalised in 1967, engaging in them was seen as a blackmail risk, so gay men could not become, say, spies or judges. From 1988 until 2003, local authorities were banned from promoting homosexuality or 'the teaching in any maintained school of the acceptability of homosexuality as a pretended family relationship'. (What was the word 'pretended' doing in that sentence?) But the tide had already begun to turn. In 2002, gay and lesbian couples were allowed to adopt children jointly. In 2005 they could enter into civil partnerships which gave them almost all the same rights and responsibilities as married couples. In 2008 a lesbian couple could agree that they would both be legal parents of a child born as a result of fertility treatment in a licensed clinic. And in 2013 gay and lesbian couples could get married.

That does not mean that all the problems have gone away. People have been protected against discrimination on grounds of their sexual orientation since 2007; but others have been protected against discrimination on grounds of their religion or belief. So the Supreme Court has twice had to think about how to balance the two. And one of the most toxic debates of all is around the rights of trans persons – in particular whether there is a conflict between the rights of trans women and the rights of born women. But there are also some people who do not want to identify as being of either sex and, even more compellingly, some people who cannot do so because they were born with the characteristics of both.

The gay couple and the Christian hotel-keepers

Steven Preddy and Martyn Hall were a gay couple, living in Bristol, who had entered into a civil partnership. They planned a short break in Cornwall. On 4 September 2008, Mr Preddy made a telephone booking of a double room for the nights of 5 and 6 September at the Chymorvah private hotel in Marazion and paid a deposit. The hotel was owned by Peter and Hazelmary Bull, a married couple who ran it with their cousin, Mr Quinn. They were devout Christians, who believed that 'the only divinely ordained sexual relationship is that between a man and a woman in marriage'. Their online booking form stated that, 'Out of a deep regard for marriage we prefer to let double accommodation to heterosexual married couples only.' They would let single and twin-bedded rooms to anyone, regardless of marital status or sexual orientation, but they would not let double-bedded rooms to couples who were not married to one another, whether they were homosexual or heterosexual.

Mr Preddy did not see the online booking form, because he booked over the telephone. When she took the booking, Mrs Bull did not ask whether the reservation was for a man and wife, as she usually did, because she wasn't well and had had to get out of bed to answer the telephone. When Mr Preddy and Mr Bull arrived at the hotel on 5 September, they were told by Mr Quinn that double-bedded rooms were only for married couples. It made no difference that the couple were in a civil partnership. Mr Quinn explained that they were Christians and didn't believe in civil partnerships so they couldn't honour the booking. He was perfectly polite about it, but there were other people present. The couple left the hotel and found other (more expensive) accommodation and their deposit was refunded, but they found the whole episode 'very hurtful'.

Mr Preddy and Mr Hall brought a discrimination claim against Mr and Mrs Bull, arguing that they had been treated unfavourably because of their sexual orientation. Mr and Mrs Bull argued that they had not been treated unfavourably because of their sexual orientation but because they were not married to one another; an unmarried heterosexual couple would have been treated in the same way. They also argued that prohibiting them from refusing double-bedded rooms to unmarried or same-sex couples would interfere with their right to manifest their religion, protected by article 9 of the European Convention on Human Rights.

What do you think?

1. Were Mr Preddy and Mr Hall denied a double-bedded room because they were gay or because they were not married to one another?
2. In 2008, gay couples could not get married. In 2013, they could. What do you think Mr and Mrs Hall would have said if Mr Preddy and Mr Hall had been married? (Does that make a difference to your answer to question 1?)
3. Do you think that people running a business offering services to the public should be able to refuse to serve a customer if to do so would offend their religious beliefs?
4. Does this apply to any customer or only those with a 'protected characteristic' such as sex, race, sexual orientation, etc.?
5. The Equality and Human Rights Commission supported the claim brought by Mr Preddy and Mr Bull. This was a case of conflicting rights. Should the commission have supported this claim? Can you think of a good reason why they should choose one right over the other?

What did the court think?

It is 'direct' discrimination when a person treats another person less favourably than they treat or would treat others because of that person's sexual orientation. In this case, three out of the five justices in the Supreme Court held that this was direct discrimination, because civil partnership was indistinguishable from marriage in law but the hotelkeepers insisted on marriage which at the time was only available to opposite-sex couples.[1] (They also limited their double-bedded rooms to 'heterosexual married couples only', so it seems likely that even had Mr Preddy and Mr Hall been married, they would have been refused the room.)

It is 'indirect' discrimination when a provider applies a 'provision, criterion or practice' which puts people of a particular sexual orientation at a disadvantage. The other two justices held that this was a criterion which put same-sex couples at a serious disadvantage compared with opposite-sex couples.

Direct discrimination can only be justified on limited defined grounds (which didn't apply here) whereas indirect discrimination can be justified if there is a good reason for the provision, criterion or practice independent of its discriminatory effect. All five of the justices would have held that this criterion was not justified. They also held that this conclusion was not incompatible with the hotel-keepers' right to manifest their religion as it was a proportionate means of protecting the rights and freedoms of others. If you provide a service to the public you must not discriminate against people with a protected characteristic.

The Christian cake-makers

Mr and Mrs McArthur and their son Daniel ran a bakery business in Belfast. They called it the Ashers Baking Company after the reference in the Bible: 'Bread from Asher shall be rich and he shall yield royal dainties.' They were devout Christians who believed that the only form of full sexual expression consistent with the Bible and acceptable to God was within marriage, and the only form of marriage consistent with the Bible and acceptable to God was between a man and a woman. But they did not make their beliefs, or the biblical connection of their name, known to the public. They had no objection to serving gay customers or to employing gay people. The bakery offered a bespoke 'Build a Cake' service to customers, who could request particular images or messages to be iced onto a cake. The leaflet which advertised this did not mention any religious restrictions.

Gay marriage had become lawful in Great Britain in 2013 but that law did not extend to Northern Ireland: it was a matter for the Northern Ireland Assembly to decide. The Assembly had just narrowly rejected a motion supporting gay marriage. QueerSpace, an organisation for the LGBT community in Belfast, was having a party to mark the end of Northern Ireland anti-homophobia week. Gareth Lee was a gay man who volunteered with QueerSpace. He decided to take a cake to the party.

He went into an Ashers shop and placed an order and paid for a bespoke cake, iced with the Muppet characters Bert and Ernie, the QueerSpace logo, and the headline 'Support Gay Marriage'. Mrs McArthur took the order and made no objection at the time, because she wanted to think about how to explain things to Mr Lee and spare him embarrassment. A few days later she telephoned Mr Lee and explained that they could not fulfil his order because they were a Christian business and could not ice the slogan he had requested. She apologised and his money was refunded. He was able to obtain a similar cake from another bakery to take with him to the party.

Mr Lee claimed that Ashers had discriminated against him on the ground of sexual orientation or on the ground of religious belief or political opinion. It is unlawful in Northern Ireland, but not in Great Britain, to discriminate on the ground of political opinion. The bakery denied this, arguing that they would have refused to supply a cake bearing that message to anyone, whether or not they were gay. They also argued that their right to freedom of expression, protected by article 10 of the European Convention on Human Rights, included the right, not only to express the views which they *did* hold, but also *not* to express the views with which they profoundly disagreed.

What do you think?

1. Did Ashers discriminate against Mr Lee or his friends because they were gay?
2. Did Ashers discriminate against Mr Lee because of his political opinion?
3. Should Ashers' right not to express views with which its owners profoundly disagreed outweigh Mr Lee's right not to be discriminated against because of his political opinion?
4. The Equality Commission for Northern Ireland supported Mr Lee's claim. This too was a case of conflicting rights. Should the commission have supported Mr Lee?
5. Mr Lee relied solely on the laws in Northern Ireland which protect against discrimination on grounds both of sexual orientation and of religious belief or political opinion. He did not complain that he had been discriminated against in his enjoyment of the

right to respect for his private life, protected by article 8 of the European Convention on Human Rights, or of the right to manifest his beliefs, protected by article 9 of the Convention, or of the right to freedom of expression, protected by article 10. Should he have done?

What did the court think?

The Supreme Court held that the bakery had not discriminated against Mr Lee – or against anyone with whom he was associated – because of their sexual orientation; the bakery would have refused to supply the cake to anyone, gay or straight; it was the message that they objected to and not the customer.[2]

It might be said that they had discriminated against Mr Lee because of his political opinion; but the relevant provision in Northern Ireland law had to be read compatibly with the McArthurs' rights under article 10 of the European Convention on Human Rights, not to be made to express an opinion with which they profoundly disagreed.

Mr Lee then complained to the European Court of Human Rights in Strasbourg that the United Kingdom had breached his right to respect for his private life, under article 8 of the European Convention on Human Rights, his right to freedom of thought, conscience and religion under article 9, his right to freedom of expression under article 10, and his right to enjoy those rights without discrimination under article 14. The Strasbourg Court held that his complaints were inadmissible.[3] It was not self-evident that the facts 'fell within the ambit' of articles 8, 9 or 10 so as to bring article 14 into play. But in any event, Mr Lee had chosen to rely on Northern Ireland's anti-discrimination laws rather than on the Human Rights Act 1998. So the UK courts had not had the opportunity of considering his rights under the Convention and balancing them against the rights of the bakery owners. 'Given the heightened sensitivity of the balancing exercise in this particular national context', the UK courts were better placed to strike this balance than was the European court. In choosing not to rely on his Convention rights, Mr Lee had deprived the UK courts of that opportunity. He had 'failed to exhaust his domestic remedies'.

A trans woman and her pension

Mark Bennett (not his real name) was born a man in 1948. In 1974, he married Susan Bennett (not her real name). But he suffered from gender dysphoria. Eventually in 1991 he began to live as a woman, Mary Bennett, and in 1995 underwent sex reassignment surgery. Mary and Susan continued living together and, for religious reasons, wanted to stay married to one another.

Until 2005, UK law did not recognise a change of sex. Then the Gender Recognition Act 2004 came into force. A person could apply to a gender recognition panel for a gender recognition certificate. This would be granted if the person had or had had gender dysphoria, had fully lived in the gender he or she wanted to acquire for at least two years, and intended to live in that gender for the rest of his or her life. Evidence had to be supplied from a doctor or psychologist practising in the field of gender dysphoria, and another doctor. This would have to give details of the diagnosis and of any treatment or surgery. The law did not require that the applicant had undergone surgery but if they had not, the report would have to explain why not.

When the Gender Recognition Act came into force, UK law did not allow marriages between people of the same sex. This meant that married people who changed sex could not stay married. They could divorce before applying for a certificate or they could be issued with an interim gender recognition certificate. This meant that their marriage could be easily annulled, after which they could have a full gender recognition certificate, which changed their sex for all legal purposes in future.

Mary did not apply for a gender recognition certificate because she and Susan wished to stay married to one another. Once civil partnership was introduced, also in 2005, they might have entered into a civil partnership after their marriage was annulled. But they had religious objections both to the ending of their marriage and to civil partnership. Apart from that, Mary fulfilled all the physical, social and psychological criteria for recognising that she was now a woman.

In 2008, Mary reached the age of sixty, which at that time was the age at which a woman could claim a State retirement pension. Her application was rejected by the Department of Work and Pensions (and by the tribunals) because, as she did not have a gender recognition certificate, she was still a man in the eyes of the law, and not entitled to a pension until she reached sixty-five. She complained that requiring her to end her marriage discriminated against her on the ground of her transgender status, as marital status is irrelevant to the entitlement to a State pension. People who have not changed sex are entitled to a State pension irrespective of whether or not they are married.

What do you think?

1. Should Mary have got her pension at the age of sixty?
2. Since the introduction of gay marriage in 2014, married people who change sex can stay married if their spouse consents. Does this make any difference to your answer to the first question?
3. Note that the evidence that a person is living fully in their acquired gender can include, for example, a driving licence or a passport which has already been issued in that gender. A passport can be issued in the acquired gender if a doctor confirms that the applicant's orientation to their acquired gender is likely to be permanent. The code on a driving licence which indicates the holder's sex can be changed on request. So what practical (as opposed to legal) difference does a gender recognition certificate make?
4. Should medical evidence be required for the issue of a gender recognition certificate? If so, what should it say? Should surgery be required?
5. In another case, the Supreme Court said this: 'Gender dysphoria is ... the overwhelming sense that one has been born into the wrong body, with the wrong anatomy and the wrong physiology. Those of us who, whatever our occasional frustrations with the expectations of society or our own biology, are nevertheless quite secure in the gender identities with which we were born, can scarcely begin to understand how it must be to grow up in the wrong body and then to go through the long and complex process of adapting that body to match the real self. But it does not take much imagination to understand that this

is a deeply personal and private matter; that a person who has undergone gender reassignment will need the whole world to recognise and relate to her or to him in the reassigned gender; and will want to keep to an absolute minimum any unwanted disclosure of the history.'[4] Do you agree?

What did the court think?

This was before Brexit, so the United Kingdom was still a member of the European Union and had to apply European Union law. In Mary's case, the Supreme Court could not decide whether the requirement that a trans person be unmarried before his or her change of sex could be recognised in UK law was contrary to the European Union law which prohibited discrimination on grounds of sex in relation to pensions. The answer was not clear.[5] Where the answer to a question of European Union law is not clear, Member States are required to refer the question to the Court of Justice of the European Union in Luxembourg, so that that court can provide an answer which will apply throughout the European Union. So the Supreme Court asked the Luxembourg court whether the directive prohibiting sex discrimination 'precludes the imposition in national law of a requirement that, in addition to satisfying the physical, social and psychological criteria for recognising a change of gender, a person who has changed gender must also be unmarried in order to qualify for a State retirement pension'. The Grand Chamber of the Luxembourg court answered that question 'yes' – it was precluded.[6] So Mary was entitled to her pension at the age of sixty.

This case was about who is a woman in European Union law. In April 2025, the Supreme Court decided a case about who is a woman in UK law.[7] The appellants challenged guidance issued by the Scottish Ministers under an Act of the Scottish Parliament, the Gender Representation on Public Boards (Scotland) Act 2018. The guidance said that 'woman' in that Act has the same meaning as in the Equality Act 2010 (a UK Act) and includes a person with a gender recognition certificate which recognises her as female. The Supreme Court held that this was wrong. The Gender Recognition Act was qualified by the Equality Act and in that Act 'man' and 'woman' and 'male' and 'female' referred to their sex at birth and not to their acquired gender. What this means for single sex spaces (which are allowed in certain circumstances but not required) is not discussed in the judgment. There are strongly differing views about this but hopefully some middle ground can be found.

Do we need a gender at all?

Christie Elan-Cane (whom for convenience and meaning no disrespect I shall call Christie) was born a girl. But when she grew up she felt revulsion at having a female body. So she underwent a double mastectomy and then a hysterectomy. Christie now identifies as non-gendered and campaigns for the legal recognition of a category of non-gendered people. 'Gender' in this context refers to a person's feelings or choice of sexual identity rather than their biological characteristics.

Passports, however, require a person to be described as 'M' or 'F'. In 1995, Christie contacted the United Kingdom Passport Authority, then the agency of the Home Office dealing with the issue of passports, and enquired whether it was possible for a passport to be issued without describing the holder as 'M' or 'F'. Christie was told that this was not possible and so was issued with a passport with the description 'F'. Later enquiries produced the same result, hence the campaign by Christie and other non-binary people for the introduction of passports with an 'X' marker, to indicate unspecified.

Since at least 2006, the International Civil Aviation Organisation has allowed countries to issue passports with an 'M', 'F' or 'X' marking. Six of the forty-seven members of the Council of Europe do so, although in three cases this is only for people born with ambiguous sexual characteristics (intersex rather than non-binary). New Zealand has done so since 2005, Australia since 2011 and Canada since 2017.

Christie complained that the UK's refusal to introduce an 'X' marking in passports showed a lack of respect for her private life, protected by article 8 of the European Convention on Human Rights, or discriminated between non-binary people and people who were content to be labelled 'M' or 'F' in the enjoyment of that right, contrary to article 14 of the Convention. The Government argued that these markers were important to national security, helping to verify the identity of passport users; that it would be expensive to change the application process; and that it would be anomalous to introduce a non-binary category of passport holders when so much of our law and administration depended on assigning people to one sex or the other.

What do you think?

1. Should Christie and other non-binary people be able to get an 'X' marking in their passports? What harm would it really do?
2. How many laws can you think of which depend upon whether a person is male or female (apart of course from the laws about acquiring or inheriting titles)?
3. What about those public services, such as schools, prisons, hospital wards and refuges, which only admit people of one sex?
4. To what extent do you think that people should be able to identify themselves as male, female or non-binary?

What did the court think?

When the case came before the Supreme Court,[8] it was not disputed that a person's identification as non-gendered was an aspect of private life entitled to respect under article 8 of the European Convention on Human Rights. The State is not allowed to interfere in the exercise of this right unless there is a good justification. But the Supreme Court held that the question was whether article 8 imposed a *positive* obligation on the State to provide an 'X' passport, as opposed to whether denying such a passport interfered with the exercise of the right. The claimant's interest in having an 'X' passport was outweighed by the State's interests in security, saving the significant costs involved, and having a coherent approach across government about whether to recognise gender categories beyond male and female.

But the court went further. As there was no European consensus on this, it was a matter within the 'margin of appreciation' allowed to Member States to decide for themselves what their law should be. An earlier case in the House of Lords had held that the courts, rather than Parliament, could sometimes decide what the UK's approach should be, especially where discrimination is involved.[9] Unlike Great Britain, the law in Northern Ireland prohibited unmarried couples from adopting a child jointly. The House of Lords held that a blanket rule to this effect discriminated against unmarried couples, whether of the same or opposite sexes, and could not be justified as there would be some cases in which it would be in the best interests of the child to allow them to adopt. The European Court of Human Rights in Strasbourg had not yet gone so far. Although there was every reason to think that they would soon do so, it was still within the 'margin of appreciation' where Member States could decide for themselves. The Law Lords stressed that it would not always be right for the courts to develop human rights within the 'margin of appreciation' – but it was the courts' role to protect minorities from discrimination because the elected majority would not always do this. In Christie's case, the Supreme Court held that this approach was wrong. If it was a matter within the margin of appreciation, only Parliament could decide what the answer should be. Is this giving proper respect to the role of the democratically elected Parliament or is it a backward step in the protection of minority rights?

Lessons learnt?

There are some very good things to come out of these stories. Businesses which offer services to the public must not discriminate against gay people because they disapprove. Nor must they discriminate against straight people. Just as the Christian hotel-keepers could not refuse to offer the same service to a gay couple as they would to a straight one, gay hotel-keepers could not refuse to offer the same service to a straight couple as they would to a gay couple. The cake is different. The sexual orientation of the customer was irrelevant. The point was free speech. We all have a right to free speech. but we don't have a right to insist that others help us even if they profoundly disagree with what we want to say.

But there are also some very disturbing things. When transgender issues first came before the courts, the focus was on people whose gender dysphoria was so acute that they were willing to go through the rigours of hormone treatment and surgery to align their bodily with their psychological identity. Who could not feel for their pain and want to recognise what they had gone through? But should women who have suffered at the hands of violent or predatory men be obliged to accept trans women as women? And when should a person who was born a man be recognised as a woman? Is self-identification ever enough? Why are we worried about the risk of a few predatory men pretending to be trans women when we are not worried at all about a few predatory women pretending to be trans men?

We have come a long way towards resolving some of these differences. But the recent furore over trans versus women's rights shows how deeply embedded our perceptions of sex and gender are. So spare a thought for people who were born with characteristics of both sexes. Their parents might well be advised to choose surgery to adapt the child to one sex or the other. But that would not necessarily align with their hormones, leaving them in a limbo between the sexes as they grew up. The law needs to cope with this problem but currently does not.

12   Workers Have Rights

What does the word 'worker' mean to you? Does it conjure up a mineworker, a steelworker, a factory worker, a shop-worker or many other kinds of worker – but always someone doing a job involving manual labour, skilled or unskilled, for someone else, a boss? In the law we used to call the boss a master and the worker a servant, reflecting that antiquated view of who was a worker and the relationship between them. Nowadays there are many workers who are not engaged in manual labour at all – unless banging computer keys can be called manual labour. They include office workers of all sorts. They also include many with professional qualifications, as doctors or nurses or other healthcare professionals; as architects or building engineers or quantity surveyors; as university professors, college lecturers or schoolteachers; and many more. These are all workers who will (or should) have a contract of employment with their employers. Master and servant have become employer and employee and the relationship between them is now very different.

At the other end of the spectrum, there are many people who work for themselves, running their own businesses, large or small, or practising their professions on their own account or in profit-sharing partnerships rather than for anyone else. These we call the self-employed and they are not regarded as workers by the law however hard they work. There is also an in-between category, people who are not employees, who don't have a contract of employment, but are obliged by contract *personally* to carry out work for another person who is not their client or customer. They must do the job themselves and they are not in business on their own account. These too are called workers.

In the olden days, the law believed in 'freedom of contract'. Employers and employees were free to agree to whatever terms they liked (provided these were not illegal, immoral or contrary to public policy). Not surprisingly, these contracts usually gave the employee very few rights. The employer was in a much stronger bargaining position. But for a long time, the law has interfered with freedom of contract to give employees many more rights. It has also given some rights – but not as many – to those in-between workers who do not have a contract of employment but are nonetheless obliged to work for someone else. It is all very technical and complicated.

Some of the present rights are derived from European Union law. Now that the UK has left the European Union, Parliament could change these at any time. But some of them, such as the right not to be unfairly dismissed, do not come from the European Union. And laws against discrimination in the workplace have been with us for a long time now. We have seen an example of how they work in chapter 4. So these are probably here to stay, although governments may want to improve them – by increasing or decreasing workers' rights, depending upon their views of what is good for the economy and the workforce. There are still plenty of interesting questions, especially on the margins – such as trafficked workers who are here illegally, part-time workers who don't have the same benefits as full-timers, older workers who can still be treated less favourably if there is a good reason. The question of who counts as an in-between worker and who is self-employed has come before the Supreme Court several times recently. And then there are office-holders, such as judges and some clergy, who don't have a contract at all but may deserve some of the same protection as workers.

The victim of trafficking

Mary Hounga came from a poor family in Nigeria. She had no education and could not read or write. From around the age of twelve, she worked as a live-in domestic servant for a well-to-do family in Lagos. When she was about fourteen, the family suggested that she might come to England to work for Mrs Allen, who was the sister of the man she worked for in Lagos. She was promised that she would also go to school and that she would be paid £50 per month as well as having board and lodging in Mrs Allen's household. Mary was particularly attracted by the promise of education in England and willingly agreed.

But in order to get her entry clearance to come to England, she took part in an elaborate deception devised by Mrs Allen's brother. She swore an affidavit that she had been born in 1986 and so was then twenty years old, but that her birth certificate had been lost. She also swore that her surname was that of Mrs Allen's mother. She was issued a Nigerian passport in that name. Then she was taken to the British High Commission in Lagos. There she produced a document in which Mrs Allen's mother, pretending to be Mary's grandmother, invited Mary to come and stay with her in England. She was given entry clearance to do so. She flew to Heathrow in January 2007. Her passport was stamped with a visitor's visa, valid for six months. Mary knew that she had gained entry to the United Kingdom on false pretences. She knew that she was not allowed to stay longer than six months. And she knew that she was not allowed to take work in the United Kingdom.

For the next eighteen months she worked for Mrs Allen as a domestic servant. She looked after Mrs Allen's three small children and she did the housework. She was never enrolled at a school and she was never paid the £50 a month she had been promised or indeed any wages at all. She was seriously physically abused by Mrs Allen. She was also threatened that, if she left the house and was found by the police, she would be sent to prison because her presence in the UK was illegal.

In July 2008, Mrs Allen, angry that the children had not eaten their supper, smacked and hit Mary; after the children had gone to bed, she attacked and beat Mary, threw her out of the house and poured water over her. Mrs Allen's husband let her back in but said that Mrs Allen could do whatever she liked to Mary; so Mrs Allen pushed her out of the house again and told her to die. Mary slept in the garden in her wet clothes. In the morning no one would open the door to her, so she made her way to a supermarket car park where she was found and taken to social services who looked after her.

Mary brought a claim against Mrs Allen in an employment tribunal. She claimed for breach of her contract of employment, unpaid wages, holiday pay and unfair dismissal. She also claimed compensation for racial discrimination in the harassment she had suffered before her dismissal and in the dismissal itself.

What do you think?

1. Mary was here illegally; she was not entitled to work for money; she had no right to her job: should she have got anything at all?
2. Or should she have got compensation for the harassment, abuse and discrimination she had suffered, but nothing for the work she had done or for unfair dismissal?
3. Both the United Nations Protocol to Prevent, Suppress and Punish Trafficking in Persons (the Palermo Protocol) and the Council of Europe Convention on Action against Trafficking in Human Beings (the Warsaw Convention) prohibit the 'recruitment, transportation, transfer, harbouring or receipt of a child for the purpose of exploitation'. Had Mary been trafficked in this way?
4. In 2012, the International Labour Organisation published eleven indicators of forced labour: abuse of vulnerability; deception; restriction of movement; isolation; physical and sexual violence; intimidation and threats; retention of identity documents; withholding of wages; debt bondage; abusive working and living conditions; excessive overtime. How many of these applied to Mary?
5. Do the victims of human trafficking or forced labour deserve compensation even if they know that they are here illegally and not allowed to work?
6. Mary claimed compensation for racial discrimination: but was she treated badly because of her race, ethnicity or nationality or because of her status as an illegal migrant?
7. Mary might have brought a claim for damages for assault in a county court. Should that have been affected by the fact that she was here illegally?

What did the court think?

The Supreme Court held that Mary could make a claim for harassment and discrimination – it was not defeated because her presence here was unlawful.¹ (Think about it – if she had been run over by a careless driver, should her claim for her injuries be denied because she shouldn't be here at all?) Ironically, however, Mrs Allen was refused permission to argue, late in the day, that Mary had not been badly treated because of her nationality or ethnicity but because of her precarious immigration status. But in two later cases, where the facts were very similar, this point was raised from the beginning, and the Supreme Court held that the discrimination was on the ground of their immigration status.² This is not a protected characteristic which can ground a discrimination claim, so they had no claim.

However, as we shall see later, Mary's case made an important contribution to the development of the law on illegality. A later decision of the Supreme Court³ (see further in chapter 15, p. 213) means that Mary might well have been able to make a claim to be paid a reasonable sum for the work she had done for Mrs Allen: the public policies in deterring illegal working and deterring trafficking in children would have to be weighed against one another and after all, Mrs Allen had benefited from the work which Mary had done for her.

The part-time firefighter

Most firefighters work full-time. They work in a structured shift system of forty-two hours a week with overtime. They have a conventional salary structure, sick pay and pensions. A typical contract lists as their main duties: to respond immediately to emergency calls; to check, test and maintain the fire station appliances and equipment so that everything is ready for immediate use; to take part in practice drills and training; to maintain the necessary high level of physical fitness; and to get to know their local area, its risks, hazards, and water supplies. They also have to carry out fire inspections and visits, provide advice for other organisations and the general public, and understand the fire authority's health and safety framework and other policies. In practice, of course, while they have to be on duty for forty-two hours a week, they will not spend all this time responding to emergencies. They will spend some time on community fire safety work, doing fire risk assessments, attending local events and giving demonstrations. And they will spend some time in the fire station waiting for an emergency call.

However, a surprisingly large proportion of firefighters do not work full-time. They are expected to turn up for two or three hours each week for training and drill, but apart from that they are not expected to turn up for a set number of hours each week. Instead they commit themselves to being on call for anything from eighty-four to one hundred and fifty-six hours each week. They are called out to emergencies and have to be able to get to the fire station within five minutes of being called. So they spend most of their duty time responding to emergencies and ensuring that the appliances and equipment are ready to do so. They spend much less time on community fire safety work, although they could do this too. They are paid an initial retaining fee, and for their regular weekly commitment, and for the times when they are called out. This pattern of working is much more common in rural areas than it is in large conurbations. But the majority of fire stations are manned in this way rather than by full-timers.

At the scene of the fire, both the full-time and part-time firefighters do exactly the same job. You would not be able to tell which was which. Whoever was the senior officer at the scene would assume command and remain in control.

The part-timers, with the support of the Fire Brigades Union, complained that they were being treated less favourably than the full-timers: specifically, there was a different and less favourable way of calculating sick pay; there was a differential rate for additional duties; and above all, they were excluded from the pension scheme.

What do you think?

1. What's your first reaction: should the part-time firefighters be members of the Fire Service pension scheme?
2. A part-time worker has the right not to be treated less favourably than a 'comparable' full-time worker. Do you think the full-time firefighters are comparable with the part-time firefighters?
3. To be comparable, part-timers have to be employed 'under the same type of contract'. By definition, part-time workers will not be employed on exactly the same terms and conditions as full-time workers. Do you think the differences here meant that it was not 'the same type of contract'?

4. To be comparable, part-timers also have to be 'engaged in the same or broadly similar work'. Do you think that the part-timers and full-timers were 'engaged in the same or broadly similar work'?
5. Part-time judges are in a very similar position. They are not on call but they are expected to turn up for training sessions and to commit themselves to sitting no fewer than a certain number of days a year. When they are in court they do exactly the same job as the full-time judges, but they do not have the additional administrative tasks which some (but by no means all) full-time judges have. Should they be entitled to a pension to reflect the number of days they have in fact sat?

What did the court think?

When the part-time firefighters' case came before the House of Lords, three of the five Law Lords held that the part-time and full-time firefighters *were* employed under the same type of contract – this referred to the same type of employment relationship rather than the same terms and conditions of employment.[4] Otherwise, part-timers and full-timers would never be comparable with one another. This would make no sense, as the law prohibits unjustified discrimination against part-time workers. Three out of the five also held that the fact that the full-timers did extra tasks would not necessarily prevent their work being the same or broadly similar to that of the part-timers: weight had to be given to the extent that their work was exactly the same – as it was on the fire ground – and the importance of that work. The case was sent back to the employment tribunal which eventually ruled in their favour.

The courts rely heavily on part-time judges to shift the workload. Mr O'Brien was a recorder, a part-time judge in the Crown and county courts. He challenged the exclusion of part-time judges from the judicial pension scheme. When his case came before the Supreme Court, the question whether judges were 'workers' at all was referred to the European Court of Justice in Luxembourg, which said that if what they did looked like what workers did then they should be treated as such. The Supreme Court held that they were workers and should not have been excluded from the judicial pension scheme – there was no justification for treating them differently from the full-time judges.[5]

The police worker nearing retirement

Terrence Homer retired from the police force at the age of fifty-one with the rank of detective inspector. He immediately began to work as a legal adviser with the Police National Legal Database (PNLD). When he began to work for the PNLD, a law degree was not required as long as he had other qualifications, which he was taken to have because of his service with the police and the exams he had passed there. The rules were later changed so that a law degree became essential but at first this did not affect him.

Then the PNLD introduced a new career structure with a view to making the job more attractive. There were three thresholds above the starting grade. Mr Homer met the first two but not the third, as he did not have a law degree, although he qualified for the third threshold in all other respects. By then he was aged sixty-two. It would take him at least four years to get a law degree by part-time study. By that time he would be over the normal retiring age of sixty-five. So he could not meet the third threshold and the benefits which went with it – a higher salary and as a result a higher pension.

Mr Homer claimed that he had been treated less favourably – discriminated against – because of his age.

What do you think?

1. Mr Homer had not been treated less favourably because he was aged sixty-two. He had been treated less favourably because he did not have a law degree. If this is discrimination, it is *indirect* – applying a criterion which is applied to everyone but puts people in the same age group as Mr Homer at a particular disadvantage compared to younger people. (The classic example is requiring employees to have a beard, which indirectly discriminates against women.) Do you think that this was indirect discrimination?
2. Mr Homer's employer argued that it wasn't his age that put him at a disadvantage but the fact that he was approaching

retirement, so he was no worse off than anyone else who was thinking of leaving the job. What do you think of that?
3. Indirect discrimination is not unlawful if the employer can show that the criterion in question is justified. This means, first, that it must have a legitimate aim. The employer's aim here was to help both to recruit *and to retain* staff of the right quality. Do you think that is a legitimate aim?
4. If the aim is legitimate, the employer must then show that the criterion is a suitable way to achieve it. Might what is suitable to attract new recruits, by offering them a career structure, be different from what is suitable to retain existing valuable staff?
5. If the criterion is suitable, the employer must then show that it is reasonably necessary to impose it. Do you think that the impact upon a person like Mr Homer could be justified by the benefit to the employer?
6. What else might the employer have done to achieve its aim without discriminating against people like Mr Homer?
7. Are you beginning to think that this is all too complicated?

What did the court think?

The Supreme Court held that Mr Homer was indeed being indirectly discriminated against because of his age.[6] It was a criterion that he simply *could* not meet because of his age. With others leaving was a choice. The aim of recruiting and retaining staff of appropriate calibre was a legitimate aim. But recruitment and retention were two different things. Was it reasonably necessary to impose the law degree requirement in order to *keep* good staff? Were there other ways of doing so? The case was sent back to the employment tribunal for them to ask themselves the right questions.

Mr Homer's case was heard at the same time as the case of a solicitor who challenged his firm's mandatory retirement age of sixty-five.[7] Unlike discrimination on other grounds, direct discrimination on grounds of age — which this was — can be justified if it is a proportionate means of meeting a legitimate aim. The firm's aims — of inter-generational fairness and avoiding unseemly debates about an older worker's capabilities — were legitimate. But was a retirement age of sixty-five a proportionate means of meeting them? Many employers have revisited their retirement policies as a result.

The Pimlico plumber

Gary Smith was a plumbing and heating engineer by trade. From August 2005 to April 2011, he worked for Pimlico Plumbers Ltd, a well-known company with a substantial business in London, under two written agreements drafted by the company. These were described by a judge as 'carefully choreographed' – on the one hand, to present their operatives to the public as part of their workforce and to exercise a 'substantial measure of control' over them, and on the other hand, to make them self-employed in business on their own account.

The first contract described him as a 'sub-contracted employee'. The second described him as 'an independent contractor of the company, in business on your own account'. The agreements and accompanying company manual provided, among other things, that he had to wear the company logo'ed uniform, be clean and smart at all times, and carry a company ID card. Normal working hours were a five-day week in which he was expected to complete at least forty hours. He had to notify the company in good time of days when he would be unavailable to work. The company was under no obligation to offer him work nor was he under any obligation to accept it. But there were restrictions on his ability to accept other work, not only while he was employed with the company but also after he left them. Customers contracted with the company and not with him. He got 50 per cent of what the company charged the customer but only after the customer had paid the company. If he couldn't do a job he had quoted for, he could arrange for another person who worked for the company to do it. He was required to pay income tax and national insurance contributions as a self-employed person, and did so.

Gary suffered a heart attack and the agreement was terminated. He brought a claim in an employment tribunal for, among other things, unfair dismissal, non-payment of wages and holiday pay, and disability discrimination.

What do you think?

1. To bring a claim for unfair dismissal, you have to be an employee. Was Gary an employee?
2. For the other claims, it is enough to be an in-between worker: someone who has contracted to perform work personally for the company, which is not his customer or client. Was Gary such a worker or was he in business on his own account?
3. Had he contracted to perform work personally when he could arrange for another Pimlico Plumbers' tradesman to do it?
4. Was Pimlico Plumbers Ltd his client or customer?

What did the court think?

The courts have long held that, in the context of employment, taking into account the relative bargaining power of the parties, the written documentation might not reflect the reality of their relationship.[8] It was necessary to look at the parties' actual agreement by examining all the circumstances and identifying the parties' actual legal obligations. The employment tribunal held that Gary was not an employee, so he was not entitled to bring a claim for unfair dismissal, but that he was an in-between worker and so he was entitled to bring the other claims. The Employment Appeal Tribunal agreed. The Supreme Court held that the employment tribunal had been entitled to reach that conclusion.[9]

The Supreme Court reached the same conclusion in respect of Uber drivers in London – customers contracted with Uber and Uber engaged the drivers to carry out the bookings; their service was very tightly defined and controlled by Uber and they had little or no opportunity to seek work elsewhere.[10] By contrast, Deliveroo riders were held (by the body which can oblige employers to recognise trade unions for collective bargaining purposes) not to be 'workers' because they did not have to do the job themselves and could also work for competitors.[11]

The whistle-blowing district judge

Claire Gilham was appointed a district judge in 2006. Before she took the job, she was sent a 'Memorandum on conditions of employment and terms of service'. This dealt with many things, including the number of days she was required to sit, sick pay, parental leave, training and outside activities. Her salary was to be taxed under what used to be Schedule E to the Income Tax Act, referring to income from an office or employment, rather than Schedule D, referring to income from self-employment. She would be regarded as an employed earner for the purpose of National Insurance contributions. Her Instrument of Appointment was signed by the Lord Chancellor, Lord Falconer of Thoroton, in January 2006, and assigned her to sit on the Wales and Chester Circuit.

She began sitting in the county court in Crewe and then transferred to the county court in Warrington. In 2010, the Cheshire courts were transferred from the Wales and Chester Circuit to the Northern Circuit. In 2011, as part of widespread cuts to the justice system, the Runcorn county court was closed and its business transferred to Warrington. Judge Gilham was concerned about the lack of appropriate and secure courtroom accommodation, the severely increased workload placed upon district judges and some administrative failures. She raised her concerns with the local leadership judges and with senior managers in the courts service.

She complained that she was badly treated as a result. There was a significant delay in investigating her grievance. She was seriously bullied, ignored and undermined by her fellow judges and court staff; she was told that her workload and concerns were simply a 'personal working style choice' – in other words that she was too conscientious; this all led to a severe deterioration in her mental health; she was signed off work due to stress from the beginning of January 2013; and she complained that she had been given inadequate support to help her return to work.

She claimed that she was a whistle-blower who had been treated badly because of her whistle-blowing activities. Her complaints had been made to the right people within the justice system. They had raised the right sort of issues – that there was a failure to comply with legal obligations, that miscarriages of justice were likely, that the health and safety of individuals was being endangered. But instead of doing something about them, the powers that be had subjected her to a number of detriments.

What do you think?

1. Whistle-blowing protection does not stem from EU law, so the question was whether Judge Gilham counted as a worker in UK law. Is a judge someone who is obliged personally to carry out work for someone who is not their client or customer? Can she delegate her sitting days to someone else?
2. If a judge is obliged personally to carry out her work, is that because she holds an office created by Act of Parliament? Or is it also because she has a contract? But if so, who is her contract with – is it with the Lord Chancellor who heads the Ministry of Justice; the Lord Chief Justice who is responsible for deploying her, training her and disciplining her if necessary; or His Majesty's Courts and Tribunals Service, which organises the courts?
3. It is an important principle of our Constitution that the judges should be free from government interference and able to do their job without fear of repercussions if the government does not like what they do. Would it be compatible with the independence of the judiciary for a judge to be employed by a government minister?
4. If judges are denied the same protection as other whistle-blowers, are they being treated less favourably than others – that is, discriminated against – in the exercise of their right to freedom of speech, protected by article 10 of the European Convention on Human Rights and the Human Rights Act?
5. Can you think of any good reason why they should be denied that protection?

What did the court think?

The Supreme Court held that Mr O'Brien (see above) was a worker because he was obliged to perform his duties as a part-time judge personally, even though his services were not provided under a contract. This was because the protection of part-time workers was required by European Union law. The protection given to whistle-blowers is not required by European Union law – only by UK law. It does apply to workers in the in-between category but they have to be obliged *by contract* personally to perform work for another party to the contract. In Judge Gilham's case, the Supreme Court held that there is no contract between a judge and the government, or the courts service, or the Lord Chief Justice as head of the judiciary.[12] However, the right to freedom of speech, protected by article 10 of the European Convention on Human Rights, was involved. Article 14 of the Convention says that there must be no discrimination in the enjoyment of the Convention rights on a variety of grounds which undoubtedly include the status of being a judge. There was no good reason for denying judges the whistle-blowing protection which was available to all other workers. The legislation had to be read and given effect so as to include them. Judge Gilham won her case.

Lessons learnt?

Freedom of contract is all very well but there have to be limits. There are some contracts which involve long-term relationships between parties who are inevitably not in an equal bargaining position. The prime examples are landlord and tenant, and employer and worker. For many years, Parliament has intervened to protect the presumably weaker party. But justice between the individual parties is not the only consequence. What did rent control and security of tenure do to the private rented housing market? But what did their removal do? What have workers' rights done to the job market? What would increasing or decreasing them do? These are socio-economic questions for the politicians rather than legal questions for the courts. Meanwhile we have seen how the law can protect workers who are often marginalised, perhaps because they work part-time or are getting near retirement. We have also seen how the courts will look to the reality of the relationship, rather than the letter of the contract written by the employer, to see what rights the worker has.

These cases all ended up in the Supreme Court, but they started in an employment tribunal, which is meant to be easy for workers to use to assert their rights. As we saw in chapter 4, it can be very far from easy, however hard the tribunal tries. The justice system is still struggling to make itself accessible to everyone who needs it. And the more complicated the law is, the more difficult that becomes. We have learned just how complicated the law on workers' rights can be – but could it be any different?

13 Women Have Rights

Before the Equal Pay Act 1970 and the Sex Discrimination Act 1975 were brought into force on the same day, it was possible for a woman to be refused a job for which she was well qualified, simply because she was a woman; it was common for women doing exactly the same work as men to be paid less for it; but it was also common for women to be segregated into 'women's work', which was typically paid much less than the jobs done by men. In 1968, the Ford Motor Company rated the work of the women sewing machinists who made seat covers for their cars as less skilled than the work done by men, and paid the women 15 per cent less than they paid the men. The women went on strike. Car production ground to a halt after three weeks because there were no more seat covers and no one else knew how to make them, thus showing how skillful their work was. The women eventually won their fight for better pay and the following year the Equal Pay Act was passed.

At long last, progress towards equal rights for women in the workplace was being made. But the fight is by no means over, as we shall see. It is still very difficult – costly and time-consuming – to prove that the work traditionally done by women is worth as much as the work traditionally done by men. And it is all too easy for women to be subject to insidious discrimination – putting down – in the workplace in ways which may seem trivial to some, but which are very far from trivial to those who have to suffer it.

But the devaluing of women's work outside the home is as nothing compared with the devaluing of women's work inside it. The law did not and does not regard the work which women do in the home – looking after the family, bringing up the children, cooking, cleaning, keeping house – as 'money or money's worth', nor does it count towards our Gross Domestic Product. Yet the assumption that a woman's work was in the home, and that she would have a husband to support her, was a large part of the reason why her work outside the home was regarded as less important than a man's. So alongside the struggle for women's equality outside the home we have to look at the struggle for women's equality within it.

I firmly believe, in the words of the Universal Declaration of Human Rights, that 'All human beings are born free and equal in dignity and rights' and that includes women as well as men. But in a variety of ways, and for a variety of reasons, our experience of life is different from that of men. We are more vulnerable to violence, to sexual assault and exploitation, to unwanted pregnancy, and the law has sometimes struggled to recognise this.

Equal pay for classroom assistants

When it was first passed, the Equal Pay Act would not have helped the Dagenham machinists, because it only required equal pay for 'like work' or 'work rated as equivalent' in a workplace study which employers had no duty to undertake. It did nothing to tackle the problem of women's work. But European Union law required equal pay for 'work of equal value' and eventually, in 1984, the United Kingdom was forced to change the Equal Pay Act to include this.

In 2006 to 2007, equal pay claims were brought by 251 classroom assistants, support for learning assistants and nursery nurses, employed in schools run by the Dumfries and Galloway Council. These jobs are mostly done by women because the hours and dates are convenient for women with child care or other domestic responsibilities. They were all based at particular schools, although the workers might be required to go to other schools.

In order to make an equal pay claim, you have to find a man, or a group of men, with whom to compare yourself. This is because, if you succeed, you will automatically be entitled, not only to the same pay, but also to the same terms and conditions if these are better than yours. So these claimants wanted to compare themselves with a variety of manual workers employed by the council, as groundsmen, refuse collectors, and refuse drivers. These men were entitled to hefty

Women Have Rights 171

bonus payments and supplements on top of their basic pay, whereas the claimants were not. The men were based at various depots from which they went out to do their work. They were not based in schools and they never would be based in schools to do the work that they did.

What do you think?

1. The women had first to show that they were 'in the same employment' – that the terms and conditions of the men would be the same wherever they were employed by that employer. Men's work is often done in different places from women's work, so should it matter that these men would never be based in schools?
2. The women would next have to provide expert evidence that their work was of 'equal value' to the men's 'in terms of the demands made on her (for instance under such headings as effort, skill and decision)'. Do you think that the work done by nursery nurses looking after very young children is of equal value to the work done by bin men?
3. If the women get over both these hurdles, the employer might still try to prove that the differences between the women and the men were 'genuinely due to a material factor which is not the difference of sex'. Rates of pay can be the same even if the days and hours worked are different. So should it matter that the women only worked during school terms and for less than thirty-five hours a week?

What did the court think?

The Supreme Court held that the men and the women were 'in the same employment' even though they did not work in the same place.[1] Otherwise, it would defeat the whole idea of 'equal pay for work of equal value' – employers could just organise things so that the women's work was done in one place and the men's in another. I said:

'It stands to reason that some very different jobs which are not or cannot be carried out in the same workplace may nevertheless be rated as equivalent or assessed as having equal value. One example is the (female) office worker who needs office equipment in a clean environment and the (male) factory worker who needs machines which create dirt and dust . . . The fact that of necessity their work has to be carried out in different places is no barrier to equalising the terms on which it is done. It is well-known that those jobs which require physical strength have traditionally been better rewarded than those which require dexterity.'

Both groups had been employed under the terms of collective agreements negotiated between employers and trade unions, the women under the Administrative, Professional, Technical & Clerical Agreement (known as the Blue Book); the men under the Scottish Council for Local Government Services (Manual Workers) Scheme (known as the Green Book). These had been replaced by a single-status agreement (known as the Red Book) but the existing pay and grading arrangements remained in force until the employers had done a job evaluation exercise.

The consultant orthodontist

Mrs Sumithra Hewage was not bringing an equal pay claim. She was complaining that she had been obliged to leave her employment with the Grampian Health Board because of sex and race discrimination against her. Mrs Hewage was born in Sri Lanka but had made a career in dentistry in the UK. Since 1993 she had been employed as a consultant orthodontist at the Aberdeen Royal Infirmary. She resigned from that position in 2003 and a year later she resigned from her employment with the board. The board accepted that she had resigned because they had treated her unfairly but they denied that this was because of her race and sex.

The trouble with sex and race discrimination claims is that you have to find someone of the opposite sex and/or a different race who is in a similar situation to you and has not been treated as badly as you have been. Mrs Hewage complained that she had been bullied and harassed by employees of the board, in particular the service manager, but the board had not taken this seriously. She compared her treatment with that of Professor Forrester, who was head of the department of ophthalmology and had experienced similar difficulties with the same service manager. He resigned as a result and refused to return to the role if she were still there. The board had taken this seriously. It led to a reorganisation in which the service manager was no longer involved in the ophthalmology department and Professor Forrester could return to his post.

Mrs Hewage also compared her treatment with that of her successor. She had long been of the view that a consultant should be involved on the interviewing panel for dental nurses. But this had been strenuously resisted by the service manager. Yet when she resigned, Mr Lamour, her successor, made the same request and it was immediately agreed to. Not only that, senior management had assured Mr Lamour that if he had any problems with the service manager he should let them know immediately. They had assured him of their support.

The board did not provide any satisfactory explanation for the differences between the way they had treated Mrs Hewage and the way they had treated Professor Forrester and Mr Lamour but they did say that the circumstances were not identical – mainly because different people had been involved in the decisions – and so she shouldn't be compared with them.

What do you think?

1. Do you think it was fair to compare how Mrs Hewage had been treated with how the two male consultants had been treated?
2. Can you think of reasons why Mrs Hewage had been treated as she was which had nothing to do with her race or her sex?
3. If you can think of other reasons, why do you think that the board did not put them forward but raised a whole heap of technical objections?

What did the court think?

The Supreme Court held that there was material on which the employment tribunal could find that Mrs Hewage had been discriminated against because of her race and sex.[2] The two white men had undoubtedly been treated better than she had been. This meant that the health board had to provide an explanation and it had not done so.

The minor differences in her circumstances and those of the men were not 'material'.

Mrs Hewage was lucky – there were two white men who had obviously been treated better than she had in comparable situations. Sometimes there are no real comparators, so the tribunal has to ask itself how a hypothetical man in the same situation would have been treated. Sometimes there may be differences in their situation which are thought material. A woman chief inspector in the Royal Ulster Constabulary (as it then was) complained that she had been prevented from doing appraisals of police constables while two male chief inspectors were still doing them. The House of Lords agreed that there was a material difference: there had been complaints about how she did the appraisals but not about how the men did them.[3] But I have always wondered whether the complaints were themselves discriminatory – because the male constables did not like being appraised by a woman.

The farming family's finances

Martin and Pamela White were married in September 1961. They both came from farming families. They carried on a successful partnership as dairy farmers. It was agreed that both had worked equally hard in that business. At the outset, they both contributed a roughly equal amount of capital, about £2,000. A year after their marriage they bought a 160-acre farm in Somerset with a fine Jacobean farmhouse in their joint names. The price was £32,000, of which £21,000 was raised on mortgage. Martin's father made them an interest-free loan of £11,000 together with a further £3,000 as working capital. He released this loan in 1974. Over time, they bought more land, increasing the size of the farm to 337 acres. By the time they divorced, in 1996, the farm was worth around £3.5 million.

They also farmed at another 300-acre farm, Rexton Farm, as part of their partnership business. This was part of an estate which Martin's father had acquired in 1971, largely with borrowed money, and later transferred into the names of himself and his three sons. Martin's share of the borrowings was paid from the Whites' farming partnership. In 1993 Martin acquired Rexton Farm, subject to a mortgage of £137,000, as his share of the estate. It was worth £1.25 million.

Together with their pension provision, and less the mortgage liabilities on both farms and other liabilities, their overall net worth was around £.4.6 million. Of this, some £2,668,000 belonged to them jointly; £193,000 belonged to Pamela alone; and £1,783,500, mostly Rexton Farm, belonged to Martin alone.

Until 1971, when a couple divorced, each would keep any property which they owned. A husband might be ordered to maintain his wife, if she needed it and had been a good wife. But the court had no power to alter the ownership of property acquired during the marriage. In 1971, the law was changed so that the court had power to share out all the property and recourses, present and future, of both husband and wife so as to provide fairly for them both and, more importantly, their children. Ownership became unimportant but the courts struggled to work out what was fair.

What do you think?

1. Pamela and Martin had been married for thirty-five years. They had three children together, one sadly killed in an air crash and the other two now grown up. They had farmed together for most of that time. Would the fair result have been to divide their property equally?
2. Or, given that there were two farms which they had farmed together, would it be fair to give one of them one farm and one the other? If so, should Martin get the more valuable farm because of the help they had received from his family?
3. Or should Pamela get a lump sum which would meet her reasonable living requirements?
4. Or does any other solution occur to you?

What did the court think?

The trial judge adopted solution 3. He thought it unreasonable of Pamela to want enough money to be able to buy a farm of her own. The existing farming enterprise should not be split up to enable her to set up on her own. She needed a home with stables and 25 acres for her horses, which would cost £425,000, plus a net annual income of

£40,000 which a capital sum of £550,000 would provide. This amounted to £980,000, slightly over one-fifth of their total assets. Martin was left with more than he required but he would be able to carry on farming. The Court of Appeal increased her share to roughly two-fifths of the total (now reduced by over £300,000 which they had spent on legal costs). Both parties appealed to the House of Lords.

The House of Lords resoundingly rejected the third solution.[4] Where there was enough money to go round, the courts had got into the habit of awarding a wife enough to meet her reasonable requirements no matter what the combined resources of the couple were. This was not only wrong in a case like this where the couple had genuinely been equal business partners. It was also wrong in more traditional families where the husband was the main breadwinner and the wife was the main homemaker. Their roles should be regarded as equal: 'There should be no bias in favour of the money-earner and against the home-maker and child-carer.'

It was going too far to say that there should be a presumption of equal division. The statute requires the court to consider all the circumstances – these include the actual and foreseeable resources of each party, their actual and foreseeable needs and responsibilities, their standard of living before the breakdown of the marriage, their ages and the length of the marriage, any physical or mental disability of either, and their respective contributions to the welfare of the family. Having done this, the court should check the outcome against the 'yardstick of equality'.

So both Martin and Pamela lost their appeals and the Court of Appeal's order stood. What some might think the obvious solution – that Martin got the more valuable farm (to take account of the contribution made by his inheritance) and Pamela got the other – was not available to an appeal court.

Cases like this, where there is more than enough to go round, hit the headlines in the law reports but do not represent the great majority. A few years later, the House of Lords followed this up in another two cases, decided together, *Miller v Miller* and *McFarlane v McFarlane*:[5] there were three principles which should guide the courts in trying to achieve a fair outcome: the needs of the parties (in practice the only principle in most cases, especially where there are young children);

compensation for relationship-generated disadvantage (e.g. if one had given up a lucrative career to look after the family); and sharing the fruits of the matrimonial relationship. The goal, I suggested, should be 'to give each party an equal start on the road to independent living'.

Single-sex facilities

Isobel Coll was now in her fifties. She had lived almost all her adult life in London. She had two adult children in their twenties and two young grandchildren, all living in the London area. Many years ago, she had been convicted of murder and sentenced to life imprisonment. The minimum term she was required to serve before being released on licence was eleven years and three months. After that expired, she was released on licence but on condition that she lived in approved premises – what used to be known as probation hostels. She was required to live in approved premises in Bedford for nine months and she was unable to get travel warrants to look for accommodation in London. So after leaving the approved premises she had to live in rented accommodation near Bedford. She was unable to return to London to be near her family.

Two laudable policies were in conflict. The idea is to reintroduce serious offenders back into the community and if possible close to their families. So male offenders are placed as close as possible to home. But female offenders are particularly vulnerable and need different facilities from men – they need safe spaces. So all approved premises are now single-sex. But there are far fewer women in prison than men. And even fewer women who have committed the sort of serious crimes that mean that they have to be eased back into society in this way. There are ninety-four approved premises for men and only six for women. None of those for women are in London. This means that women are far more likely than men to be sent to approved premises which are a long way from their homes and families. Isobel Coll and women like her are obviously at a disadvantage compared with men.

It is allowed to provide separate but equal services or separate and different services for women and men if a joint service would be 'less effective' and this is 'a proportionate means of achieving a legitimate aim'.

What do you think?

1. Did the policy discriminate against women? How should the justice system cater for the needs of women prisoners when there are so few of them?
2. Should there be safe spaces for women in (a) prisons, (b) approved premises, (c) refuges from domestic violence and abuse, (d) hospital wards, (e) gyms and swimming pools, (f) anywhere else?
3. Should safe spaces for women be open to (a) people born male who have fully transitioned to female, (b) people born male who are living as female on the way to being legally recognised as female, (c) people born male who have declared themselves to be female?

What did the court think?

The Supreme Court held that the provision of approved premises by the Secretary of State for Justice did discriminate against women because it meant that many of them had to be placed far away from their homes and communities when men did not.[6] The Ministry of Justice had not thought about the possible impacts upon women, the disadvantages and what might be done to mitigate them, and so could not show that the policy was a proportionate means of achieving a legitimate aim.

Questions (2) and (3) did not arise but, as we saw earlier (in 'A trans woman and her pension' in chapter 11, p. 149), the question of 'Who is a woman?' has recently come before the Supreme Court. The judgment does not discuss the practical consequences for single sex spaces and services of their decision that 'man' and 'woman' in the Equality Act 2010 refer to sex at birth.

The victims of rape

Women are particularly vulnerable to sexual assault and exploitation, especially when they are out at night. But one place where they might expect to feel safe is in the back of a London black cab – unless they had the misfortune to get into the cab owned and driven by John Worboys. Between 2002 and 2008, he assaulted well over a hundred women in the back of his cab. His method was simple. He would pick up a woman passenger wanting to get home after a night out, engage her in conversation, explain that he had recently won a large sum of money and invite her to have a drink of champagne with him to celebrate. He was very insistent. But if she agreed, he laced her drink with drugs which would rapidly make her unconscious, and unable to resist his assaults. Not only that, the drugs he used would also lead to memory loss, so that she would remember little if anything about what had happened.

Many of the women whom he attacked did not complain to the police at the time. But two of those who did complain brought an action against the Metropolitan Police, claiming that the police had failed to investigate their complaints properly.

One of the women, whom I shall call Donna, was put into the cab by her friends in Soho in the early hours of 7 May 2003. The driver was given an address in Hornsey which turned out not to be quite right. When they got there, Donna was slumped on the floor of the taxi, covered in vomit, mumbling and slurring her words. Kevin, who lived at that address, did not know her but suggested that they take her to the nearest police station. The front desk reception staff did not record any of the relevant details, including the number of the cab. They called an ambulance and Donna was taken to hospital. When she woke up there a few hours later, she had reason to believe that she had been drugged and raped and her boyfriend reported this to the police. The police failed to take her complaint seriously. They did not interview Kevin or examine CCTV footage. They viewed her as a drunk or addict rather than a potential victim of serious crime. They did examine her and her possessions but they made no serious attempt to trace the cab driver. Worboys went on to commit many more assaults using the same methodology. A few of them were reported to the police but the connections were not made.

If they had been, it is likely that Worboys would have been caught and the other woman claimant, whom I shall call Nora, would not have been attacked at all. She hailed Worboys' cab in Holborn at about 2.00 a.m. on 25 July 2007 to take her home to her student residence in Eltham after a night out with friends. The cab arrived there about two and a half hours later. She got out of the cab in an unsteady state, the driver rummaged in the back of the cab, 'embraced' her and then quickly got back in his seat. She managed to get to her room and woke up several hours later, with reason to believe that she had been the victim of a sexual assault by the driver. She called the police. This time the police did examine CCTV footage and identified Worboys. But they did not conduct a prompt search of his home, giving him time to clear up any traces and hide the 'rape kit' which the police found a few months later, after they had at long last put two and two together and linked up the complaints that they had received by then. They interviewed Worboys before they had done a search or interviewed Donna properly or thoroughly reviewed the CCTV. They failed to establish the time when she hailed the taxi or to inquire why it had taken such a long time to get her home. They closed the case and Worboys went on to commit further assaults until he was eventually arrested and prosecuted in 2008.

The police accepted that Worboys had subjected the women to 'inhuman and degrading treatment' within the meaning of article 3 of the European Convention on Human Rights. Worboys was liable to compensate them for the assaults. But were the police liable to compensate them for the psychological harm that they had suffered as a result of the police failure to investigate their cases properly?

What do you think?

1. Article 3 of the European Convention on Human Rights requires the State to have systems in place to protect people from torture or inhuman or degrading treatment or punishment; to investigate allegations effectively; and to punish those responsible. But the Convention mainly aims to protect people from actions by the State and its officials. Should it also protect people from the actions of private individuals such as Worboys?
2. The Convention recognises that the police have a difficult job and too much should not be expected of them. Do you think that they had fallen short of what could reasonably be expected?
3. Did Donna and Nora deserve to be compensated, not only by Worboys for the assaults which he had committed upon them, but also by the police for the psychological harm they had suffered through the police's failure to take them seriously?
4. Why do you think that the police did not take them seriously?

What did the court think?

The trial judge found that there were multiple failures by the police – both in handling the individual complaints and in their systems for dealing with such cases. The officers in question had not been properly trained and so did not take steps which they should have taken and which could have identified Worboys and verified the women's claims. Their supervising officers had not been properly trained either. And they were under pressure from the top not to focus on sexual assaults. Proper records were not kept and so strikingly similar complaints were not linked up. They failed to gain the trust of victims, many of whom did not report the attack to the police because they did not think that they would be believed. They didn't allocate sufficient resources to the investigation. He held them liable to compensate both Donna and Nora, awarding them £22,500 and £19,000 respectively. The police appealed on the ground that they were not liable under the Human Rights Act for failing to prevent inhuman and degrading acts perpetrated by private citizens.

The Supreme Court upheld the judge's decision.[7] The State had an obligation under the Human Rights Act rigorously to enforce the laws which prohibited inhuman and degrading treatment and this required that complaints of such treatment be properly investigated even where agents of the State were not responsible for inflicting the harm. We should not expect too much of the police, but here there had been serious failures, both in the general systems and in the response to individual cases.

Wrongful pregnancies

Rape is a risk run by both men and women, although far more often by women. But pregnancy is a risk run only by women. Sometimes it is the result of medical negligence.

Catherine McFarlane was born in Scotland in 1992. Her parents already had four children and decided that they didn't want any more. They had moved to a larger house and taken on a larger mortgage. Her mother returned to work as a night carer to help pay for it. Her father decided to have a vasectomy, cutting the duct which carries the sperm through the penis. This was done at a hospital run by the Tayside Health Board. There is a risk that the duct will repair itself enough to let sperm through. So patients are advised to continue to use contraception until samples of semen are tested for live sperm. Mr and Mrs McFarlane were advised that the tests were negative and they could stop using contraception. That advice was wrong and negligent. Catherine was conceived. Her mother decided not to have an abortion and to keep the baby when she was born. But Mrs McFarlane had of course to go through the pregnancy and childbirth and to give up her job. And her parents had to look after Catherine and bring her up.

Catherine was a healthy child, but Scott Parkinson was not. He was born in Leeds in 1995. His parents already had four children and were living in a cramped two-bedroomed house. His mother planned to go back to work, so that the family could afford to move to larger accommodation. She decided to have a sterilisation. This was done at a hospital in Leeds, but negligently. A clip was not properly attached to one of her fallopian tubes and two other clips were left in her abdomen. She became pregnant about ten months later and was advised that the baby might be disabled. And so he was. He had severe learning difficulties and behavioural problems. His mother could not go back to work so the family could not move. The strain on the marriage was too much and his father left before he was born.

But what if it is the mother rather than the child who is disabled? Anthony Rees was born in Darlington in 1997. His mother was nearly blind, severely visually impaired. She felt that she would not be able to look after a child properly and so was determined not to have children. She too had a sterilisation, which was done at a hospital in Darlington, but negligently, and Anthony was conceived. His mother was bringing him up herself with the help of her mother and other relatives who lived nearby, but it was a struggle.

Mr and Mrs McFarlane, Mrs Parkinson and Ms Rees all sued the hospitals where the vasectomy and sterilisations had been performed. The general rule is that if somebody negligently causes you a personal injury – harm to your body – they must compensate you for the 'pain, suffering and loss of amenity' caused by that injury, and also for any financial loss you suffer as a result. So if you lose your leg in a road accident, you will be compensated, not only for the loss of the leg, but also for any resulting loss of earnings, pensions and the like.

What do you think?

1. Is having a child you never meant to have a personal injury?
2. If so, should the mother get damages for the pain, suffering and loss of amenity involved in the pregnancy and childbirth?
3. Does it make any difference if she could have had a lawful abortion?
4. Should the mother, or the mother and father if they are both bringing up the child, get damages for the financial consequences of having another child to look after? Or does a child bring incalculable blessings and joy which outweigh those consequences?
5. Should it make any difference if (a) the child is disabled, or (b) the mother is disabled, and so the costs of bringing up the child are greater than they would otherwise be?
6. Should it make a difference that the parents might have put the child up for adoption?

What did the court think?

In the case of Catherine McFarlane, the House of Lords held that Mrs McFarlane was entitled to damages for the 'pain, suffering and inconvenience' of pregnancy and childbirth, and for the associated extra medical expenses, clothing and loss of earnings. But it was not 'fair, just and reasonable' to impose liability for the cost of bringing up a healthy normal child.[8] The birth of a healthy normal baby was a blessing and not a detriment so the benefits outweighed any loss.

In the case of Scott Parkinson, the Court of Appeal of England and Wales held that if the unwanted child was disabled, the mother could get the *extra* costs of bringing him up.[9] I pointed out that:

'The right to bodily integrity is the first and most important of the interests protected by the law of tort . . . Included within that right are two others. One is the right to physical autonomy: to make one's own choices about what will happen to one's own body. Another is the right not to be subjected to bodily injury or harm.'

I went on to explain at length how getting pregnant, having a baby, and the responsibility for bringing up a child interfere in a woman's life. The defendant hospital did not appeal.

In the case of Anthony Rees, the Court of Appeal held that the disabled mother could get the extra costs of bringing up a healthy child.[10] This time the hospital did appeal. The mother tried unsuccessfully to persuade the House of Lords to overturn the McFarlane case. But she did persuade them that she should get more than nominal damages for the gross invasion of her autonomy. Three of the Law Lords would have agreed with the Court of Appeal that she could get those extra costs; four decided that it was still wrong to give damages for bringing up a healthy child, but that the mother should have a 'conventional' sum, put at £15,000, for the wrongful invasion of her right to live her life as she had planned.

Lessons learnt?

We have come a long way since 1970. Women's rights in the workplace outside the home have improved dramatically. Theoretically they should have equal pay for work of equal value and not be discriminated against, either on account of their sex or on account of their pregnancy. But equal pay claims for large groups of workers take a long time to resolve. And individual claims may be difficult to pursue – as we saw in chapter 4, they can be very complicated and legal aid is not available.

At the same time, women's rights to be regarded as equal partners in marriage, even if they have largely devoted themselves to working inside the home, have been greatly enhanced, at least when the marriage has broken down. But it is an odd situation: husband and wife are treated as separate individuals, with separate property rights, and no right to know about the other's property or earnings, until the marriage breaks down, when everything is up for grabs and it can be very costly and difficult, both to find out what the assets are and then to distribute them fairly. And currently the law does nothing to help unmarried couples when their relationship breaks down – they still have to sort out who owns what.

We have also seen how the criminal justice system still has some way to go in recognising the needs of women – both when they are victims of crime (as a perhaps surprisingly high proportion of us are) and when they are perpetrators of crime (as a perhaps surprisingly small proportion of us are).

But at least the courts have recognised that it is indeed a woman's right to decide for herself whether or not to have a child and she deserves some compensation for the wrongful invasion of that right – even if not the same compensation that she would get if she were negligently run over by a bus.

14 Patients Have Rights

Sick or injured people are very vulnerable. They need professional help to make them better. But they don't always know what help they need or how to get it. They are very reliant on what the healthcare professionals tell them. But what if they are given the wrong information? Or not given enough information? And what if the treatment they are given is not the right treatment? But what if they don't want the treatment the professionals think that they need? Can they be forced to have it? On the other hand, what if the professionals don't want to give them the treatment that they or their loved ones want them to have? The stakes can be very high – sometimes life-changing injuries and sometimes even life or death. But this means that the healthcare professionals are also very vulnerable – mistakes can have catastrophic consequences for them too. These problems would be difficult enough in any healthcare system, but they are made even more acute in a National Health Service which is under so much pressure and would much prefer to spend its limited resources on patient care than on costly lawsuits and compensation.

Waiting in A & E

One afternoon in May 2010, Mike Darnley, then aged twenty-six, was hit on the head: we don't know who did it and we don't know why it was done. We do know that Mike Darnley rang his friend Robert Tubman and told him that he had been hit on the head, that he had a headache and that it was getting worse. So Robert drove him to A & E at the local hospital in Croydon. He was clocked in at 20.26. He told the receptionist that he had been hit on the back of his head, that he was feeling very unwell and his head was hurting. Both Robert and

Mike told the receptionist that they were worried that Mike had a head injury and needed urgent attention. The receptionist was not helpful. She told Mike that he should go and sit down and that he would have to wait for up to four to five hours before being seen. Mike was feeling too unwell to stay in A & E, so at 20.45 they left and Robert drove him to his mother's house where he went to bed. But at 21.30 he became very distressed and an ambulance was called. An ambulance arrived at 22.05 and took him back to A & E. There it was found that he had a large blood clot on his brain. He was transferred to another hospital and at 1.00 in the morning he was operated on to drain the blood clot. But it was too late. He suffered permanent brain damage which left him paralysed down one side of his body and severely disabled.

In fact he should have been told that he could expect to be seen by a triage nurse within half an hour. That was the system in the hospital at the time. It was the normal practice of the receptionists to explain this. If they had done so, Mike would have stayed. His decision to leave was at least partly based on the length of time he had been told that he would have to wait before being seen. If Mike had collapsed at 21.30 while in the hospital, he would have been transferred to the other hospital and had the operation much earlier. If that had happened, he would have made a very nearly full recovery from his injury. It was foreseeable that if someone was given misleading information about having to wait such a long time to see a doctor, they might leave the hospital when they wouldn't have done if they'd been told that a nurse would see them much earlier. And it was foreseeable that someone who left A & E without being seen might suffer harm as a result.

Mike sued the A & E hospital for compensation for his injuries. He claimed that they had been negligent in giving him misleading information.

What do you think?

1. Should a hospital have a duty to people who turn up at A & E not to give them misleading information?
2. Should it make any difference that the information is provided by receptionists rather than healthcare professionals?

3. Should it make any difference that the compensation in a case like this will be enormous?
4. Waiting times in A & E have become a lot longer since 2010. Is it enough if the hospital gives accurate information to patients? Or should there be a legal duty to see people within a certain time? And should that time be different according to the type of problem they present with?

What did the court think?

In Mike's case, both the trial judge and the Court of Appeal thought that it was 'not fair, just and reasonable' to hold the hospital liable. The Supreme Court disagreed.[1] The 'fair, just and reasonable' test had been devised for new kinds of case, outside the established categories of blame. It did not apply to well-established cases. It had been the law for a long time that people should not cause physical harm by their careless acts or by their careless words. Doctors should not treat their patients carelessly or give them careless advice. The same applied to other hospital staff. A & E providers owed a duty to take reasonable care not to cause physical injury to people who presented themselves complaining of illness or injury even before they had been admitted as inpatients to the hospital. An averagely competent receptionist in A & E would not give misleading information to a would-be patient. So it had been a breach of the duty of care to do so. And it was foreseeable that this would cause the patient physical harm. It had been a reason why he left and this caused the delay which resulted in the harm. So the hospital was liable. It made no difference that what some might think a relatively small slip would lead to a very large sum in damages.

The obstetric disaster

Nadine Montgomery is an intelligent and well-educated woman. She has a science degree and has worked for a pharmaceutical company. Her mother and sister are both doctors. She is also an insulin dependent diabetic, short and slight. In 1999 she was expecting her first baby. It is well known that these are high-risk pregnancies, because diabetic women are likely to have larger than normal babies. Usually, the widest part of a baby's body is the head. So if this descends successfully into the birth canal, the rest of the body will follow too. But if the mother is diabetic, the widest part of the baby's body may be the shoulders. This can mean that the head descends into the birth canal but the shoulders get stuck. This is known as shoulder dystocia. There is a 9 to 10 per cent risk of this happening to a diabetic mother.

It is a major obstetric emergency. There are various ways of resolving it: widening the pelvic gap or trying to dislodge the baby's shoulders; pushing the baby back into the womb so that an emergency Caesarean section can be performed; or cutting through the bone joining the two halves of the mother's pelvis. There are risks to the health of the mother and to the life and health of the baby even if the emergency is handled properly.

Mrs Montgomery's obstetrician (a woman) was determined that this baby would be born by a normal vaginal delivery if at all possible. The baby's size was monitored and it was decided to induce labour early before the baby got too big. But the baby was bigger than estimated and his shoulders got stuck when his head was halfway out. The obstetrician decided not to try and push the baby back in but to cut the pelvis and pull him out. This she eventually managed to do. But for the twelve minutes between the baby getting stuck and the baby getting out the umbilical cord was squashed and he was deprived of oxygen. As a result, he suffers from cerebral palsy and a paralysed arm. The risk of either of these happening is very small, respectively 0.1 per cent and 0.2 per cent. If he had been born by Caesarean section, he would not have been injured at all. The risk to the mother of a Caesarean section is now so low that the National Institute for Health and Clinical Excellence (NICE) advises that it should be offered to any woman requesting it if, after discussion and offers of support, a vaginal birth is still not 'acceptable'. The risk to the baby is nil.

Mrs Montgomery was not told of the risk of shoulder dystocia. She was worried about her ability to deliver such a large baby vaginally but she had not specifically asked what the risks to her and her baby were. The obstetrician did not routinely volunteer this information. She thought that any woman told of the risk of shoulder dystocia would ask for a Caesarean section. And she thought that it was 'not in the maternal interests for women to have Caesarean sections'. They should give birth vaginally if possible.

Mrs Montgomery sued the hospital for compensation on behalf of her son. She argued that the doctor had a duty to warn her of the risks and discuss the options with her.

What do you think?

1. Should a doctor's duty to inform patients depend upon current medical practice or upon what a reasonable patient would want to know?
2. Whose values are important here – the doctor's or the patient's?
3. Should it have mattered that the risks of catastrophic injury to the baby were so low?
4. Do you think that a 9 to 10 per cent risk of shoulder dystocia is significant?
5. Do you think that the doctor's failure to warn Mrs Montgomery of the risks caused the baby's injury?

What did the court think?

There had been an earlier case in the House of Lords[2] holding that doctors' decisions about what to tell the patient were to be judged by the same test, known as the Bolam test, as decisions about what treatment to give:[3] there is no liability if a 'responsible body of medical opinion' would support the doctor's decision even if an equally responsible body would not.

But in Mrs Montgomery's case, the Supreme Court disagreed with the House of Lords.[4] The Bolam test did not apply. Giving information was different from giving treatment. It was the patient's right to decide what was done with his or her own body. The patient's consent was necessary before any treatment interfering with bodily integrity was undertaken. So a doctor was under a duty to take reasonable care to ensure that the patient was aware of any material risks involved in any recommended treatment and of any reasonable alternatives. The obstetrician should have warned Mrs Montgomery of the risk of shoulder dystocia and discussed the alternative of Caesarean section with her. Where there are choices, it is the patient's rather than the doctor's values which count. On the doctor's own evidence, if properly advised, Mrs Montgomery would have chosen a Caesarean section and her son would not have been harmed. So the hospital was liable. This brought the law into line with the good practice advice which the General Medical Council was already giving to doctors.

The mentally disabled patient

Mrs Montgomery was perfectly well able to make decisions for herself if she was given the information she needed to do so. But what if the patient is not able to make his own decisions? A man whom I shall call Jimmy (not his real name) was autistic and suffered from severe learning disabilities. He was unable to speak, had very little understanding and no sense of danger. From the age of thirteen he had lived in a hospital. But after more than thirty years, he left the hospital to live with foster parents, whom I shall call Mr and Mrs Brown (not their real names). They became very fond of him and he was regarded as one of their family. He attended a day centre regularly. One day in July, he became particularly agitated there, hitting himself on the head with his fists and banging his head against the wall. The day centre could not contact Mr and Mrs Brown so they called a local doctor who gave Jimmy a sedative. They also contacted his social worker. She recommended that he be taken to the hospital. He was taken there in an ambulance. At the hospital a psychiatrist assessed that he needed inpatient treatment so he was readmitted to the hospital. Jimmy appeared to be fully compliant with this and did not attempt to leave.

Mr and Mrs Brown, however, did not agree that Jimmy should be in hospital and wanted him to come home to them. The hospital agreed that this should be the plan. But in the meantime they refused to allow Mr and Mrs Brown to visit Jimmy, for fear that he might want to leave with them before the hospital thought that he was ready.

There are special procedures under the Mental Health Act 1983 for detaining and treating patients with mental disorders in hospital if this is in the interests of their own health or safety or for the protection of other people. (This is known as sectioning.) They need the approval of a specialist mental health professional and two doctors and are subject to review by an independent mental health tribunal. But because Jimmy did what he was told and did not attempt to run away, it was decided that these procedures were not necessary: he could be admitted to hospital and kept there informally.

Mr and Mrs Brown decided to challenge this. From medieval times the writ of habeas corpus has been used to obtain the freedom of people who are unlawfully detained. The person doing the detaining is ordered to 'bring up the body' of the person being detained and provide lawful authority for the detention. If there is no lawful authority, the person must be released. In October, the Court of Appeal decided that Jimmy was being unlawfully detained by the hospital. The hospital promptly sectioned him under the Mental Health Act, so his detention was now lawful. Happily, the hospital was soon able to agree that he should be reunited with Mr and Mrs Brown and he was discharged from detention in December.

However, the Court of Appeal's decision caused consternation amongst mental health professionals. They thought it a good thing, rather than a bad thing, if patients who did not object could be admitted to hospital and treated there without the formalities and potential stigma of sectioning. So the hospital was allowed to appeal against it to the House of Lords, then the highest court in the United Kingdom. The case eventually ended up in the European Court of Human Rights in Strasbourg.

What do you think?

1. Remember all those stories of sane people being put away in mental hospitals for the convenience (or worse) of their relatives: do we need safeguards against such abuses?
2. But does that mean that no one should be admitted to a psychiatric hospital without their active consent or some special procedure to safeguard against abuse?
3. How do you feel if you learn that someone has been sectioned under the Mental Health Act? Is there a stigma associated with it?

4. What about someone like Jimmy: he wasn't able to consent but he didn't actively object. Is it kinder or crueller not to section him?
5. Jimmy was mentally disabled from an early age. What about all those older people who suffer from dementia and are unable to agree to their living arrangements? Is it kinder or crueller not to section them?
6. Jimmy was legally free to go; the ward was not locked; the hospital was acting in what was believed to be his best interests. But he was kept under sedation at all times; he was not allowed to see Mr and Mrs Brown for fear that he might want to leave with them; if he had tried to leave, he would have been stopped and then sectioned straight away. Was he really free to go?
7. Do you think that there should be some safeguards so that people like Jimmy, and people with dementia, are not kept in living arrangements – hospitals, care homes or other places – which are not in their best interests?
8. If so, what should those safeguards be?
9. What about children who, because of their mental problems, are allowed less freedom than is normal for children of their age? Do they need safeguards too?
10. What do you think the European Court of Human Rights decided in Jimmy's case?

What did the courts think?

The House of Lords held that Jimmy had not been unlawfully detained when he was admitted to hospital.[5] The Mental Health Act 1983 envisaged that people who were unable to make the decision for themselves, but who did not object, could be admitted to hospital without being sectioned. The House of Lords had held in an earlier case that it was lawful to treat people who were unable to decide for themselves if this was in their best interests.[6] Three of the Law Lords also thought that Jimmy had not been detained. Two of them thought that he had – Lord Steyn described the idea that he was free to leave the hospital as a 'fairy tale'.

A complaint was made on Jimmy's behalf to the European Court of Human Rights in Strasbourg, arguing that the United Kingdom had violated his rights under article 5 of the European Convention on Human Rights. Article 5(1) says that 'No one shall be deprived of his liberty' except in one of a number of defined circumstances and 'in accordance with a procedure prescribed by law'. The Strasbourg Court agreed with the two Law Lords who had held that Jimmy had been deprived of his liberty, i.e. detained. Article 5(1)(e) does allow the 'lawful detention . . . of persons of unsound mind'. But lawfulness requires procedural safeguards to protect a person against the arbitrary deprivation of liberty and here there were none. There was also a breach of the requirement in article 5(4) that everyone deprived of their liberty must be able to challenge their detention in a court: habeas corpus was not enough because it could not look into whether there were in fact sufficient grounds for his detention.[7]

This meant that Parliament had to introduce safeguards (known as the Deprivation of Liberty Safeguards, colloquially DOLS) to protect people who could not decide their living arrangements for themselves against the risk of being wrongly deprived of their liberty, not only in a hospital but also in a care home, when this was not in their best interests. Few would now deny the need for such safeguards – but there are still debates about how elaborate they should be.

How does this apply to children? Parents regularly deprive their young children of their liberty. This is not against the law: quite the reverse. But if, because of their mental disabilities, young people have to be subject to more restrictions on their liberty than is normal for people of their age, then however well-meaning this is, safeguards are needed to make sure that it is indeed in their best interests. As I put it, 'a gilded cage is still a cage'.[8]

The suicidal patient

Melanie Rabone was twenty-four years old. She was the much-loved daughter of her parents, Mr and Mrs Rabone. But she suffered from clinical depression and needed treatment. In March 2005, she tried to commit suicide by tying a pillowcase around her neck. She was admitted to hospital and diagnosed as suffering from a severe episode of a recurrent depressive disorder. She was discharged from hospital after eleven days and went on holiday to Egypt with her family. Soon after getting back, she cut both her wrists with broken glass but there were no mental health beds available at the hospital. In April she tied lamp flex round her neck. A hospital doctor assessed her as having a severe depressive episode with psychotic symptoms and being at high risk of deliberate self-harm and suicide. She agreed to be admitted to hospital informally. Her father told the hospital staff how concerned he was about her and urged them not to allow her to come home or to leave the hospital too soon. Her parents repeated their anxieties to staff several times.

After a week in hospital, Melanie asked to come home on leave. Her mother told the psychiatrist that she was worried about this. But he agreed to her going home for the weekend. There was no formal risk assessment or support plan, other than the care of her parents, who thought that she should not come home. If the psychiatrist had not agreed, Melanie would not have insisted on leaving the hospital, even though she was legally free to do so. She went home on the Friday. She spent most of Saturday with her mother. In the late afternoon, she told her mother that she was going to see a friend. In fact, she went to a local country park and hanged herself from a tree. There was an inquest in which the coroner returned a verdict of suicide.

Melanie's parents brought a claim on behalf of her estate – that is, the claim which she could have brought herself if she had lived. They argued that the hospital had been negligent, and that it had breached its duty of care towards her, resulting in her death. An independent expert agreed (applying the Bolam test, see 'The obstetric disaster' in chapter 14, p. 188, above) that no reasonable doctor would have allowed her to go home when he did. The hospital agreed to pay her estate £7,500 in damages: roughly £1,500 for the funeral expenses and the rest for her pain and suffering.

The Act of Parliament which gives some people a claim for 'bereavement damages' does not apply to parents who are bereaved by the death of an adult child, so Melanie's parents brought proceedings under the Human Rights Act 1998 for the anguish they had suffered because of her death. They claimed to be victims of the hospital's breach of the right to life protected by article 2 of the European Convention on Human Rights: 'Everyone's right to life shall be protected by law.' This means not only that the State authorities (which include the NHS) must not intentionally take life, but also that there must be systems of law or regulations to protect life, and 'in certain circumstances', where a public authority (including a hospital) knows or ought to know of a real and immediate risk to the life of an individual, it must take reasonable steps to prevent this risk materialising.

What do you think?

1. The duty to protect the lives of individuals includes a duty to protect certain people from committing suicide: this applies to prisoners detained in prison and to psychiatric patients detained in hospital. Should it also apply to psychiatric patients in hospital who are not detained (but could be if they threatened to leave against medical advice)?
2. If the duty does apply, did this hospital know that there was a real and immediate risk to Melanie's life? Or should it have done?
3. Could the hospital reasonably have prevented her committing suicide, given that she could but would not have left the hospital against the advice of her psychiatrist?
4. If there was a breach of a duty to protect Melanie's life, can her parents be regarded as its victims?
5. If Melanie had been under eighteen, her parents would have been able to claim £3,500 in bereavement damages. If they were the victims of a breach of article 2, what would you have given them in damages? £3,000? £7,000? £10,000? Or what?

What did the court think?

The Supreme Court held that the hospital had breached the rights of Mr and Mrs Rabone under article 2 of the European Convention on Human Rights.[9] Although Melanie was not a compulsory patient, she could have been, and she was extremely vulnerable, having been admitted to hospital precisely because she was a suicide risk. So the hospital knew that there was a real and imminent risk to her life if she was allowed to leave. And they could easily have prevented this. Mr and Mrs Rabone, who had lost their daughter because of the hospital's breach of duty, were also victims of a violation of their rights under article 2. They were each entitled to £5,000 damages.

To treat or not to treat?

David James was a talented professional musician, having spent over fifty years in the music business. In 2001, he suffered from cancer of the colon. During the course of his treatment, he had a stoma – an opening in his abdomen to connect his colon to the outside of his abdomen. In May 2012, when he was around sixty-eight years old, he was admitted to hospital because of a problem with his stoma. This was soon solved but he picked up an infection. He also developed chronic obstructive pulmonary disease (COPD), a lung condition which affected his breathing, as well as an acute kidney injury and persistent low blood pressure. He was admitted to the critical care unit and placed on a ventilator. After that, his condition fluctuated. He had a stroke, which left him with right-sided weakness and tightening of the muscles and joints in his legs. He suffered a cardiac arrest which needed six minutes of cardiopulmonary resuscitation (CPR) to bring him back to life. He had more infections, which led to septic shock and multiple organ failure. But in between he could be taken off the ventilator and put onto a less intrusive form of help with his breathing. Even so, because he had been immobile for so long, he could not sit or stand for himself. He was fed and watered through a naso-gastric tube. In short, he was very disabled. His chances of leaving the critical care unit, let alone the hospital, were very low.

Since July, he had also been considered to lack the mental capacity to make decisions about his medical treatment. There was severe neurological damage. But he recognised and was pleased to see his wife and his family who visited often. He kissed his wife when she leaned in to him. He mouthed what seemed to be words in reply to her and hospital staff. He was a devoted family man, with three children, three grandchildren and many friends. Family and friends visited him regularly in hospital. His daughter felt that he got a lot of enjoyment from this. She herself was there for four hours every day. He turned the pages of a newspaper, smiling while he did so, put on and took off his glasses, and appeared to enjoy watching videos on his son's phone.

There was no question of stopping the help with his breathing or the artificial feeding and watering. But the hospital wanted not to have to do three things, if his condition deteriorated to the point where he needed them: one was to administer strong drugs to correct episodes of dangerously low blood pressure (which had been done in the past); another was filtering his blood through a machine to make up for a lack of kidney function (which had not yet been done); and the third was CPR – restarting his heart if it stopped beating, whether by drugs, by electric shock therapy or by physical compression of the chest and inflating the lungs (which had been done when his heart stopped in August). The clinical team thought that these would not be in his best interests. Originally, they also wanted to stop giving him intravenous antibiotics, but they did not pursue this.

The family disagreed. They thought that every time he had had an infection he had pulled through. The gaps between infections were becoming longer. While he would never regain his previous quality of life, he got a lot of enjoyment from seeing his family and close friends. He himself would want to pull through his current predicament as he had been determined to beat his cancer.

The hospital applied to the Court of Protection for permission to withhold those three treatments should he need them. The Official Solicitor was appointed to safeguard Mr James's interests. He backed the clinical team.

What do you think?

1. Everyone has the right to decide what is to be done to their own body. If a person who has the capacity to decide for himself refuses permission for treatment – even treatment which will save his life – it cannot be given. So is the right question, not whether it would be lawful *not* to give certain treatments but whether it would be lawful to *give* them should the need arise?
2. But what if a person lacks the ability to decide for himself? How should the decision be made? Should it be made by the doctors responsible for his treatment and care? Or should it be made by his nearest and dearest? Or if they disagree, should an independent outsider (such as a judge) decide what is in his best interests?

3. Would it be in Mr James's best interests to receive each of the three treatments in question if they were necessary to keep him alive?
4. Should keeping him alive be the only test or are there circumstances when it would not be in a patient's best interests to be kept alive?
5. Is it relevant that the patient would have wanted those treatments if he had been capable of making the decision for himself?
6. Is it relevant that the patient was never going to get back to how his life had been before he went into hospital?
7. Is it relevant that the patient appeared to enjoy the life that he did have, limited though it was?

What did the court think?

The hospital had applied for a declaration that it would be *lawful to withhold* the three treatments.[10] The Supreme Court pointed out that this was the wrong question. The court cannot order the hospital to provide the treatments, any more than the patient could do. The question was whether it would be *lawful to administer* them. This depended upon whether this was in the patient's best interests. The starting point is a strong presumption that it is in a person's best interests to stay alive. But decision-makers have to consider the best interests of this particular patient at this particular time; looking at his welfare in the widest sense, not just medical but also social and psychological; considering the nature of the treatment, what it involves and its prospects of success, and the likely outcome for the patient; putting themselves in the place of this particular patient and asking what his attitude is or is likely to be; and consulting his carers and others who are interested in his welfare. Recovery did not mean a return to full health but a return to a quality of life that the patient would think worthwhile. The burdens involved in the treatment had to be weighed against the benefits of continued existence. When a patient was suffering from an incurable illness, disease or disability, it did not make sense to talk of recovering a state of good health. The trial judge had been right to refuse the hospital's application, because it was too soon to say that the treatments in questions were *not* in Mr

James's best interests. But the judge had applied the right tests. By the time the case got to the Court of Appeal, Mr James's condition had deteriorated dramatically, so it was not in his best interests to give the treatments. In fact, he died shortly afterwards but the Supreme Court heard his widow's appeal because of the importance of clarifying the law.

Lessons learnt?

Once again, we can see the importance of the Human Rights Act in safeguarding life and liberty – particularly the liberty of people who, because of mental disability, are unable to make decisions for themselves. But we can also see the importance our law has always attached to autonomy and bodily integrity. We must all take reasonable care to prevent bodily harm to a person we can foresee may be harmed if we don't take care. We must not invade another person's bodily integrity without their consent. We must take reasonable care to give them the information which they might reasonably want to know before asking for their consent. It is up to them whether to say yes or no.

These cases do not touch the biggest question of all: should someone who wants to die be allowed to have help to end their own life? The autonomy principle means that it is lawful for someone to refuse treatment which is necessary to save or prolong their life. It is also lawful for someone to refuse food and water and so starve themselves to death. It is also lawful for someone to take active steps to commit suicide. But it is unlawful to help someone to do so. In a case concerning two very severely disabled people who wanted help to end the lives which they found intolerable, two Supreme Court justices thought that this was incompatible with their human rights – to decide the time and manner of their own death; three justices thought that it might be, but this was not the time or the case in which to say so; and four thought that it was a matter solely for Parliament: only Parliament could change the law against assisting suicide and only Parliament could properly debate the issues and form a view about it.[11] As I write, Parliament is currently struggling to do this.

We shall turn in Part Three to the different ways in which Parliament and the courts make the law.

Part Three

MAKING LAW FOR EVERYONE

Introduction

There are three ways in which law is made in the United Kingdom: in Parliament, in the government and in the courts. Parliament is at the top of the tree. Most countries in the developed world have a written Constitution which sets out how the country is governed, who makes the laws and who enforces the laws. We don't have a written Constitution in this country. But we do have a bundle of laws, customs and conventions which cover the same ground. And the guiding principle of that Constitution is the sovereignty of Parliament, summed up in the adage that 'Parliament can make or unmake any law'. The government, the courts and everyone else have to obey the laws which Parliament has made. Parliament can make a law which obliges the government to act in a certain way or empowers it to act in a certain way or prevents it from acting in a certain way. But the one thing which Parliament cannot do is make a law which prevents a later Parliament from acting in a certain way. Parliament cannot bind its successors.

Written Constitutions are very different. In a written Constitution some laws are entrenched. This means that they cannot be changed as easily as other laws. It may need a so-called super-majority – say two-thirds – in two Houses of Parliament. It may need a referendum of the people. In a federation such as the United States of America, it may need the agreement of all or most of the Member States. There are many variations. But it does mean that a Parliament cannot always do what it likes. And it also means that there has to be a body independent of Parliament to tell Parliament when it cannot do what it likes. In countries in the English-speaking world, that body is usually a Supreme Court, which sits at the top of the ordinary justice system. In other countries with legal systems based on those of continental Europe, that body may be a special Constitutional Court, which sits outside the ordinary justice system. The United Kingdom is very unusual: we have no court which can tell Parliament that it cannot do what it wants to do. Even our Supreme Court cannot strike down provisions in an Act of the UK Parliament. But, as we shall see, even though our Parliament can in theory do what it likes, there are some things which it really shouldn't do.

Laws contained in an Act of the UK Parliament are known as primary legislation. But there is another type of legislation, known as delegated or secondary legislation. It is called delegated because Parliament has given the power to government ministers, or to other public bodies such as local authorities, to make it, usually in the shape of rules, regulations or by-laws. Parliament decides the scope of what can be done, and what the power should be used for, but leaves the details to be worked out in government. This type of law is also called secondary, because here the courts do have a role. These laws have to be within the scope of the power which Parliament has given to whomever made them. And they have to be made for the purposes for which Parliament gave the power. If a rule or regulation is found to be outside that scope or purpose – what is known as *ultra vires* – then the courts can and do strike it down as invalid. We shall see a couple of examples of this in chapter 16 on making law in government.

Primary legislation is controversial because it can do anything. Secondary legislation is also controversial. This is partly because there is so much of it – volumes and volumes of rules and regulations are made every year. This makes a mockery of the principle that everyone is presumed to know the law – during the Covid-19 pandemic, for example, you could be prosecuted for breaking a rule which you did not know existed. But secondary legislation is also controversial because of the lack of democratic control. Primary legislation made by Parliament has to go through a complicated process of approval by democratically elected politicians – as we shall see. Secondary legislation is usually (though not always) made by democratically elected politicians – ministers in central government or councillors in local government. But it is subject to much less parliamentary scrutiny. Some of it is subject to no parliamentary control at all. Some of it has to be laid before Parliament. Sometimes this is just for information. Sometimes Parliament can disapprove of it by passing a negative resolution. Sometimes it has to be positively approved by an affirmative resolution in each House of Parliament before coming into force. It all depends upon what the parent Act which delegated the power requires. But even if Parliament could in theory disapprove or refuse to approve a particular piece of delegated legislation, this hardly ever happens – even when it uses what are known as Henry VIII powers. These are powers given to government ministers to amend provisions in an Act of Parliament by secondary legislation. So a law which has been made by Parliament – for example, about how the Supreme Court justices are chosen – might be changed by regulations made by a government minister.

There is another type of secondary legislation. These are the laws made by the Scottish Parliament, the Northern Ireland Assembly and the Welsh Senedd. The UK Parliament gave these devolved parliaments the power to make laws for their own part of the United Kingdom. Their powers are carefully defined in the Scotland Act 1998, the Northern Ireland Act 1998 and the Government of Wales Act 2006. So their laws can be challenged in the courts for being outside the scope of their powers – not only by the people who object to them but also by the governments of the UK or the other parts of the UK. But the courts are more reluctant to strike down these laws because they have gone through a much more rigorous process of democratic scrutiny than have the laws made by central or local government.

Both primary and secondary laws can claim a degree of democratic legitimacy. They have been made or approved by politicians who have been elected by the people. How real this is can be debated. Many of these laws have not been promised or even foreshowed in the manifestos which the mainstream political parties publish before a general election. But at least if the people do not like what the Members of Parliament or the government have done, they can vote them out at the next general election. The same is true of the by-laws made by local authorities for the areas they govern.

The courts are different. They have three different roles in lawmaking. Although they cannot strike down provisions in primary legislation, they can decide what those provisions mean – and sometimes this can lead to results which might surprise the Parliamentarians who made them. We shall see an example of this in chapter 15 on making law in the courts. They can also decide what secondary legislation means and whether it is outside the powers which Parliament gave to whomever made it. We shall see examples of this in chapter 16 on making law in government. And they can make law themselves, through their own decisions in those many areas of the law which are not – or not yet – governed by legislation of any sort.

The courts perform an essential role but they cannot, and do not, claim the same democratic legitimacy as Parliament and government. Our judges are not elected by the people. These days they are not even chosen by the government. Politics do not come into it. They are chosen, in England and Wales, by the Judicial Appointments Commission; in Scotland, by the Judicial Appointments Board; and in Northern Ireland, by the Judicial Appointments Commission for Northern Ireland. These bodies are at arm's length from government. They conduct the selection processes and recommend the people selected to the government. The government can in theory reject any particular recommendation, or ask the commission to think again, but in practice it does not do this. And once appointed, judges hold office 'during good behaviour'. They can only be removed from office with difficulty and by special procedures.

The independence of the judiciary is another fundamental principle of our Constitution. Judges have to be free – both to make decisions without political interference of any kind and on occasions to hold the government to account. But although the judges are not elected, they are also accountable: to the people who appear in front of them and their lawyers; to the public and media who observe and can criticise what they do; to the higher courts which can overturn their decisions if they are wrong; and ultimately to Parliament which can overturn judicial decisions which it does not like: we shall see an example of this in chapter 16 on making law in government.

So should we have a written Constitution? I am often asked this question, particularly when Parliament passes or plans to pass legislation which challenges fundamental principles. The Safety of Rwanda (Asylum and Immigration) Bill, as we shall see, did just that. Surely, it is said, there should be some laws which Parliament cannot make, still less authorise others to make, without special processes. Surely, every person must have some fundamental rights which cannot easily be taken away. Surely, the courts cannot be prevented from scrutinising the legality of what government has done. Surely, almost every other country in the developed world has a written Constitution so why shouldn't we?

As I see it, there are at least three reasons why the chances of its happening here are vanishingly small. First, it would mean that Parliament, and in particular the House of Commons, would have to vote to limit its own powers. Turkeys and Christmas spring to mind.

Second, it would mean that the unelected judges would have power to strike down the laws passed by the elected Parliament of the day. I know of no judge in the United Kingdom who would welcome such a power, not least because it would lead to the politicians taking a much greater interest in who is appointed as a judge, particularly in the higher courts, than they currently do. Contrast the United States of America, where the Supreme Court can strike down laws made, not only in any of the states, but also in the Congress of the United States. Its judges are nominated by the President and approved by the Senate. Not surprisingly, presidents are inclined to nominate judges whose politics coincide with their own. I can honestly say that that doesn't happen here: my first two appointments were recommended by Conservative Lord Chancellors, my next two by Labour Lord Chancellors, and my final two by independent appointment commissions. Many people think that it is a good thing that our judges are not currently appointed for political reasons.

Third, it almost always takes a constitutional moment for a country to decide that it must have a written Constitution – a moment such as the seizing of independence from the colonial overlord, as in the United States of America in 1776; or a seismic revolution, as in France in 1789; or the progressive granting of power to colonial territories, leading ultimately to independence, as in most of the rest of the British Empire during the twentieth century; or the reconstruction of a country after a catastrophic war, as in most of continental Europe after the Second World War.

We had our constitutional moment in 1688, when James II abandoned the throne and William and Mary were invited by Parliament to take it over – but only on Parliament's terms, terms to which they agreed and which were embodied in the Bill of Rights of 1689. But we have not had one since – we have not had to break free of a colonial overlord, we have not suffered a violent popular revolution, we have not lost a war on our own territory. However much we might want a written Constitution, I doubt whether we would want to descend into the turmoil and strife of the seventeenth century ever again – which takes us back to turkeys voting for Christmas.

In what follows, I look at examples of lawmaking by the courts, by the government and by Parliament. I look at how the courts develop old principles or devise new ones to cope with new situations, at how they interpret the laws made by Parliament and government, at how they try and ensure that the laws made by the government are within the powers which Parliament has given, and at how Parliament itself passes new laws. Lawmaking is all about stories and the stories are very varied – from human trafficking, to cheating at cards, to regulating all our lives during the Covid-19 pandemic, to telling us all that we must treat Rwanda as a safe country to which to send would-be asylum seekers, whether or not it is or remains a safe country. I hope you find them as interesting as I do.

15 Making Law in the Courts

It is quite an awesome thought, when you become a High Court judge, that your decisions may be making law. It is a big responsibility, but it is only carrying on the centuries-old tradition of judge-made law. For most of our history, up until the nineteenth and twentieth centuries, Parliament did not make many laws which affected the whole population. They made private laws which affected only the individuals or enterprises to which they applied. Most of the law which affected the whole population was made by the decisions of the judges. They were applying the principles which had been developed in the courts over many centuries. Much of the law which applies today is still judge-made law. What makes an agreement binding upon the people or enterprises who made it? When can someone who causes harm to another person or his property be made to pay compensation for it? What does the criminal law mean by words such as 'intentionally', 'recklessly', or 'dishonestly'? The basic principles of the law of contract were devised by the judges, although Parliament has intervened to regulate certain types of contract, usually because of an imbalance of power between the parties, such as landlord and tenant, employer and employee, supplier and consumer. The basic principles of the law of tort, wrongfully causing harm to another individual or enterprise, were devised by the judges. Once again, Parliament has intervened on specific points, such as the liability of occupiers of land towards people who come onto the land, because it was thought that the judges had got it wrong. The basic principles of blameworthiness in the criminal law were devised by the judges, although most of the specific offences, such as theft or burglary, are now defined in legislation. The basic principles of the ownership of land were devised by the judges, but Parliament decided that they had made such a mess of it that since

1925 most of the land law has been covered by legislation. The basic principles of the ownership of many other forms of property are still those devised by the judges. Above all, perhaps, the basic principles of the High Court's power to review the legality of actions and decisions by lower courts and tribunals or by government – known as judicial review – were devised by the judges.

The judges have to decide how these basic principles apply in the modern world, where the context may be very different from when they were first developed, or when completely new situations come along which have never been decided before. But it is not a free-for-all. There are recognised techniques for deciding such questions. But as we shall also see in the examples which follow, some judges are more adventurous than others in developing the law to produce the solutions which they think are just. The problem with judge-made law is that judges, however learned in the law, are human beings with their own values and experiences. They do not always agree where justice lies.

There is also a hierarchy among the judges, designed to promote certainty and continuity. At the top is the Supreme Court of the United Kingdom, whose decisions are binding – that is, they lay down how other cases raising the same legal issue must be decided – on all the courts and tribunals in the United Kingdom. The Supreme Court is not bound to follow its own previous decisions, or those of its predecessor, the Appellate Committee of the House of Lords; but it will normally do so, unless convinced that justice requires a different approach. Next down come the Courts of Appeal in England and Wales, Scotland and Northern Ireland (in Scotland, the Court of Appeal is called the Inner House of the Court of Session). Their decisions are binding on the courts and tribunals below them in their respective parts of the United Kingdom. The Court of Appeal in England and Wales is also generally bound by its own previous decisions. Next down come the High Courts in England and Wales, Scotland and Northern Ireland (in Scotland, the Outer House of the Court of Session or, in criminal cases, the High Court). Their judges' decisions are binding on the lower courts and tribunals in their part of the United Kingdom but not on one another. If there are conflicting High Court decisions, the High Court and the lower courts can choose between them. The decisions of lower courts, the county courts and magistrates' courts in England and Wales and Northern Ireland, the sheriffs and magistrates courts in Scotland, are not binding on anyone (except the parties to the particular case). In the tribunal system, the decisions of the Upper Tribunal and the Employment Appeal Tribunal are binding on the First-tier Tribunal and the employment tribunals.

Binding decisions are called precedents, because they have to be followed in future cases, according to where they sit in the hierarchy. Non-binding decisions do not create precedents in the technical sense, because they do not have to be followed in future cases. But they are sometimes called precedents, because they may be a useful indicator of the way the judicial wind is blowing. Generally, judges regard the decisions of other judges, even if not binding, as 'persuasive'. They require good reasons to take a different view.

We are talking here about decisions on points of law – arguments about what the rules are. It's surprising how many of these there still can be. Decisions on points of fact – what actually happened or what the state of affairs is – stand, unless and until they are set aside by an appeal court (or, very exceptionally, by Parliament). Many decisions on points of law are about the precise meaning of the words used in an Act of Parliament or secondary legislation. But many are still about the judge-made law. So let's look at four recent decisions of the Supreme Court to illustrate the range and the methodology. How does the fact that someone has been involved in unlawful activity affect their legal rights and liabilities? When can one landowner object to what a neighbouring landowner is doing with his land? What do we mean by dishonesty? And when – if ever – can Parliament prevent the courts from deciding whether the decision of a public body is lawful? I was involved with three of these cases, so of course I have a view about whether we got it right.

Visiting the Supreme Court of the United Kingdom

The highest court in the land used to be a committee of the House of Lords, the upper House of Parliament. This was an accident of history. Nowhere else in the world is the top court part of the body which makes legislation. Their roles are different and should be kept separate. So in 2009 the Supreme Court of the United Kingdom was set up to take over the role of the Appellate Committee of the House of Lords. The Law Lords who used to sit there became the Justices of the Supreme Court. We moved out of the Houses of Parliament and into a handsome building across Parliament Square, known as the Middlesex Guildhall, because it was built in 1913 as the home of Middlesex County Council.

It was the ideal size and the ideal location – on Parliament Square, opposite the Houses of Parliament, with the Treasury (the most powerful government department) on one side and Westminster Abbey (representing God and the monarch) on the other. All the elements of the Constitution ranged around the square. Its original wealth of exuberant decoration – in stone and wood and glass – was restored, and new features – such as carpets and curtains in vibrant patterns and colours – were introduced. The idea was to create a beautiful, friendly and welcoming place, open to all, but where serious work could be done.

We walk in from Parliament Square, under an elaborate stone-carved frieze which includes King John sealing the Magna Carta in 1215. We are greeted by friendly security guards who direct us through the discreet security arch to the right. Dividing the entrance hall between the unsecured and the secured areas is a glass screen embellished with the very moving words of the judicial oath: 'I will do right to all manner of people after the laws and usages of this realm, without fear or favour, affection or ill-will.' I have sworn that oath many times (with each new judicial appointment) and it always brings home to me the enormous responsibility of being a judge – trying to do the right thing, trying to treat everyone fairly, trying to put away 'fear or favour, affection or ill-will'. On the other side of the screen are the doors into the court's library, bearing a facsimile of the 1227 version of Magna Carta with the famous words 'to no one will we deny, to no one will we delay, right or justice' picked out. There is also a reception desk where we can pick up a variety of leaflets, including a self-guided tour of the public parts of the building. When the court is sitting, we can also pick up a sheet of paper which will tell us what the case is all about and who the judges are. Anyone can pop into any of the courtrooms: there is no need to book.

The illegality defence

One of the ancient principles devised by the judges, which is now firmly embedded in the law, is summed up in the Latin phrase *ex turpi causa non oritur actio*, no cause of action arises from a wicked source, explained by Chief Justice Mansfield in 1775 like this: 'No court will lend its aid to a man who founds his cause of action upon an immoral or illegal act'.[1] But what does this mean? We are in Court Number 1 in the Supreme Court to find out.

Court Number 1 used to be the council chamber for Middlesex County Council. It has a magnificent ceiling bedecked with wooden flying angels. The benches on which the councillors used to sit have been turned into seats for the general public, with wooden bench ends and armrests carved with kings and creatures. The floor has been flattened. There is a curved bench at one end of the room which is designed for nine justices (although it can hold eleven at a pinch). Facing the justices are two curved benches for the advocates and their teams. So we are all sitting round a notional oval table, nothing like a traditional courtroom. There are nine justices hearing this case, headed by the President, Lord Neuberger of Abbotsbury, and the Deputy President, Baroness Hale of Richmond (me). Also on the panel are two justices who have espoused very different approaches to the problem, Lord Sumption and Lord Toulson.

The facts are simple. Mr Patel paid a total of £620,000 to Mr Mirza. The purpose was to bet on the price of shares in RBS (the Royal Bank of Scotland) using insider information which Mr Mirza expected to get from contacts within RBS, and to share the profits. This was a conspiracy to commit illegal insider dealing. If the plan had gone ahead and profits had been made, Mr Patel would not have been able to sue to get his share of them. No court would lend its aid to a man who founded his cause of action on such an unlawful act. But the information was not forthcoming and the plan did not go ahead. There was no insider dealing. So Mr Patel wanted his money back. Mr Mirza refused, pointing out that the agreement they had made was for an illegal purpose.

Should Mr Patel get his money back? He had paid it over for a purpose which had wholly failed. If you pay over money for goods which never arrive or a service which is never given you are entitled to get your money back. Normally, therefore, it would be unjust for Mr Mirza to hang on to the money. It would be an unmerited windfall. But the purpose was illegal. And Mr Patel could not explain why he had paid the money over, and why he wanted it back, without explaining the purpose. That sounds very like Lord Mansfield's proposition – the court would be lending its aid to a man who founded his cause of action on an illegal act.

Over more than two centuries since Lord Mansfield stated the principle, there have been hundreds of cases trying to work out what it means in practice. Some of them tried to devise some clear rules – most notably that if a claimant has to rely on an illegal act or transaction in order to make his claim, then his claim will generally fail, but if he can make his claim without relying on the illegal act or transaction, then he will generally succeed. This rule was affirmed by the House of Lords in a case called *Tinsley v Milligan*.[2] Two women bought a house together, both contributing to the purchase price and both understanding that they owned it in equal shares. But it was put into the name of only one of them so that the other could make false claims for welfare benefits. When they fell out, the legal owner tried to claim the whole property but the other woman was allowed to get her share. She did not have to rely on the illegal reason why the property was put into only one name. She could rely on her contribution to the purchase and the common understanding that they would share equally.

A rule like this may be clear, but it is likely to operate in an arbitrary fashion. Many lawyers argued for a more flexible approach, balancing the competing legal policy considerations applicable to the particular case. No one seriously expected Parliament to sort it out by enacting some clear rules – it is very difficult to translate principles like this into the sort of precise language used in Acts of Parliament. The Law Commission, an independent body set up by Act of Parliament to promote the reform of the law, recommended that the judges could develop the law to solve the problem.

Matters came to a head in 2014 when three cases reached the Supreme Court. The first was *Hounga v Allen*,[3] the case of the fourteen-year-old girl brought here to work for a Nigerian family (described earlier in 'The victim of trafficking' in chapter 11, p. 155).

The court did not ask itself whether her claim was based on an illegal act. Instead, it asked on the one hand, what was the policy underlying the prohibition of employment? And on the other hand, were there aspects of public policy going the other way? Compensating her for the injury to her feelings caused by the discrimination was not allowing her to profit from her unlawful employment or to evade a penalty imposed by the criminal law. Refusing the claim would allow people like her employers to believe that they could get away with their behaviour. Public policy favoured protecting the victims of people trafficking such as this.

Later in 2014, the Supreme Court heard two other cases, *Les Laboratoires Servier v Apotek Inc* and *Bilta (UK) Ltd v Nazir*,[4] in which the illegality defence was raised, although it was dismissed as irrelevant in both of them. But the justices voiced some very different views about it. As Lord Neuberger put it in *Bilta*, 'The debate can be seen as epitomising the familiar tension between the need for principle, clarity and certainty in the law and the equally important desire to achieve a fair and appropriate result in each case.' In *Les Laboratoires Servier*, four out of the five justices, led by Lord Sumption, agreed with the rule-based approach in *Tinsley v Milligan* but without considering *Hounga*. (The Supreme Court sits in panels of at least five judges, and one panel does not always know what another panel is doing.) One of them, Lord Toulson, who had been chairman of the Law Commission while it was considering the illegality defence, strongly disagreed. In *Bilta*, two of the seven justices, including Lord Sumption, continued to support the rule-based approach, while two of them, including Lord Toulson, took the *Hounga* view, and three of them sat on the fence. Lord Neuberger said that the proper approach needed to be addressed by the Supreme Court, conceivably with a panel of nine justices, 'as soon as appropriately possible'.

So that is why nine justices sat to hear the case of *Patel v Mirza*.[5] That case too could have been decided without resolving the difference of approach. The plan had not been carried out. Mr Mirza had no right to the money he was hanging on to. Letting Mr Patel have it back was not enforcing the illegal agreement or letting him profit from it. Nevertheless, Lord Neuberger thought that it was a suitable case in which to resolve matters. And six of the justices agreed with the more flexible approach espoused by Lord Toulson, while

Lord Sumption continued to disagree. Lord Toulson explained his approach like this:

'The essential rationale of the illegality doctrine is that it would be contrary to the public interest to enforce a claim if to do so would be harmful to the integrity of the legal system . . . In assessing whether the public interest would be harmed in that way, it is necessary (a) to consider the underlying purpose of the prohibition which has been transgressed and whether that purpose will be enhanced by denial of the claim, (b) to consider any other relevant public policy on which denial of the claim may have an impact and (c) to consider whether denial of the claim would be a proportionate response to the illegality, bearing in mind that punishment is a matter for the criminal courts.'

So Mr Patel could sue for his money back. Indeed, if Mary Hounga's case had been heard in a lower court after *Patel v Mirza*, she would probably have been awarded a fair sum to compensate her for the value of the work she had been forced to do for the Allen family without reward – not allowing her to enforce the illegal contract of employment but not allowing the Allen family unfairly to profit from her services.

This is a tough example with which to begin an exploration of judicial lawmaking. Mary Hounga's case is a good illustration of the advantages of the new policy-based approach – weighing the various reasons why she should, or should not, have a remedy against the Allen family. The aim is to arrive at the most just result in each case. But of course, there are value judgments involved. Some judges might attach more importance to deterring trafficking in child labour even if this means punishing its victims. Once such value judgments are brought into it, the results in any given case may be even more unpredictable than they were under the old approach. A simple and clear rule, like that in *Tinsley v Middleton*, begins to look more attractive. I was in the majority in *Patel v Mirza*, so I agree with the new approach. But that doesn't mean that I cannot see both sides of the argument.

Private Nuisance

Just as ancient as the defence of illegality is the tort of private nuisance. A tort is an interference with the rights of another person – an individual or an enterprise – for which the law has decided to give a remedy. The best-known example is the tort of negligence – if I can reasonably foresee that my acts or omissions may cause actual harm to another person if I do not behave carefully, then I have a duty to take reasonable care. That general principle was laid down by the House of Lords less than a hundred years ago in the case of *Donoghue v Stevenson*.[6] Allegedly (because the case was dealt with as a preliminary point of law before the facts were decided) the claimant went to a café with her friend and the friend bought her a bottle of ginger beer. The bottle glass was opaque, so she couldn't see that it contained the decomposed remains of a snail. She drank the ginger beer, and suffered shock and severe gastroenteritis as a result. She could not sue the café for supplying faulty goods because she had not bought them. So she sued the manufacturer. The House of Lords held that the manufacturer might be liable in negligence. It deduced a general principle from a number of well-established instances of liability for failing to take sufficient care. As Lord Atkin put it, comparing the law of negligence with the parable of the Good Samaritan:

'The rule that you must love your neighbour becomes in law, you must not injure your neighbour; and the lawyer's question, Who is my neighbour? receives a restricted reply. You must take reasonable care to avoid acts or omissions which you can reasonably foresee would be likely to injure your neighbour. Who, then, in law is my neighbour? The answer seems to be – persons who are so closely and directly affected by my act that I ought reasonably to have them in contemplation as being so affected when I am directing my mind to the acts or omissions which are called in question.'

That is why you are liable to pay compensation if you injure someone or damage his car by driving carelessly. But there have to be limits. The foreseeable consequences of failing to take reasonable care could be endless. Bodily injury or property damage are one thing. But what about psychiatric injury or financial loss unrelated to any bodily injury? The courts are still working out how far the duty to prevent these goes.

The tort of private nuisance goes back a lot further than the tort of negligence. No doubt this is because it protects rights of property. It consists of wrongly preventing or interfering with the exercise of another person's rights over his land. Some cases are obvious – blocking a private right of way or stopping the flow of water to which the claimant has a right. Less obvious are the cases where the use to which one person puts his land interferes with the use to which another person puts his land. This could be from physical invasions, like Japanese knotweed or cricket balls, but more often it comes from intangible things such as fumes, noise, vibration or smells. But what is it that turns one person's use of his land into a wrong to which another person can object? The principle which has been quoted time and again was stated by Baron Bramwell in *Bamford v Turnley* well over a hundred years ago:[7]

'... those acts necessary for the common and ordinary use and occupation of land and houses may be done, if conveniently done, without subjecting those who do them to an action.'

So it's an unusual use which makes the interference wrongful. But that can depend upon where you are. What is 'common and ordinary' in one area may not be 'common and ordinary' in another. In *Bamford v Turnley*, the defendant was making bricks and the claimant complained that the fumes given off by the brick kilns made his home 'unfit for healthy or comfortable occupation'. So it all depended upon whether the defendant's use was 'common and ordinary' in the area. Baron Bramwell went on:

'[This principle] is as much for the advantage of one owner as of another; for the very nuisance the one complains of, as the result of the ordinary use of his neighbour's land, he himself will create in the ordinary use of his own, and the reciprocal nuisances are of a relatively trifling character. The convenience of such a rule may be indicated by calling it a rule of give and take, live and let live.'

But what is ordinary and what is not? What does 'live and let live' entail? In 2023, the Supreme Court had to consider these questions in a novel context. The Tate Modern art gallery was created from the disused Bankside Power Station on the south side of the river Thames opposite St Paul's Cathedral. In 2016 a striking new extension was added to the complex, the Blavatnik building. A popular feature was a viewing gallery which ran round all four sides of the top floor, giving 360-degree views over London. Unfortunately, this included views into some of the nearby flats at Neo Bankside, which had been completed in 2012. These (very expensive) flats also had a striking design. The walls of the living area were made entirely of glass. This meant that visitors to the Tate's viewing gallery could see right in: 'Some look, some peer, some photograph, some wave. Occasionally binoculars are used. Many photographs showing the interiors of the flat have been posted on social media.' Thousands of people had seen these posts. The gallery attracted hundreds of thousands of visitors each year (estimated at 500,000 to 600,000) and originally was open whenever Tate Modern was open, from 10.00 a.m. to 6.00 p.m. on Sundays to Thursdays and 10.00 a.m. to 10.00 p.m. on Fridays and Saturdays. These hours were slightly reduced when the flat-owners complained and notices were put up asking visitors to respect their privacy. These efforts were regarded as pretty feeble and the flat-owners sued: *Fearn v Board of Trustees of the Tate Gallery*.[8]

The first question was whether visual intrusion like this could be an actionable nuisance at all. We all have to put up with being overlooked by our neighbours to some extent – more so in cities and towns than in villages and the countryside. The trial judge, who heard all the evidence and visited the site, concluded that if it was bad enough, visual intrusion could amount to a nuisance.[9] The Court of Appeal held that it could not.[10] However, the trial judge also held that this particular intrusion did not amount to a nuisance because the Tate's use of the top floor as a viewing gallery was reasonable and the flat-owners were to some extent the authors of their own misfortune – for buying flats with glass walls and not remedying matters by lowering the blinds or installing net curtains. Had it been necessary for them to do so, the Court of Appeal would have agreed with him on this point.

The claimants appealed to the Supreme Court. It is an indication of how difficult the justices found the case that they heard the arguments over two days in December 2021 and did not deliver judgment until February 2023. The five justices all agreed with the trial judge that visual intrusion could amount to an actionable nuisance but were split three to two over whether it did so in this case.

The majority, led by Lord Leggatt, found the application of the legal principles to the facts of the case 'quite straightforward'. The viewing and photography taking place from the Tate caused a substantial interference with the ordinary use and enjoyment of the flat-owners' homes. The locality was described by the judge as 'a part of urban south London used for a mixture of residential, cultural, tourist and commercial purposes'. But the Tate had not alleged that operating a public viewing gallery was necessary for the common and ordinary use and occupation of their land as an art gallery. 'Inviting members of the public to look out from a viewing gallery is manifestly a very particular and exceptional use of land. It cannot even be said to be a necessary or ordinary incident of operating an art museum.' So the Tate could not rely on the principle of give and take.

The minority, led by Lord Sales, took a different view. They agreed that the Tate's use of its land was not common and ordinary, but neither was the flat-owners' use of their property (most people do not live in glass houses). Where the use of its land by both claimant and defendant fell 'outside existing standards of common and ordinary use of land' there was no reason 'why the unusual use of land by the defendant should give way to unusual use of land by the claimant without any attempt to balance the competing interests'. Indeed, linking matters to the 'common and ordinary use' of land was 'too conservative as regards the development of land' and conflicted with the general policy of the law that a landowner should be free to use his land as he wishes – including building on it what he wanted. Landowners might succeed – either as claimants or as defendants – even if their use was not common and ordinary. It was necessary to have recourse to 'a more general principle of objective reasonableness' informed by the standards of the locale. The judge had found that the operation of the viewing gallery was not inherently objectionable in the neighbourhood. Had the claimant's flats been more conventionally constructed, with walls and windows, there would have been no nuisance. The Neo Bankside flat-owners 'could not turn the operation of the viewing gallery into a nuisance by reason of the development of their own property according to a design which was out of line with the norm for the area'.

You may be wondering about planning permission. Both developments had planning permission. But both sides agreed that this was irrelevant. Planning control protects the public interest in the orderly development of land. Private nuisance protects the land-holders' interest in the use and enjoyment of their land.

Although the majority decided that this was an actionable private nuisance, the Supreme Court did not decide what the remedy should be. There was a debate to be had: should the Tate be ordered to close part of the gallery to prevent the intrusion or would the payment of compensation be enough? If the parties could not agree on a solution, the High Court would have to decide. The gallery had in fact been closed since the beginning of the Covid-19 pandemic in 2020. In October 2023 it was reopened but with access restricted to three sides of the building. The south side looking into the Neo Bankside flats was closed. This appears to have been a solution negotiated between the parties after the Supreme Court's judgment.

On one view, this was not a point of law at all, but a point of fact: were the parties' respective use of their properties common and ordinary for the area or were they not? But there were points of law. Is visual intrusion capable of being an actionable nuisance at all? Is common and ordinary use the test? What if neither use is common and ordinary? What if the defendant's use is not common and ordinary but it is reasonable to expect the claimant to put up with it? What if the claimant's use is not common and ordinary but the defendant's interference is such that the claimant should not be expected to put up with it? I doubt very much whether the Bankside case will be the end of the story. The majority may have been right in their interpretation of the multitude of past decided cases but the minority were proposing a more dynamic and forward-looking approach for the future – not unlike the more dynamic and forward-looking approach to the illegality defence in *Patel v Mirza*.

Dishonesty

The purpose of the civil law is to vindicate the rights of an individual or enterprise – usually by compensating them for past violations of their rights but sometimes, as in the case of private nuisance, by preventing invasions in the future. The purpose of the criminal law is to punish people who have offended against the interests of the whole community by committing crimes. Most criminal offences are defined in Acts of Parliament, such as the Offences against the Person Act 1861, the Theft Act 1968, or the Sexual Offences Act 2003, or in Regulations, such as those dealing with road traffic offences. But the general principles of blameworthiness – of what makes it right and just to punish someone for what he has done – are still mostly laid down in judge-made law. Most offences require not only a prohibited deed (an *actus reus*) but also a 'guilty mind' (a *mens rea*) – this will depend upon the offence in question, but may involve intention, recklessness or carelessness.

You might think that intention, recklessness or carelessness were easy to define, but believe me they are not. Not only that, some offences require a more specific intent – murder requires an intention to kill or to cause really serious bodily injury; causing really serious bodily injury short of death carries a heavier sentence if done with intent to do serious injury than if done without such intent; and so on. Theft requires the intentional taking of someone else's property but the taking must be dishonest. So what do we mean by dishonesty?

The term is sitting there in the Theft Act 1968 and the drafters gaily assumed that everyone knew what it meant and could recognise it when they saw it. But the judges had to decide how juries and magistrates were to be advised what it meant. Was it to be judged by the objective standard of what ordinary honest people would think dishonest? Or was it to be judged by the subjective standard of what the defendant thought that ordinary honest people would think dishonest? The question came before the Supreme Court in one of the most entertaining cases I have ever heard: *Ivey v Genting Casinos (UK) Ltd (trading as Crockfords Club)*.[11]

A little-known heiress from China called Cheung Yin Sun, with a fondness for gambling, had a grudge against an American casino. She resolved to get back at them in an unusual way. She mastered the art of edge sorting. Many packs of cards for ordinary domestic use have pretty pictures on the back with an obvious top and bottom, so that you know which way up it is. This is fine for family games of Snap and Beggar My Neighbour but not fine for games such as Bridge when signals may be sent by turning a card the wrong way up. So the packs of cards used by serious card players and in casinos have either completely plain backs or overall symmetrical patterns, with no right or wrong way up. However, when cards are produced by machines the patterns may not be reproduced entirely symmetrically. This means that if certain cards are rotated through 180 degrees a sharp-eyed person will be able to detect them.

Ms Cheung teamed up with another high-rolling gambler, Phil Ivey, to use edge-sorting in a version of Baccarat called Punto Banco. It's a very simple game. The croupier deals two (or in certain circumstances three) cards in turn to each of Punto and Banco and players bet on which total is closest to nine. If the first card dealt is a 7, an 8 or a 9, that side is likely to win. So the first time the croupier went through the shoe of cards, Ms Cheung would persuade the croupier to turn the important cards through 180 degrees, claiming it was a Chinese superstition. Casinos like to pander to punters' superstitions. Mr Ivey persuaded them to use the same shoe of cards in the following deals. The next time the shoe was played, Ms Cheung was able to recognise the important cards and tip the wink to Mr Ivey which way to bet.

Over a day and a half of gaming in Crockfords casino in London, they won £7.7 million. That is not supposed to happen. With such a large win, it was Crockford's practice to have a post-mortem before paying up. With the help of CCTV, they worked out what had been happening and refused to pay. So Mr Ivey sued them for the money. He could not have done this before 2005, because the Gaming Act 1845 made all gambling contracts illegal (see above). This led to all sorts of dubious practices to collect the money won. So the Gaming Act 2005 introduced a scheme for licensing gambling providers and made gaming contracts between licensed providers and gamblers enforceable. Both Crockfords and Mr Ivey agreed that there was an implied term in the gaming contract that the gambler would not cheat. But the trial judge found that Mr Ivey genuinely did not think that what he had done was cheating. Every casino gives itself a house edge, an improved chance of winning, so in his view they were fair game and he had various ways of getting round the house edge. To Mr Ivey, this was legitimate gamesmanship. The trial judge held that it was still cheating and dismissed the claim.[12]

Nothing daunted, Mr Ivey appealed to the Court of Appeal, which also dismissed the claim but only by a majority.[13] Still undaunted, Mr Ivey appealed to the Supreme Court and we were happy to take the case. The question was whether it had to be shown that Mr Ivey was dishonest. If it did, the definition of dishonesty which had been adopted in the criminal courts up until then meant that Mr Ivey was not dishonest – he genuinely believed that what he was doing was legitimate. So another question was whether that definition was correct. In fact, we decided that cheating did not necessarily involve dishonesty – there are many other forms of interfering in the normal course of a game or sport, such as tripping up another runner, taking performance-enhancing drugs or (as every Rubber Bridge player knows) deliberately slowing down play when time is limited. But this form of cheating – persuading the casino to turn the cards and reuse the shoe – did involve dishonesty. So the Supreme Court went on to decide that dishonesty did not mean what the Criminal Division of the Court of Appeal had said that it meant.

The original idea had been that a jury of ordinary people, or a bench of lay magistrates, could recognise dishonesty when they saw it. But then came the case of *R v Ghosh*.[14] Dr Ghosh was a surgeon acting as a locum consultant. He claimed fees for carrying out operations or acting as anaesthetist when either another surgeon had done the work or it had been done under the NHS so no fees were payable. He denied that he had been dishonest and claimed that the fees were legitimately payable to him. The jury found him guilty. The trial judge had directed them that it was for them to decide whether he had been dishonest by applying contemporary standards of honesty or dishonesty. The Court of Appeal held that this was not enough. There were two questions. First, was what the defendant had done dishonest by the standards of ordinary reasonable and honest people? But second, did the defendant realise that ordinary honest people would regard his behaviour as dishonest? (In fact, the court decided that even if the jury had been given this direction, they would still have convicted Dr Ghosh, so the conviction was upheld.)

That is why Mr Ivey was not necessarily dishonest. He did not think that what he had done was cheating. But the second question meant that 'the more warped the defendant's standards of honesty are, the less likely it is that he will be convicted of dishonest behaviour'. It rewarded people whose moral compass did not accord with that of 'ordinary, reasonable and honest people'.

So the Supreme Court decided that *Ghosh* was wrongly decided and that dishonesty was to be judged by the objective standard of what ordinary, reasonable and honest people would think was dishonest, not what this person thought was dishonest. Mr Ivey lost again. And although this was a civil case, the criminal courts decided that they had better follow what the Supreme Court had said. So Mr Ivey, with his extraordinary persistence, has done the criminal law a great service, making it much easier to prosecute financial crime in particular. But the other lesson is that ordinary English words such as 'dishonestly' are not always easy to define. Which brings us to another, much more difficult, case about the precise meaning of what look like ordinary words.

Judicial review and the rule of law

After the Norman Conquest of England in 1066, the kings were anxious to assert their authority over all the kingdom and to impose a common system of law to take over from the local laws being administered by the local lords. The first common law court was the King's Court, or *Curia Regis*, established by William the Conqueror. Its power gradually spread and spread as it travelled round the country with the King. An essential part of that power was to correct and supervise the decisions of all other courts and judges in the King's name (that is why judicial review cases are brought in the name of the King or Queen, albeit on the application of the person who wants the error corrected). The King's Court became known as the King's or Queen's Bench and became part of the High Court in 1873. It is still part of the High Court and it still has power to correct and supervise the decisions of other courts and tribunals. The principle is that those other courts and tribunals have limited powers and so there has to be a higher court which can ensure that they stick within those powers. (Judicial review of this sort is different from a right of appeal which might be on a question of fact or law.)

These days, those other courts and tribunals will have been created by Parliament and their powers defined by Parliament. So the High Court is respecting the will of Parliament in keeping them within their powers. But what if Parliament has tried to exclude the role of the High Court? After all, the courts are not always popular with politicians and their interference can sometimes be a nuisance. Attempts to do this are known as ouster clauses. The High Court has always taken a very dim view of them because they are seen as a threat to the rule of law – the principle that everyone and everybody, including judicial decision-making bodies, must abide by the law. The question in *R (Jackson) v Attorney General*[15] was whether the Hunting Act 2004 was a valid Act of Parliament. (It was.) But there was some discussion about whether there were any limits to what an Act of Parliament could do. Three of the Law Lords speculated that maybe it couldn't oust the powers of the courts to decide upon the legality of government action. I remarked that, 'the courts will treat with particular suspicion *(and might even reject)* any attempt to subvert the rule of law by removing governmental actions affecting the rights of the individual from all judicial scrutiny.' (Paragraph 159, italics supplied.) The words in italics have excited law teachers and law students ever since but were roundly condemned by Lord Bingham, retired senior Law Lord, in his book *The Rule of Law*. They have never been put to the test, but a case which came close to doing so was *R (Privacy International) v Investigatory Powers Tribunal*.[16]

The Investigatory Powers Tribunal (IPT) was established under the Regulation of Investigatory Powers Act 2000. It examines whether the use of investigatory powers – phone tapping, bugs, intrusive surveillance, computer hacks and the like – by public authorities, including the Security Service, the Secret Intelligence Service, the Government Communications Headquarters (GCHQ), the police and others – is lawful. The 2000 Act has an ouster clause which reads as follows:

'*Except to the extent that the Secretary of State may by order otherwise provide*, determinations, awards, orders and other decisions of the tribunal (including decisions as to whether they have jurisdiction) shall not be subject to appeal or be liable to be questioned in any court.' (Italics supplied.)

The words in italics give the Secretary of State power (by delegated legislation) to allow some or all of the decisions of the IPT to be challenged in court. But the Secretary of State has not done this. So what does this ouster clause mean? Does it mean what it seems to say – no challenges at all – or is it more complicated than that?

Privacy International is a UK-based charity whose object is to promote the right to privacy throughout the world. It wanted the IPT to rule on whether, if GCHQ did conduct computer hacking operations which might affect the charity, it would be lawful. These activities require a warrant from the Secretary of State, who has to be satisfied that they are lawful, necessary and proportionate. This is some sort of protection against their over-broad use. So the legality of the activity in question would depend upon whether the Secretary of State's warrant authorising it was lawful. Specifically, the concern was that the warrant might authorise computer hacking in respect of a broad class of property rather than in more narrowly defined terms. (A warrant to hack, for example, in any premises where GCHQ wanted to hack would obviously not be much protection against unjustified use of the power.) The IPT ruled that 'the warrant has to be as specific as possible in relation to the property to be covered by the warrant, both to enable the Secretary of State to be satisfied as to legality, necessity and proportionality and to assist those executing the warrant, so that the property to be covered is objectively ascertainable'.

Privacy International wanted to bring judicial review proceedings in the High Court to argue that this interpretation was wrong in law. This is obviously a matter of considerable public interest. It could affect us all. How precise do the reasons have to be before GCHQ is given the power to hack into our computers? But did the ouster clause prevent the question going to court? The High Court and the Court of Appeal held that it did. The Supreme Court, by a majority of four to three, held that it did not.

The starting point is the fundamental common law presumption, going back centuries, that the supervisory role of the High Court can only be excluded by clear and explicit words. You might think that the words of this ouster clause were clear and explicit. But there was a House of Lords precedent in the famous case of *Anisminic Ltd v Foreign Compensation Commission*.[17] Anisminic's property had been taken over by the Egyptian authorities during the Suez crisis of 1956. The company claimed compensation under an Order in Council made under the Foreign Compensation Act 1950. The Foreign Compensation Commission (FCC) refused the claim. The company wanted to argue that the FCC had misinterpreted the legislation it was applying. But the 1950 Act contained an ouster clause:

'The *determination* by the commission of any application made to them under this Act shall not be called in question in any court of law'. (Italics supplied.)

The House of Lords held that 'determination' meant a *valid* determination. The ouster clause did not apply to a determination which was invalid because the commission had misconstrued the legislation defining its powers. In other words, a determination which was based on a wrong interpretation of the commission's powers was not a determination at all and so was not covered by the ouster clause. This meant that it could be questioned in a court of law like any other decision of a public body. (It is a tribute to the independence of the judiciary that this markedly anti-government decision was made by an Appellate Committee presided over by Lord Reid, who had been a Conservative Member of Parliament before he became a Law Lord.)

Ah, it was argued in *Privacy International*, but *Anisminic* only applied to determinations which were outside the powers (jurisdiction) given to the FCC, not to determinations which were inside their powers but depended upon a mistake of law. That is why the ouster clause for the IPT expressly covered errors of jurisdiction too. The majority of the justices had two answers to this. First, as later decisions had made clear, the *Anisminic* ruling applied both to so-called jurisdictional errors and to errors of law in deciding a question within the FCC's jurisdiction. (It is very difficult to decide whether the matter complained of is one or the other – it's a pretty meaningless distinction.) Second, what was complained of here was an error of law – so the reference to 'whether they have jurisdiction' was irrelevant.

That was enough to decide the case. The ouster clause did not apply to decisions of the IPT which were not decisions at all because they were wrong in law. But Lord Carnwath, who gave the leading judgment for the majority, went on to discuss whether, if it got the language right, an Act of Parliament could ever oust the supervisory powers of the High Court over courts and tribunals with limited jurisdiction. His conclusion was that, consistently with the rule of law, it was for the court to decide the extent to which an ouster clause should be upheld, 'having regard to its purpose and statutory context, and the nature and importance of the legal issue in question; and to determine the level of scrutiny required by the rule of law'. In other words, if it's doing something simple, like setting a time limit for challenges, it may be valid. But if it's allowing a fundamental question, like the extent of the Secretary of State's power to authorise computer hacking, to go unchallenged, it may not be valid. Lord Kerr and I agreed with his judgment. Lord Lloyd Jones agreed with him on the main issue but declined to express a view on the wider question.

Lords Sumption, Reed and Wilson disagreed. Rights of appeal and review are quite frequently subject to limitations (time limits, permission requirements and prohibiting second-tier appeals are obvious examples). It was open to Parliament to give the IPT power to determine the meaning of the legislation which it was applying and that is what the ouster clause had done. There is no constitutional right to an appeal of any sort. The European Court of Human Rights has held that the right to a fair trial, in article 6 of the European Convention on Human Rights, does not necessitate a right of appeal.

I agree that there must sometimes be limits on the power to challenge the decisions of courts or tribunals, whether by appeal or judicial review. The system is overloaded as it is. And there are some people who will go on for ever if they are allowed to do so. But the idea that a court or tribunal is free to decide the meaning of the law which it has to apply, without any possibility of its being challenged in a higher court, goes against the grain. Some questions are so important that it ought to be possible to take them to the highest court in the land – and the scope of warrants to hack into people's computers feels like one of those.

Lessons learnt?

The judges are not making it up as they go along. They are building on centuries or at least decades of judicial thinking. No fewer than sixty-six previously decided cases are referred to in the two judgments in the *Tate Modern* case. The oldest was *Semayne's Case* in 1604, in which it was famously declared that 'the house of everyone is to him as his castle and fortress, as well for his defence against injury and violence, as for his repose'.[18] But different judges may sometimes draw different conclusions from those earlier cases, especially when trying to apply them to a new set of facts.

The judges are trying to state principles in a way which can be applied in other cases. It is not enough to say, 'We think the Tate should win,' or 'We think the Tate should lose.' There has to be a reason and the reason has to be one which is capable of applying in future cases where essentially the same issue arises. The 'common and ordinary use' principle is a good example. But, as *Tate Modern* shows, it only takes us so far.

When the existing principles have got the law into a mess, or do not seem capable of producing just results, then the judges can 'develop' or adapt them. That is what the minority were trying to do in *Tate Modern*, because they thought that the principle of common and ordinary use did not apply. That is also what the majority in *Patel v Mirza* were doing – to a much greater extent – because they thought that the *Tinsley v Milligan* principle was not capable of doing justice. It could be an accident whether the claimant had to rely on the illegality in order to make the claim.

However, it is not surprising that existing principles can get the law into a mess. The criminal law is used to looking at the defendant's subjective state of mind: did he intend to do what he did? Did he genuinely believe that his life was in danger? It's not until you get a case like *Ivey v Genting* that you realise that dishonesty cannot be a subjective state of mind – otherwise the most dishonest people will get away with theft and deception while more honest people won't.

Good judges are genuinely trying to do justice – to get the right result between the parties in a civil case and to get the right result between the State and the individual or enterprise in a criminal or public law case. But it is not always easy to see where justice lies, perhaps especially in public law cases. And so sometimes the judges' own experiences of life, their background and their values, may influence their thinking. I know at least one judge who did not think that what Mr Ivey did was cheating. Fortunately, I also know a barrister who used to be a professional Poker player and who definitely thought that it was. That is why we need judges with a variety of backgrounds, experiences and values on the bench.

16 Making Law in Government

If you walk round Westminster and Whitehall you will pass the head offices of many government departments. Beavering away in many of these will be government lawyers whose job it is to draft the myriad detailed rules and regulations which turn the broad-brush provisions in Acts of Parliament into operable rules – some of them 'mind-numbingly boring' (according to a civil servant drafting some benefit rules), many of them incomprehensible to the ordinary reader, most of them hard to find unless you know how and where to look. It would be tempting to leave out this type of lawmaking, as too detailed to be interesting, but this would give a false picture of what the law is all about. So much of the law that affects all of us every day is contained in these rules and regulations – think about the rules governing traffic on the roads, entitlement to pensions and other social security benefits, town and country planning, the fees that can be charged for taking your case to a court or tribunal, or the things we couldn't do during the Covid-19 epidemic.

Roughly 3,500 of these rules and regulations are made every year. But they get very little scrutiny in Parliament – even those which Parliament could veto (by a negative resolution) or has to approve (by an affirmative resolution). The House of Lords has a Secondary Legislation Scrutiny Committee, which can draw the attention of the House to measures which Parliament can do something about (by negative or affirmative resolution). The grounds include 'that it is politically or legally important or gives rise to issues of public policy likely to be of interest to the House'. An example was the 2023 Special Development Orders allowing the conversion of former RAF bases to house asylum seekers. Parliament is always interested in asylum seekers and other migrants. There is also a Joint Committee of both

Houses of Parliament whose job is to scrutinise and report, not on the merits of what is being done, but on whether the proper processes have been complied with. This includes where 'there appears to be doubt about whether there is power to make [the rule or regulation] or that it appears to make an unusual or unexpected use of the power to make it'.

It is an important feature of the rule of law that government ministers, and other public bodies, should only do what they have power to do: a government minister should not be making rules and regulations, which look to all intents and purposes like the law of the land, will be taken to be the law of the land by anyone involved, and may well lead to criminal penalties if they are broken, if he has not been given the power to do so by an Act of Parliament. This is where the courts come in. Their job is to see that people (or enterprises) are not being made subject to rules and regulations which there was no power to make. That is why this type of lawmaking has to be included even if the details are mind-numbingly boring (though of course I do not think that they are).

Terrorism and the United Nations

It's a pretty drastic thing to have your assets frozen – to be told that you cannot spend the money you have to support yourself or your family as you wish and that you cannot earn or make any more. It is worse still if you have no means of finding out why this has been done or of challenging it before an independent court or tribunal.

In 2006, the Treasury made an Order (the Terrorism Order) to implement a resolution of the United Nations Security Council.[1] It laid down a very onerous regime for denying economic resources to, and freezing all the assets of, people designated under it – these included people designated by the Treasury if it had reasonable grounds for suspecting that they were or might be involved in terrorism. Also in 2006, the Treasury made another Order (the Al-Qaida and Taliban Order) applying a similarly onerous regime to people on a list compiled by the United Nations' Sanctions Committee. The Treasury then used these powers against the five appellants in three cases: *Ahmed and others v Her Majesty's Treasury*.[2]

The three Ahmed brothers were subjected to the Terrorism Order regime because the Treasury took the view that it had reasonable grounds for suspecting that they facilitated acts of terrorism. It was said that an operative linked to Al-Qaida had identified two of them as East London-based Al-Qaida facilitators and that two of them had travelled to Pakistan to deliver money to contacts there and take part in terrorist training. Mr al-Ghabra was made subject to the Terrorism Order regime for the same reason, but he was also told that he was on the United Nations list. This was because the United Kingdom had asked for his name to be put on the list. He was not told why: the reasons were said to be so sensitive that they could not be disclosed. Mr Youssef was made subject to the Al-Qaida and Taliban Order regime because he too was on the United Nations list, but at the request of another Member State. He was not told which that Member State was or why it had made the request. The impact of the asset-freezing regime on all of these men – and on their families – was devastating but what could they do about it?

Mr al-Ghabra and Mr Youssef had no way of challenging the basis for their inclusion on the United Nations list, and their chances of being removed from it seemed slim indeed (as all the members of the Sanctions Committee had to agree to do this). In practice, it was almost impossible for the Ahmed brothers to challenge the basis for the Treasury's view of them. So all five argued that the Treasury had no power to make either the Terrorism Order or the Al-Qaida and Taliban Order.

This was the very first case to be heard by the newly created Supreme Court of the United Kingdom in October 2009. As our President, Lord Phillips of Worth Matravers, observed, this was particularly appropriate, because it concerned the separation of powers: had Parliament really delegated to the government the power to make such draconian Orders?

The Treasury had made both of these Orders under section 1(1) of the United Nations Act 1946:

'If . . . the Security Council of the United Nations call upon His Majesty's Government in the United Kingdom to apply any measures to give effect to any decision of that Council, His Majesty may by Order in Council make such provision as appears to Him necessary or expedient for enabling those measures to be effectively applied . . .'

This appeared to give the government the power to do whatever was needed to give effect to what was required of the United Kingdom by the United Nations Security Council. The United Nations was set up by charter in 1945 with the aim of saving succeeding generations from the scourge of war. Primary responsibility for the maintenance of international peace and security is placed on the Security Council (of which the United Kingdom is a permanent member). The Security Council has power to decide what measures are necessary to give effect to its decisions and to call upon Member States to apply such measures. Member States are bound to carry out the decisions of the Security Council.

The Security Council has done its best to respond to the threat to international peace and security posed by international terrorism. At first its efforts were directed to what Member States themselves should or should not do. But eventually it began to require Member States to take action against individuals. In the wake of the bombing of the United States embassies in Nairobi and Dar es Salaam in 1999, Security Council Resolution (SCR) 1267 required Member States to freeze funds derived from resources of the Taliban. It established a sanctions committee (known as the 1267 Committee) to oversee this. In 2000, this regime was extended to Usuma bin Laden and his associates, including Al-Qaida. A list of individuals, groups, undertakings and entities whose assets were to be frozen was created – but although people on the list could apply to be taken off it, there was nothing they could do to challenge being put on it the first place: there was no due process involved.

Then came the atrocities of 11 September 2001. The Council passed SCR 1373, which applied to anyone involved in or associated with terrorism. Among other things, it required Member States to freeze the assets of 'persons who commit, or attempt to commit, terrorist acts or participate in or facilitate the commissions of terrorist acts'.

So did the 1946 Act give the government power to implement these Security Council resolutions by making the Terrorism Order and the Taliban and Al-Qaida Order (neither of which could be challenged in Parliament)? This depended upon the approach to be adopted to interpreting legislation which might affect the fundamental rights of individuals.

There is a long-standing principle in the interpretation of legislation that fundamental rights cannot be overridden by general or ambiguous words. If Parliament wants to give the government (or anyone else) the power to interfere in the fundamental rights of individuals it must do so in clear and unambiguous terms. It must be obvious to parliamentarians what it is that they are doing so that they can understand the political consequences and 'take the flak'. These Orders interfered with the fundamental right to the peaceful enjoyment of one's own property – long before the Human Rights Act 1998, the law recognised that 'an Englishman's home is his castle' which cannot be invaded without a clear legal justification which can be challenged in court – and the same applies to other forms of property, such as goods and bank accounts. The words in the United Nations Act were very general: they could not be taken to have authorised this. (Indeed, when it was passed, it was assumed that Security Council measures would be directed at Member States rather than at individuals.) The Terrorism Order also went further than required by the SCR because it allowed the Treasury to act on reasonable suspicion rather than the actuality of involvement in terrorism. The automatic inclusion of people on the Sanctions Committee list in the Al-Qaida and Taliban Order deprived the listed people of any possibility of challenging the interference with their fundamental rights. So to that extent the Supreme Court held that the Orders in Council were invalid, as was the action taken under them.

Access to justice

The problem faced by the Ahmed brothers, Mr al-Ghabra and Mr Youssef was that they had no means of challenging this drastic interference with their rights. But even if there is a means of asserting your rights, there may also be ways of making this meaningless in practice. One such way is by setting the fees for taking your case to court so high that it makes no sense for you to even try to do so.

Employment tribunals (as we have seen in chapter 4) were set up to provide an 'easily accessible, speedy, informal and inexpensive' way for employees and other workers to assert their rights against their employers – rights which they have mostly been given by Acts of

Parliament, for example, to redundancy payments, compensation for unfair dismissal or discrimination, to equal pay, to a written contract of employment, to rest periods, or to unpaid wages. Originally, workers did not have to pay a fee to bring a claim. But the Tribunals, Courts and Enforcement Act 2007 gave power to the Lord Chancellor to prescribe fees in respect of anything dealt with by tribunals, including employment tribunals.

It is no secret that under the policy of austerity introduced by the coalition government after 2010, government departments had to look for ways to save money. One obvious way to cut the cost of providing employment tribunals was to charge fees. The declared aims were to transfer some of the cost from the taxpayer to the people who used the system. It was also thought that it would encourage people to resolve disputes by agreement and deter weak or vexatious claims. It was thought hard to predict whether it might also deter meritorious claims.

The Employment Tribunals and Employment Appeal Tribunal Fees Order was approved by both Houses of Parliament and came into force in July 2013. Claims were divided into Type A and Type B, according to the time and trouble they took up in tribunals, rather than how much the claim might be worth. Type A were the simpler claims for such things as a written contract of employment or unpaid wages. Type B were the more complicated claims for unfair dismissal, equal pay, discrimination or the like. In each case, there was an issue fee payable to bring the claim and a hearing fee payable to take the case to a hearing. For Type A claims, the issue fee was £160 and the hearing fee £230, a total of £390. This would make it completely uneconomic to bring a claim for a written contract of employment, which has no monetary value, or for a small sum in unpaid wages. The poorest people would be likely to be bringing the lowest-value claims. For Type B claims, the issue fee was £250 and the hearing fee £950, totalling £1,200. This again might make it completely uneconomic to bring a claim – over half of race discrimination claims, for example, resulted in awards of less than £5,000, and what woman unfairly dismissed because she was pregnant would want to take the risk of bringing a claim at such a precarious moment? There was a remission scheme for claimants, but only if their income and savings were very low (and their partners' income and savings were taken into account).

Not surprisingly, after the Fees Order came into force, there was a 'dramatic and persistent fall' in the number of claims brought in employment tribunals – of between 66 per cent and 70 per cent. The fall was particularly marked in lower-value or non-monetary claims. The Ministry of Justice's own *Review of the Introduction of Fees in the Employment Tribunals* (2017) concluded that 'there has been a sharp, substantial and sustained fall in the volume of case receipts as a result of the introduction of fees'. This was said to be 'troubling'.

While the deterrent effect upon claimants was clear, it did not look as if the introduction of fees was very successful in meeting its original three objectives. It had been forecast that fees would recover roughly a third of the cost of claims, but the actual recovery rate was around 13 per cent. The revenue derived from supplying a service is not maximised by maximising the price, but by charging the right price, a price which potential claimants will see as value for money. It had also been hoped that fees would deter unmeritorious claims, but the proportion of successful claims had actually fallen since the introduction of fees. It had been hoped that fees would encourage earlier settlements, but settlements had slightly decreased since the introduction.

That all might suggest that it wasn't a very good policy. But was it unlawful? The trade union UNISON brought judicial review proceedings claiming that the Fees Order was unlawful on various grounds. But by the time the case reached the Supreme Court in 2017, the main argument was that the Order was an unlawful interference with the right of access to justice, which has 'long been deeply embedded in our constitutional law': *R (Unison) v Lord Chancellor.*[3]

Lord Reed gave the leading judgment, with which we all agreed. It is a classic exposition of why the right to go to court matters to us all. 'The constitutional right of access to justice is inherent in the rule of law.' He goes on to explain what that means:

'At the heart of the concept of the rule of law is the idea that society is governed by law. Parliament exists primarily to make laws for society in this country. Democratic procedures exist primarily in order to ensure that the Parliament which makes those laws includes Members of Parliament who are chosen by the people of this country and are accountable to them. Courts exist in order to ensure that the laws made by Parliament, and the common law created by the courts themselves, are applied and enforced. That role includes ensuring that the executive branch of government carries out its functions in accordance with the law. In order for the courts to perform that role, people must in principle have unimpeded access to them. Without such access, laws are liable to become a dead letter, the work done by Parliament may be rendered nugatory, and the democratic election of Members of Parliament may become a meaningless charade.'

So the courts do not provide a service like any other public service. Their users are not the only beneficiaries. The service they provide is of value to the whole community. This is most obvious when they decide points of law of general public importance, laying down the law for us all. But it is more than that: 'People and businesses need to know, on the one hand, that they will be able to enforce their rights if they have to do so, and, on the other hand, that if they fail to meet their obligations, there is likely to be a remedy against them. It is that knowledge which underpins everyday economic and social relations.' (And, I would add, it is the knowledge that crimes will be punished, but only after a fair trial in which the wrongly accused may defend themselves, which keeps most of us law-abiding.) Access to courts and tribunals, if necessary, means that laws are mostly observed without the need to go to court.

The constitutional right of access to the courts goes back a long way, at least as far as Magna Carta of 1215: 'to no one will we deny, to no one will we sell or delay, right or justice'. There are many modern cases deciding that the right can only be taken away or interfered with if Parliament has authorised this in clear language. Parliament had not given any indication of what the power to impose tribunal fees could be used for – it had certainly not authorised its use to prevent some people from having access to justice. But this is what it did. Fees had to be set at a level which everyone could afford but these were not – low- to medium-income households could only afford them by sacrificing 'ordinary and reasonable expenditure for substantial periods of time'. And the time limits for bringing proceedings were so short that they would not have time to save up for the fees. Quite apart from affordability, the fees might make it futile or irrational to bring a claim – no sensible person would spend £390 to bring a claim worth £500 unless virtually certain, not only that they will succeed, but also that the fees will be reimbursed and that the award will be met in full.

So the Fees Order effectively prevented access to justice and was unlawful. It had to be quashed.

The Covid-19 pandemic

When the severity of the threat posed by the new coronavirus (technically SARS-CoV-2 but known as Covid-19) became impossible to ignore, the government acted swiftly to impose draconian restrictions on our everyday lives. As from 23 March 2020, the simple message was 'you must stay at home'. Trips out were only allowed for limited purposes. Most shops, schools, businesses, places of worship and places of entertainment were closed down. The only consolation – at least for those of us who had access to open spaces or the countryside – was that the weather that spring was glorious.

How could the government impose such measures so quickly? There were three Acts of Parliament under which it might have acted, two of them more obviously designed for the situation, but both of these containing limitations which may have been thought inconvenient. The Civil Contingencies Act 2004 provides for very wide-ranging emergency regulations if the government is satisfied that an emergency has occurred, is occurring or is about to occur. An emergency is widely defined and includes events or situations which threaten serious damage to human welfare in the UK. But it is expressly stated that the regulations must be compatible with the Human Rights Act 1998. The Coronavirus Act 2020 was rushed through Parliament that March, and contains powers relating to potentially infectious persons, but not powers relating to everyone, whether or not potentially infectious, and powers to issue directions relating to specific events, gatherings and premises.

Instead of using either of these, the government acted under powers inserted into the Public Health (Control of Disease) Act 1984 in 2008 with a view to catering for the SARS epidemic and similar outbreaks. The Secretary of State for Health is empowered to make regulations 'for the purpose of protecting against, controlling or providing a public health response to the incidence or spread of infection or contamination in England and Wales . . .' On the face of it, and unlike the powers in the Coronavirus Act, the power is not limited to infectious or potentially infectious people, or to prohibiting specific events, but could apply to anyone: regulations may impose, or enable others to impose, restrictions or requirements on or in relation to persons, things or premises in the event of, or in response to, a threat to public health.

The only express limitation is that the person making the regulations or imposing the restriction or requirement must think that it is proportionate to what is sought to be achieved by imposing it – reasonable grounds for thinking this are not required. However, the Human Rights Act 1998 still requires the minister making the regulations, and the public authorities and officials enforcing them, to act compatibly with the rights contained in the European Convention on Human Rights, so the regulations must not be incompatible with those rights.

As a general rule, regulations under the 1984 Act require the approval of an affirmative resolution in each House of Parliament. However, this does not apply if the minister making the regulations declares that he or she is of the opinion that, by reason of urgency, it is necessary to make them without such prior approval. In that case, the regulations lapse unless approved within twenty-eight days, but in counting the twenty-eight days, no account is taken of the time when Parliament is dissolved, prorogued or adjourned for more than four days. The regulations which provided for the first lockdown, although it was due to begin on 23 March, were not in fact made until 26 March, by which time Parliament had gone into recess: Lord Sumption, a former Justice of the Supreme Court, has suggested (in a lecture given in Cambridge in October 2020) that this was a deliberate device to avoid parliamentary scrutiny for several weeks. Thereafter the regulations were frequently changed or superseded. Parliament did have time to debate them but was not required to approve them in draft, because the Secretary of State always stated his opinion that, because of the urgency, it was necessary to make them without prior approval.

That made it very difficult for the courts to consider the validity of the regulations while they were in force. Simon Dolan and others applied for judicial review to challenge the validity of the first lockdown regulations. By the time the trial judge reached his decision in July 2020, those regulations had been revoked and replaced by others. So the judge held that the case was academic and refused permission to bring it. The Court of Appeal agreed that the challenge was academic but thought that it was necessary to decide whether the regulations were indeed within the power granted by the Public Health Act, because this would allay doubts about the validity of things done under them and of subsequent regulations.[4] But they firmly rejected the argument that the regulations had to relate to specific individuals or groups rather than the entire population – the whole purpose had been to enable an effective public health response to a widespread epidemic.

Having decided that, the Court of Appeal refused permission to challenge the regulations on human rights grounds – but nevertheless expressed an opinion about them. Article 5 of the Convention prohibits the deprivation of liberty except in certain defined circumstances and with certain procedural safeguards. The claimants argued that the requirement to stay at home amounted to a curfew or house arrest and thus a 'deprivation of liberty'. The court said that 'it is unarguable that what happened under these regulations amounted to a deprivation of liberty'. Article 8 of the Convention guarantees the right to respect for private and family life. But interferences may be justified if 'in accordance with the law' and a proportionate means of achieving one of the defined legitimate aims, which include the protection of health. The court said that 'the interference was unarguably proportionate'. Arguments based on article 11, freedom of assembly and association, article 1 of the First Protocol, the right to peaceful enjoyment of possessions, and article 2 of the First Protocol, the right to education, met a similar fate.

So the regulations were valid. That did not, of course, mean that individuals could not claim that in their particular circumstances, their human rights had been infringed, but that is a different question.

Lessons learnt?

There are many advantages in delegating the power to make detailed laws. It means that Bills before Parliament can be restricted to the essentials. This saves parliamentary time and enables Parliament to concentrate on the principles. There is no need to work out all the fine details before promoting a Bill in Parliament. They can be tailored to the different circumstances that may arise. The rules can be amended or replaced much more easily than an Act of Parliament. This gives flexibility to adapt to changing circumstances without having to go back to Parliament.

However, there are many obstacles to effective parliamentary scrutiny of delegated legislation, even when this is required by the parent Act. Even instruments which require approval by affirmative resolution cannot be amended. There is no realistic prospect of a particular piece of delegated legislation being rejected in the House of Commons, which devotes very little time to debating them. The House of Lords devotes more time and energy to scrutiny and can sometimes persuade ministers to think again. But it will hardly ever vote it down. Above all, the sheer volume of delegated legislation and its suffocating detail make it very difficult for individual members of either House to get to grips with its defects. It is, therefore, important that the validity of delegated legislation of all types can be challenged in the courts. But this is slow and expensive – think of all the people who might have brought cases in the employment tribunals had they not been deterred by fees which turned out to be unlawful. Not only this, the law in question may have been replaced by another law before the challenge gets to court. This happened with the rapidly changing regulations made to deal with the Covid-19 pandemic. And the courts can only enquire whether the powers given in the parent Act cover what has been done. They may get some help from the principle of legality and the requirement, since the Human Rights Act 1998 came into force, that ministers and other public authorities act compatibly with the Convention rights. But they cannot generally inquire into the wisdom or merits of the delegated legislation in question, any more than they can inquire into the wisdom or merits of an Act of Parliament.

The sheer pace and volume of all this lawmaking means that it is very hard for individual members of the public, or affected bodies, to know what the law is at any given time. Yet everyone is presumed to know the law – ignorance of the law is no defence to a criminal charge. And many of the regimes prescribed in regulations – from road traffic to health and safety – are backed up by criminal sanctions. Perhaps the time has come to reconsider the presumption that we all know all the law?

The problem is made worse if the publicity given to the law fails to distinguish clearly between what is law and what is simply government guidance on how the law should be applied. This was a particular problem during the Covid-19 pandemic. Many people, including the police, thought that the advice contained in government guidance was actually the law contained in the regulations. Under the first lockdown regulations, leaving home was prohibited except for a defined list of purposes. But it was only a criminal offence if done 'without reasonable excuse'. So perhaps there was a reasonable excuse for driving a small child some 270 miles so that he could be looked after by relatives, but not for driving some 20 miles to test the driver's eyesight?

17 Making Law in Parliament

Now we have arrived at the top of the lawmaking tree, the Parliament of the United Kingdom. It's not a very welcoming arrival. There's this huge, grand, but crumbling stone building surrounded with barriers to stop vehicles crashing into it. There are many police officers, some of them quite friendly and welcoming, but some of them carrying sub-machine guns and looking decidedly unfriendly. There is a queue for the visitors' entrance, which is down a ramp past the statue of Oliver Cromwell, the man who led the Parliamentarians in their battles with the King in the seventeenth century but was for many years reviled as a traitor. Once through the inevitable security checks, visitors are led into the massive and beautiful space which is Westminster Hall, built by King William II in 1097, with a magnificent wooden hammer beam roof added two hundred years later by Richard II. It must be one of the coldest rooms in England, so it is not a place to linger. The visitor goes up the steps and turns left to go through St Stephen's Hall into the main lobby which sits at the centre of the main Victorian building. There are murals depicting St George for England, St Andrew for Scotland, St David for Wales and St Patrick for Ireland. To the left is a wide corridor leading to the House of Commons lobby and chamber, quite plain with green leather benches facing one another. To the right is another wide corridor leading to the House of Lords lobby and chamber, very grand with red leather benches and a golden throne from which the monarch speaks at the beginning of every session.

As we have already seen, the governing principle of our unwritten Constitution is the sovereignty of Parliament. Parliament can make or unmake any law. But as we have also seen, another governing principle is the rule of law – that we are governed by rules and not by the dictates of powerful individuals who form the government. Closely allied to that is the principle that we must have a justice system which is independent of government and can enforce the rules 'without fear or favour, affection or ill-will' against anyone who breaks them, including the government. It is sometimes forgotten that the government and Parliament are not the same thing. The government ministers are chosen because they or their political party have the support of the majority of the members of the House of Commons. But that does not mean that they are the Parliament.

We are about to observe the passage through Parliament of the Safety of Rwanda (Asylum and Immigration) Bill 2024 – one of the most controversial Bills ever to pass, and controversial because it offends against every principle of the Constitution except the principle that Parliament can make any law it chooses. It shows Parliament at its best and also at its worst.

The Safety of Rwanda (Asylum and Immigration) Bill

Before a Bill receives the Royal Assent and becomes an Act of Parliament, it has to go through several stages in each House of Parliament. There is the first reading, a pure formality, at which the Bill is printed and introduced without a debate. There is the second reading, at which the general principles of the Bill are debated. There is then a committee stage, at which the Bill is examined in detail and amendments debated, sometimes in a smaller committee and sometimes in a 'committee of the whole House'. After the committee stage comes the report stage when the committee reports back to the House and any amendments are agreed. Then there is the third and final reading. After this, the Bill goes off to the 'other place' to go through the same process there. Then it comes back for decisions to be made about which amendments made in the other place will be accepted. This can be quite exciting, as we shall see. Then comes the Royal Assent. This is a pure formality. The last monarch to refuse Royal Assent was Queen Anne in 1708 and she did that because her ministers advised it.

The background to the Bill

One of the oldest international human rights treaties is the United Nations Convention on the Status of Refugees, the Geneva Convention of 1951. This was originally designed as a short-term measure to deal with the refugee crisis in Europe following the Second World War, but was extended to cover the whole world permanently in 1966. This was at a more optimistic – and perhaps a kinder – time, when the perils of armed conflict, of economic inequality, and of climate change did not loom as large as they now do. Meeting our obligations under the Convention has become more burdensome and less popular.

The Convention is there to protect people who have a well-founded fear of persecution in their home country. Member States must grant them refugee status. They are also prohibited from sending people back to a place where they may face persecution or torture – the principle of 'non-refoulement' which is a general principle of international law as well as a specific obligation in the Convention. Most people who claim refugee status in the UK arrive or stay here without the permission required by our immigration laws. They used to come in the backs of lorries or by stowing away on trains coming through the Channel tunnel or by over-staying the limited permission they had to be here. Then a few years ago they began coming across the Channel in small inflatable boats which are quite unsuitable for the journey. People die. But the people smugglers make a great deal of money. The Conservative Government decided that the solution was to 'break the business model' of the people-smuggling networks by deterring their customers. Not everyone thought that blaming the victims was a good idea even if it would work. Not everyone thought that it would work.

The process of turning the policy into law began with the Nationality and Borders Act 2022, which allowed (but did not require) the Government to refuse to entertain asylum claims from people connected to a 'safe third State', that is, a State which is neither theirs nor ours. The people coming across from France are coming from a safe third State. The Illegal Migration Act 2023 took this much further. People who arrived in the UK without the required permission were prohibited from making a claim for refugee status. The Government had a duty to detain them and remove them to another country. They had only very limited rights to go to court to challenge this. But this plan meant that there had to be another country to which they could safely be removed. Until that could be arranged, the 2023 Act could not be brought into force. Most of the people who cross the Channel in small boats originate from countries to which they cannot be sent back. So, as part of the scheme, in 2022, the Government entered into a 'Migration and economic development partnership' with the Government of Rwanda. In return for large sums of money in development aid and to pay the costs, Rwanda agreed to take in the people relocated there and to process their asylum claims in Rwanda. If granted asylum they would stay in Rwanda. (This was unlike, for example, the Australian scheme to determine asylum claims off-shore in Nauru, where successful claimants are granted asylum in Australia.)

Even before the scheme was brought into force, people earmarked for removal to Rwanda challenged it in the UK courts. The European Court of Human Rights issued an urgent notice prohibiting the UK Government from removing people to Rwanda until the legal challenges here had been resolved. The challenges failed in the High Court but succeeded in the Court of Appeal which held that 'the deficiencies in the asylum system in Rwanda are such that there are substantial grounds for believing that there is a real risk that persons sent to Rwanda will be returned to their home countries where they faced persecution or other inhumane treatment when, in fact, they have a good claim for asylum. In that sense Rwanda is not a "safe third country".'[1] Hence the Government's policy was unlawful. On 15 November 2023, the Supreme Court unanimously upheld that decision.[2] It noted, for example, evidence from the United Nations High Commissioner for Refugees of 'serious and systematic defects in the Republic of Rwanda's procedures and institutions for processing asylum claims' and that Rwanda had previously 'failed to comply with an explicit undertaking to the Government of Israel to comply with the principle of non-refoulement' – that is, their duty not to return people to places where there was a real risk of persecution or torture.

The Government's response to the Supreme Court's decision was twofold. First, the Memorandum of Understanding with Rwanda was turned into a treaty which is binding on both countries in international law and strengthened its protections against refoulement. The treaty was made on 5 December 2023 and laid before Parliament the following day. That same day the Government published its Safety of Rwanda (Asylum and Immigration) Bill which was given its first reading on 7 December 2023. The basic aim of the Bill was to require all decision-makers – from ministers, to immigration officers, to courts and to tribunals – conclusively to presume that Rwanda is indeed a safe place to which to send people, whether or not that is in fact the case now or remains the case in the future. This was new. Parliament does not usually (if ever) make statements of fact which are binding on the people who have to decide real cases about real people. Parliament usually makes rules or gives people and organisations powers. It leaves the facts to be decided on a case-by-case basis, depending upon the evidence available at the time.

The Bill also severely limited the rights of individuals to challenge the decision to remove them to Rwanda. They could not complain that removal would breach their fundamental rights under the European Convention on Human Rights – the Human Rights Act 1998 was disapplied. Yet removal might well breach their rights not to be subjected to inhumane or degrading treatment or to respect for their private or family lives. They could not complain that Rwanda is not a safe country either in general or for people like them – because, for example, they happen to be gay or lesbian. They could not complain that Rwanda will or may remove them to another State in breach of its obligations in international law (non-refoulement in particular). They could only complain that Rwanda is not a safe country for them individually 'based on compelling evidence relating to the person's particular individual circumstances'. And they could only get an Order to prevent their removal before that claim is heard if they would 'face a real, imminent and foreseeable risk of serious and irreversible harm' if removed to Rwanda in the meantime. And if they persuaded the European Court of Human Rights to require the UK Government to prevent their removal pending determination of their claims, 'it is for a Minister of the Crown (and only a Minister of the Crown) to decide whether the United Kingdom will comply'. The Government was being given the right to pick and choose which of its obligations in international law it would respect. This was new.

The Human Rights Act 1998 requires a government minister who sponsors a Bill in Parliament to state that in his view the provisions of the Bill are compatible with the rights protected by the European Convention on Human Rights. Alternatively, if he cannot do that, he must state that the government wishes Parliament to proceed with the Bill despite that. Not surprisingly, the Home Secretary was unable to make a statement that the Illegal Migration Bill was compatible with the Convention rights and was now unable to make a statement that the Rwanda Bill is compatible with the Convention rights. This too was new: a deliberate decision to press ahead with a policy which may very well result in breach of the fundamental rights of thousands of people.

The Bill passes the Commons

So here we are on 12 December 2023 at the second reading debate in the House of Commons. The Home Secretary, James Cleverly, asserts that 'the actions we are taking, while novel and very much pushing at the edge of the envelope, are within the framework of international law'. The Rwanda Treaty and Bill are 'game-changing'. Permitting the swift removal of people arriving irregularly would 'deter illegal migration'. It would 'break the business model of the most evil and perverse trade that we currently can see: the trade in vulnerable people'.

The Shadow Home Secretary, Yvette Cooper, begins by criticising the enormous cost of the policy – the sums already sent to Rwanda could have been spent on thousands more border police, on clearing the backlog of asylum claims, and on ending the use of hotels to house them – and much more will be required to support the scheme in the future. Yet the policy is 'only ever likely to cover a few hundred people – less than 1 per cent of those claiming asylum last year'. (So what is to happen to the rest?) The government is 'effectively admitting that they are creating legal fictions . . . rather than following the facts, the courts will have to follow those fictions instead'. The Scottish Nationalist Party and the Liberal Democrats also oppose the Bill.

Ironically, another critic is Robert Jenrick MP, an immigration minister until he resigned over the government's decision to press ahead with the Bill – not because he thinks that it goes too far but because he thinks that it does not go far enough. Individuals should not be able to challenge the plan to send them to Rwanda on any ground whatsoever. Interim measures from the European Court of Human Rights aiming to prevent removal should never be respected. Former Home Secretary Suella Braverman had earlier said much the same thing. This is taking the attack on the rule of law to new lengths. The idea that the Government could single out people for removal to Rwanda with no possibility of claiming that a mistake has been made is truly frightening.

After six and a half hours of debate, the House votes to give the Bill a second reading by 313 votes to 269. There are 650 members of the House of Commons, of whom 342 are Conservatives. Clearly, not all of them vote in favour and some of them vote against.

The committee stage comes before a committee of the whole House on 16 and 17 January 2024. The most exciting amendments are those tabled by rebel Conservatives. These aim to reduce the possibility of legal challenges virtually to vanishing point. They are comfortably defeated but supported by around 60 MPs. With no amendments approved, there is no report stage. The Bill has survived the House of Commons unscathed. It is given a third reading on 17 January by 320 to 276 votes. Eleven Conservative MPs vote against the Bill at third reading, including Suella Braverman, Robert Jenrick and Sir William Cash.

The stage is set for a battle royal in the House of Lords – at a press conference the following day, the Prime Minister asks, 'Will the Opposition in the appointed House of Lords try and frustrate the will of the people as expressed by the elected house? Or will they get on board and do the right thing?' But by no means all the Conservatives in the House of Lords agree that this is the right thing to do. And a YouGov poll published in January suggests that a majority of the British public do not support the Bill or think it good value for money. So what do we mean by 'the will of the people'?

The Bill is challenged in the House of Lords

The House of Lords is very different from the House of Commons. The members of the House of Commons are all elected. What the majority of those elected representatives decides to do is said to be the will of the people. But of course it is not. We could only discover the will of the people on any particular issue if we took a vote on it. They are, however, accountable to the electorate. When Parliament is dissolved in preparation for a general election, members of the House of Commons lose their seats. They are no longer Members of Parliament.

Members of the House of Lords, over 800 of us, are still members, because we are there for life (if that is what we want – retirement is possible). That is why we don't have a vote in general elections. But also we are not accountable to the electorate. The House of Lords used to consist mainly of hereditary peers – dukes, marquesses, earls, viscounts and barons (with a few female equivalents) who inherited their titles from their ancestors. Most of them were deprived of the right to sit in the House of Lords by the House of Lords Act 1999. But as an interim measure ninety-two of them were allowed to stay – two ex officio (the Earl Marshal and the Lord High Chamberlain) and the rest by election among their peers (either by members of the party to which they belong or sometimes by the whole House – the rules are complicated). There is currently a Bill to remove them. This is sad for the individuals who have done so much good. But it is hard to resist in principle, except that it means that almost all the members are and will be appointed by the Prime Minister of the day.

There are also the Lords Spiritual, twenty-six Church of England bishops, always including the Archbishops of Canterbury and York, and the Bishops of London, Durham and Winchester. Of course, the Church of England is not the force in the land that it used to be. Of course, there is a good case for many other faith leaders to be represented in the Lords. But once the hereditary peers have gone, these will be almost the only members who are not the product of the Prime Minister's patronage.

Most of the remainder are life peers, appointed under the Life Peerages Act 1958. Life peers are appointed by the Crown on the advice of the Prime Minister, some in the regular honours lists that appear at each New Year, the King's official birthday, the dissolution of Parliament and the resignation of a Prime Minister, and some when the Prime Minister finds it convenient – for example, when Lord Cameron of Chipping Norton was appointed Foreign Secretary in 2023. (To be a minister in the government, he had to be a Member of Parliament, but he had resigned his seat in the House of Commons in September 2016 following the Brexit referendum.) The leaders of the other main political parties also make nominations to the Prime Minister. Nominations are vetted by the House of Lords Appointments Commission, but their powers are very limited. The commission has also appointed a few 'people's peers' from people who have applied.

And there are oddities like me. Until the Supreme Court of the United Kingdom was set up in 2009, the top court in the whole United Kingdom consisted of members of the House of Lords, known as Law Lords. Apart from former Lord Chancellors, we were appointed as Lords of Appeal in Ordinary under the Appellate Jurisdiction Act 1876, but we were also allowed to sit in the House of Lords for life. I was appointed in January 2004. When the Law Lords became Justices of the new Supreme Court in 2009, we were disqualified from sitting in the House of Lords, but we were entitled to return to the House of Lords once we retired. That is why it took me nearly twenty years to make my maiden speech there – in November 2013 in a debate about mental health services for young people.

The House of Lords has grown enormously in recent years – Prime Ministers do like making appointments – but its political balance is very different from the Commons. Of the 834 members when Parliament was dissolved before the general election on 4 July 2024, there were 261 Conservative, 168 Labour, and 84 Liberal Democrat. There were a handful from other parties but the Scottish National Party does not take part. These are the peers who take a party whip – in other words, they are kept informed of parliamentary business by their leaders and told which way they should vote on some issues. But unlike members of the House of Commons, there is not much the party can do if they fail to follow their instructions. They do not stand to lose their seats at the next general election. This means that the party whips have much less power in the House of Lords than in the House of Commons and must get their way by persuasion rather than threats.

There is also a very substantial group, around 180, of cross-bench peers who do not take any party whip – this includes many people who have been appointed because of the expertise they can bring to the House or the previous offices they have held. There are doctors, lawyers, scientists, academics, people who achieved high rank in the armed forces or police, for example, and retired judges like me. We sit on the cross benches – so called because they run across the chamber, facing the Lord Speaker on the Woolsack, while the party politicians are ranged on either side facing one another as they do in the House of Commons (but the House of Lords does not need red lines painted on the floor to keep them a sword's length apart).

It is all very civilised. The Lord Speaker sits on the Woolsack and announces the business and the votes, but he or she does not control the proceedings in the way that the Speaker of the House of Commons does. There are speakers' lists for some debates but otherwise people get up to speak in turn, with some very light direction from the Leader of the House.

Second reading of the Rwanda Bill in the House of Lords is down for 29 January 2024. But before that, the House of Lords' International Agreements Committee (chaired by Lord Goldsmith, a former Labour Attorney General) has been scrutinising the Rwanda treaty. On 16 January, the committee reports that, 'The Government has presented the Rwanda treaty to Parliament as an answer to the Supreme Court judgment and has asked Parliament, on the basis of the treaty, to declare that Rwanda is a safe country. While the treaty might in time provide the basis for such an assessment if it is rigorously implemented, as things stand the arrangements it provides for are incomplete. A significant number of further legal and practical steps are required under the treaty which will take time.' It then gives a long list of what needs to happen, including 'a system for ensuring that non-refoulement does not take place'. On 24 January, the House debates the report and resolves that 'the government should not ratify the UK–Rwanda agreement on asylum partnership until the protections it provides have been fully implemented . . .' A warning – Parliament cannot prevent the government from ratifying (confirming) the treaty – but it could prevent the government's Bill from going through, if it wants.

On 9 February, the House of Lords Select Committee on the Constitution publishes a damning report on the Bill. Deeming a country to be safe usurps the judicial function, replacing a factual assessment of the court with a deemed factual assessment expressed in the judgment of Parliament: 'Courts have long-established procedures to evaluate evidence to determine the facts. These are not replicated in the legislative process.' Even if Parliament is sovereign, it is constitutionally inappropriate to use legislation to jeopardise the rule of law and the separation of powers (see earlier). Limiting the ability of individuals to challenge decisions to remove them reduces access to justice and the protection of rights. Disapplying the Human Rights Act undermines the universal application of human rights. Respect for the rule of law requires respect for international law. Legislation that undermines the UK's international obligations threatens the rule of law. Strong stuff, all of which is said, time and time again, in the debates which follow, but to no avail.

A fatal motion

The second reading debate takes place on 29 January 2024. The Government, in the hapless shape of the Advocate General for Scotland, Lord Stewart of Dirleton, a serious lawyer but not an experienced parliamentarian, moves that the Bill be read a second time. The Liberal Democrats move a fatal motion refusing to give the Bill a second reading, which would kill the Bill. The Labour Party do not support this – ostensibly because they see the role of the House as a revising rather than a wrecking chamber but also because they expect to win the next general election and don't want the Conservative Opposition to make too much trouble for them when they are in power.

The convenor of the cross-bench peers, the hereditary Earl Kinnoull, refers to the Salisbury/Addison convention: that a government Bill with manifesto characteristics will be given a second reading. He thinks this Bill does have manifesto characteristics, though many others do not. It is, to say the least, an uncertain concept. Lord Butler, a former Cabinet secretary, points out that such a Bill was not in the Conservatives' manifesto for the 2019 election, but thinks the fact that it passed the Commons without amendment does give it manifesto characteristics. Nevertheless he thinks that the House will not be wasting its time in debating amendments – even though the amendments required to make the Bill unobjectionable will not be acceptable to the Government. The House has a right and a duty to pass amendments removing the objectionable and dangerous features of the Bill, even though this would be a 'kamikaze operation' (why is not clear – the House will not go down in flames as a result). Lord Wilson of Dinton, a former permanent secretary at the Home Office, is also against the Bill, as is Lord Lisvane, a former clerk to the House of Commons. He speaks of a 'surrealism verging on the point of being comic', points out that 'phrases such as the will of the people are not appropriate, as well as being, in terms, manifestly untrue'. He points out that these exchanges are not between the Lords and the Commons, but between the Government and Parliament.

The Archbishop of Canterbury speaks movingly of the dignity of the individual which is at the heart of all global faiths and humanism and the Christian tradition of welcoming the stranger – as well as the danger to our international reputation of picking and choosing which of our international commitments to honour. The Bishop of Durham speaks with feeling of Rwanda as a country he knows and loves but which will not be able to provide the people sent there with the support and opportunities needed for them to rebuild their lives. The Bishop of London points out that the Bill decides who is and is not entitled to human rights – has history not taught us the risk of that? The Bishop of St Edmundsbury and Ipswich speaks of 'victimising the victims'.

Lord Blunkett, a former Labour Home Secretary, sees the fatal motion as an elephant trap – if the Lords fall into it the Government will be able to blame them for failing to stop the boats. But he is outraged that people whose claims to be refugees succeed in Rwanda will have to stay there rather than come back here. Lord Davies of Brixton, another Labour peer, on the contrary thinks that the House should use the power that it has under the Parliament Acts – to delay legislation passed by the House of Commons for at least a year.

From the cross-benches, Lord Hennessy of Nympsfield, Peter Hennessy, the well-known and deeply respected historian, is eloquent: 'For those of us fortunate enough to have been nurtured within the bounds of our cherished archipelago in the cold northern seas, the rule of law has a fair claim to be the most lustrous of our values, almost talismanic in its properties . . .' and this Bill threatens that value. Lord Etherton, now retired as Master of the Rolls, the second most senior judge in England and Wales, laments that 'there are so many impermissible aspects of the Bill that it is difficult to know where to start'. He is particularly concerned about the fate of homosexuals in Rwanda. Lord Anderson of Ipswich and Lord Carlile of Berriew, both senior lawyers who used to be independent assessors of the terrorism legislation, also speak against. Baroness O'Loan, a lawyer and former Police Ombudsman in Northern Ireland, is concerned that the Bill breaches our international obligations against human trafficking and modern slavery, as well as the Good Friday Agreement and the Windsor Framework assurances about protecting human rights in Northern Ireland.

The bishops, the cross-benchers and the non-affiliated peers are mostly against the Bill although only a few support the Lib Dems' fatal motion. These include the two Green Party peers. Most of those who take a party whip support their party's stance. But there are a few notable Conservatives who do not support the Government – Lord Clarke of Nottingham, Kenneth Clarke, a former Home Secretary, Chancellor of the Exchequer and Secretary of State for Justice; Viscount Hailsham, Douglas Hogg, son of Lord Hailsham, the minister and Lord Chancellor who long ago warned against the 'elective dictatorship' inherent in our constitutional arrangements; Lord Kirkhope of Harrogate, a lawyer and former MP who led the Conservative group in the European Parliament; and Lord Marlesford, former lobby correspondent for *The Economist*.

All in all, there are far more speeches against the Bill than in its favour. I may be wrong, but Lord Sharpe, the Home Office minister winding up for the Government, does not sound very convinced by his own arguments. I decide to cast my very first vote as a member of the House of Lords in favour of the Lib Dems' fatal motion – finding my way to the content lobby alongside Baroness Chakrabarti, who is cheerfully breaking the Labour whip in order to support it. As expected, the motion is lost by 84 votes to 206. The Bill is read a second time and committed to a committee of the whole House. Now for the hard work of trying to amend it.

Trying to amend it

Committee stage is a series of short debates, spread over 12, 13 and 19 February, on the proposed amendments. Baroness Chakrabarti is proposing several, supported by the Archbishop of Canterbury, Viscount Hailsham, and me – a coalition of Labour, Spiritual, Conservative, and Cross-Bench peers. The clerks have cleverly arranged the amendments in groups so that they can be sensibly debated. Our main amendment is to restore the power of all decision-makers – ministers, officials, courts and tribunals – to decide whether Rwanda is indeed a safe country, either in general, or for the individual concerned or for a group to which that individual belongs. I make a little speech in favour. Lord Deben, John Selwyn Gummer, formerly a Conservative Cabinet minister, makes a very powerful speech in favour: 'The separation of powers is crucial for the freedom of all our people.' 'The price of liberty is inconvenience.' 'By doing it to these people, we do it to ourselves.' The Labour Party has (and at long last, some might think) decided to support us. The Advocate General for Scotland, closing for the Government, is repeatedly interrupted by peers pointing out that Rwanda is not, and will not, be safe until all the measures provided for in the treaty are up and running – so how can it be said that the requirements of the Supreme Court have been met and the courts denied the opportunity to say otherwise? I begin to feel quite sorry for him.

But no votes are taken in the Lords at committee stage. That happens at report stage on 4 and 6 March. The Lords agree to ten amendments (some propositions required more than one amendment). Lord Hope of Craighead, my predecessor as Deputy President of the Supreme Court, supported by Lord Anderson of Ipswich; Baroness D'Souza, a former Lord Speaker; and Lord German, a Liberal Democrat, proposes that Parliament cannot judge Rwanda to be a safe country until the Rwanda treaty not only has been, but continues to be, fully implemented. Lord Anderson of Ipswich, supported by Lord Carlile of Berriew, the Bishop of Manchester and Lord Clarke, proposes that the presumption that Rwanda is safe can be rebutted by credible evidence to the contrary. Baroness Chakrabarti, supported by Viscount Hailsham, the Bishop of St Edmundsbury and Ipswich, and me, proposes to restore the power of decision-makers – ministers, immigration officers, courts or tribunals – to decide that Rwanda is not a safe country for the person in question or a group to which he belongs and to grant an interim remedy to prevent removal in the meantime. Baroness Lister of Burtersett, Labour, who was director of the Child Poverty Action group – supported by Lord Dubs, a former director of the Refugee Council; the Bishop of Chelmsford, herself a refugee from Iran; and Rabbi Julia Neuberger – proposes to restore the ability of courts and tribunals to suspend removals of people claiming to be under eighteen. Baroness Butler-Sloss, former President of the Family Division of the High Court – supported by the Bishop of Bristol; Lord Randall of Uxbridge, vice chair of the Human Trafficking Foundation; and Lord Coaker, the Labour front bench spokesman – proposes to prohibit the removal of people found to be victims of modern slavery and human trafficking. Finally, Lord Browne of Ladyton, a former Labour Secretary of State for Defence – supported by Lord Houghton of Richmond (my Richmond), a former Head of the Armed Forces; Lord Stirrup, also a former Head of the Armed Forces; and Lord Kerr of Kinlochard, formerly British Ambassador to the United States and Permanent Secretary at the Foreign and Commonwealth Office – proposes to prohibit the removal of agents, allies and employees of the UK overseas, and their families. They are thinking especially of the people whose lives or liberty are at risk because they worked for the British in Afghanistan and other conflicts overseas. All these amendments get substantial majorities, not least because the Labour Party has come off the fence and supports them all, along with two more innocuous ones of its own, requiring the Government to observe international as well as national law and asking for numbers of those actually deported under the new regime.

Ping-pong

What happens next? The Commons have to consider these amendments and decide whether to accept them. If they don't, the Lords have to decide whether to press ahead with them or something similar. If they do, the amendments go back to the Commons, and so on. The process is known as ping-pong. We are fully expecting the Government to arrange for ping-pong to be completed before Easter, but they don't. Lord Coaker comments that it can't be as urgent as they were suggesting after all.

The Commons debate our ten amendments for six hours on 18 March. Generally, their contributions are on predictable party lines – and some members have to be reminded to stick to discussing the amendments rather than ranging more broadly. Some of the senior lawyer members – Sir Jeremy Wright, a former Attorney General; Sir

Robert Buckland, a former Lord Chancellor and Secretary of State for Justice; and Sir Bob Neill, Chair of the Commons Justice Committee are clearly troubled, especially by Lord Hope's amendments. But in the end, all the Lords' amendments are rejected.

The Lords consider the Commons' reasons for disagreement on 20 March. We approve seven amendments, six of them slight variations on the previous drafts and the one on victims of human trafficking in exactly the same terms. Then we all go off for the Easter recess.

The Commons consider these seven amendments on Monday 15 April and reject them all, including the one protecting victims of human trafficking. But they do substitute an anodyne amendment requiring the Home Secretary to lay an annual report before Parliament about the operation of the Act as it relates to the modern slavery and trafficking provisions in the treaty – article 13 of the treaty requires Rwanda to 'have regard' to any special needs a relocated individual may have as a result of their being a victim of modern slavery or human trafficking. Small comfort.

We consider this the next day, Tuesday 16 April, and narrow the amendments down to four: conformity with international law; Lord Hope's mechanism for ensuring that Rwanda meets and continues to meet its treaty obligations; ours on rights of legal challenge; and Lord Browne's on our Afghan and other allies – which got the largest majority.

The Commons consider them on Wednesday 17 April. The minister says that two of them are unnecessary and the other two 'worse than unnecessary'. They are all rejected.

So when the Bill comes back to the Lords later that day, we continue to vote for those two amendments in a slightly modified form. Both seem unanswerable. The Government admits that Rwanda cannot be presumed safe until all its obligations in the treaty are fulfilled – so why not wait until then? And it is apparent to everyone that things can easily change – so why not have a mechanism for displacing the presumption of safety if they do change, without having to go through the whole rigmarole of a new Act of Parliament? The unfortunate minister argues that the Government is not obliged to send anyone to Rwanda and if things change, removals can be paused. But the Illegal Migration Act requires the minister to remove migrants who arrive without permission. And the Rwanda Bill obliges everyone, ministers included, to presume that Rwanda is safe. So how can he be right? Both amendments are approved.

The Commons do not return to the Bill until the following Monday, 22 April. For an hour from 4.15 p.m., they debate the two remaining amendments. Both Sir Jeremy Wright and Sir Robert Buckland support Lord Hope's amendment – it's not the perfect way to cater for changes in Rwanda but if the Government can't come up with anything better, they will support it. There is even more outrage from the Opposition parties about our Afghan helpers. But both amendments are defeated.

So it is back to the Lords at 7.15 p.m. Lord Hope cannot be there so Lord Anderson has taken over his amendment. He still has Labour and Lib Dem support. There are lighter moments. Lord Hodgson of Astley Abbotts, Conservative, compares Lord Coaker to Harrison Ford, 'slashing his way through the Parliamentary undergrowth' (and indeed he does have a touch of Indiana Jones about him) but Baroness Chakrabarti, perhaps worried that Lord Hodgson will spend valuable time comparing peers to Hollywood actors, suggests that this is not the best use of the time available (though she stops short of accusing him of filibustering). The amendment is passed yet again.

Lord Browne does not press his amendment. The Government has made a concession on the Afghans – those who have credible links to Afghan specialist units who are already here will not be removed. This goes nowhere near as far as the amendment would have gone – it doesn't deal with family members or with Afghans stranded in Pakistan with no safe and legal route to get here. But Lord Browne's persistence has at least got somewhere . . .

So back to the Commons at nearly 10.00 p.m. The opposing parties continue to support what is now the Anderson amendment, but to no avail. The Government gets its way. Sir Robert Buckland does not vote against the Government this time, but he does point out that getting ourselves into the position of having four rounds of ping-pong on a Bill as short as this 'is not a great place to be'. It might have been avoided if the Government had been prepared to make concessions sooner. Alison Thewliss, for the Scottish National Party, remarks that 'this Westminster system is broken when the supposed revising Chamber has been ignored throughout'.

Back to the Lords at 11.45 p.m. Lord Sharpe, the hard-working Home Office minister, moves the motion that the House does not insist on the one remaining amendment. Lord Anderson gracefully concedes that 'the time has now come to acknowledge the primacy of the elected House and withdraw from the fray. We do so at least secure in the knowledge that the so-called judgment of Parliament was not the judgment of this House and we tried our hardest to achieve something a little more sensible.' Lord Coaker hopes that, if there is a change of government, the Conservative Opposition will in the end defer to the elected House. Lord True, Leader of the House, refuses to be drawn. Lord Sharpe has the last word and the House adjourns at 12.08 a.m.

Technically, the House of Lords could have insisted on its amendments. If so, the Bill would have failed. Since 1911, there has been a way of passing a Bill to which the Commons have agreed but the Lords have not (under the Parliament Act 1911 as amended in 1949). It has to be passed by the Commons in an identical form in two successive parliamentary sessions and at least a year has to have elapsed between the second reading in the Commons in the first of those sessions and its passing the Commons in the second. Suppose then that the Lords stood their ground on 22 April 2024; Parliament was instantly prorogued – suspended – for a few days so that a new session could begin; the Bill was reintroduced in the new session, finished its passage through the Commons after 12 December 2024, the mandatory year's lapse, and again rejected by the Lords. But the next general election is looming. This Parliament has to be dissolved – i.e. broken up – on 17 December 2024 at the very latest.[3] So the Bill could only have got through if the Government had been prepared to wait until the last possible moment to call a general election.

But none of that is necessary as the Lords have given in gracefully. The Bill is given Royal Assent and becomes an Act of Parliament on Thursday 25 April 2024. But it is not yet in force and the Labour Party have promised to repeal it.

Lessons learnt?

So was it all worthwhile? Can anything be learned from the saga of the Safety of Rwanda (Asylum and Immigration) Bill? The first lesson is that the Government of the day controls the business in the House of Commons – literally, it decides the agenda and the timetable. It was regarded as revolutionary when, in 2019, the House of Commons voted to control its own business in the run-up to Brexit. That didn't last long. This power, coupled with the power of the party whips, means that the Government can almost always get its way. The larger the majority, the easier this is. In practice also, the House of Commons does not devote much time or energy to scrutinising the Bills which come before it – what's the point, unless the Government wants to improve its own Bill (as does happen)?

The next lesson, therefore, is that the House of Lords does a much better job of scrutinising proposed legislation. It tried very hard to improve the Rwanda Bill. Although it did not succeed, there are many less fractious Bills where it can bring about improvements if the Government is prepared to listen and accept amendments. One of the reasons for this, perhaps paradoxically, is that the Lords are not elected. This means that even those who take a party whip are not as amenable to party discipline as are Members of the House of Commons. They cannot be dropped at the next general election. It also means that there are many Lords who do not take any party whip and are free to speak and vote as our experience, expertise and conscience dictate. And the fact that we can be there for life brings not only a degree of independence, but also a variety and longevity of experience which the Commons may sometimes lack. Against that, it does mean that the average age is much higher than in the Commons – we may look very out of touch with the modern world, a look not helped by the extraordinary grandeur of our surroundings.

Next, as the Rwanda Bill shows, the House of Lords will always, in the end, give way to the wishes of the House of Commons, in practice the wishes of the Government. Technically, we could have insisted on our amendments and waited to see whether the Government would invoke the procedures in the Parliament Act to try and get the Bill through before the next general election (see above). Some members take the view that this is the constitutional position and they are entitled to rely on it if the stakes are high enough. But only a handful of Bills have been passed under the Parliament Act since 1949 – the most notable being the Hunting Act 2004. Further, as the Rwanda Bill also shows, there is a convention that the Lords will defer to the Commons on any Bill which was promised in the Government's manifesto. This convention may even extend to Bills with 'manifesto characteristics' – whatever that may mean. This is all very well, but I doubt whether most people read the party manifestos before an election, still less that their voting decisions are motivated mainly by what the parties are promising. But it is the closest we can get to divining the will of the people without resorting to referendums on many more issues than we do at present.

But even if the House of Lords does do quite a good job in scrutinising proposed legislation, how can the existence of an unelected chamber be defended in a democracy? Removing the ninety-two remaining hereditary peers will mean that, apart from the bishops and the oddities like me, all the members have been appointed by a Prime Minister. Way back in 1911, the Parliament Act promised 'a Second Chamber constituted on a popular instead of hereditary basis' and to limit and define its powers. But this has never happened. Proposals have been made from time to time to make the Lords wholly or partially elected but would the Commons, led by the Government, ever agree to this? An elected Lords might be far more willing to challenge the elected Commons. The Government of the day might not have a majority in both Houses. It would be harder to get its business through.

There is much that could be done to reform (and reduce) the membership of the House of Lords without resorting to elections – such as giving the House of Lords Appointments Commission more power to scrutinise and to reject nominations; adopting a convention that members should retire, either at a certain age or after a certain (long) number of years' service; or requiring a minimum attendance and participation record.

Last, but by no means least, the Rwanda Bill shows that Parliament can indeed 'make or unmake any law', however constitutionally objectionable it may be. And it shows how the House of Lords can sometimes stand up for the fundamental principles of our Constitution when the Commons does not – the separation of powers between the rule-makers and the fact-finders, the protection of the fundamental rights of each individual, and the independence of the courts and tribunals whose job it is to decide upon the facts and the rights of individuals.

How could we get to the position where a young person trafficked here for domestic slavery could be sent off to Rwanda without the right to challenge that in the courts? We ought to be very worried indeed that Parliament can make a law which offends against so many principles of our Constitution.

The answer lies, not in the pipe dream of a written Constitution, but in the power of each and every one of us – to understand how much the law means to each and every one of us, how the law and the justice system are indeed on our side, and how we must stand up for it. That is what this book is all about.

Afterthoughts

'Ah, it's all very well,' you may say, 'telling us how important the law and the justice system are for all of us. But what about the times when the justice system gets it wrong? We all know about famous miscarriages of justice in the criminal courts, but some of us have personal knowledge of things going wrong in the civil and family courts too – families being wrongly evicted from their homes, women being wrongly deprived of their children, people with unpopular opinions being wrongly prevented from speaking. What have you got to say about that?'

Only the day after I'd been going through the process of copy-editing this book, I heard of just such a case, less dramatic than some but typical of the sort of thing that can happen. The management board of a block of flats was in dispute with two of the leaseholders. The judge seemed to take against the chairman of the board, a woman, referring to her by her surname alone whereas the leaseholders were referred to as 'Mr' this and 'Mr' that. He found for the leaseholders, not only on the financial calculations which were in dispute, but also on the interpretation of the leases, which obviously had serious implications for all the tenants in the block, who will be seriously disadvantaged if it prevails. So what do I say about a story like that? Several things.

First, if what I am told about the judge's attitude to the witnesses is correct, there can be no excuse for such impolite and apparently misogynistic behaviour. Gone are the days when judges could behave as badly as they sometimes did when I was a baby barrister in the 1960s. This is not only because it is plain rude. It is also because it gives an appearance of bias – of a pre-disposition in favour of one side rather than the other. But judges are human beings and often they are overworked, with too many cases in their list and not enough time to prepare properly for them, and under-resourced, with not enough back-up from the office. We all have our off days. So do bear that in mind.

Second, I have only heard one side of the story. Typically, so will you. It is difficult to form a judgement about whether the court has got it right or wrong without hearing both sides of the case. Admittedly, some cases are clear-cut. Some decisions are plainly wrong. If so, there should be an appeal court to put it right. But you may have picked up from all the stories in this book – stories from many different courts and tribunals, stories of many different kinds of legal dilemmas – that if a case gets to court it is often because the answer isn't as obvious as each side may think it is. This is true whatever is in dispute: whether it is the facts, or the law, or which of the possible ways forward will be best for a family. Where the answer is obvious, the aim should be to resolve the case without having to fight it out in court. Only where there is real doubt or dispute should a case end up in court.

Third, and most important of all, think about what life would be like if there weren't courts to resolve our disputes, enforce our obligations, punish our crimes. They are only a back-up but they are a necessary back-up. Think about gambling debts. The high-rolling Mr Ivey, whose case is described in chapter 15, believed that he had won £7.7 million at Crockfords. Crockfords refused to pay and he was able to sue them for what he believed he was owed. In the olden days, gambling debts were not enforceable in the courts. They were enforced in other, much less civilised, ways. More important than that, the fact that ultimately there is a justice system to enforce our obligations or vindicate our rights means that it is usually unnecessary. Debts are paid. Rights are respected. It is the essential under-pinning of commercial life and a civilised society. We cannot do without it.

Notes

The case reports referred to in the notes can be found at www.bailii.org

2 Inside a County Court

1 Section 57, Criminal Justice and Courts Act 2015.

7 Inside a Crown Court

1 *R v A, B, C and D* [2021] EWCA Crim 128, [2021] QB 791.
2 *R v Atkinson and others* [2021] EWCA Crim 1447.

8 Inside the Old Bailey

1 *R (Elgizouli) v Secretary of State for the Home Department* [2020] UKSC 10, [2021] AC 937.

9 Skoolkids Have Rights

1 *In the matter of an application by JR17 for Judicial Review* [2010] UKSC 27, [2010] HRLR 27.
2 *Isle of Wight Council v Pratt* [2017] UKSC 28, [2017] 1 WLR 1441.
3 *R (SB) v Governors of Denbigh High School* [2006] UKHL 15, [2007] 1 AC 100.
4 *R (Williamson and others) v Secretary of State for Education and Employment* [2005] UKHL 15, [2005] 2 AC 246.

10 Disabled People Have Rights

1 *Paulley v First Group plc* [2017] UKSC 4, [2017] 1 WLR 423.
2 *Archibald v Fife Council* [2004] UKHL 32, [2004] ICR 954.
3 *Aster Communities Ltd v Ackerman-Livingstone* [2015] UKSC 15, [2015] AC 1399.

4 *Humphreys v Revenue and Customs Commissioners* [2012] UKSC 18, [2012] 1 WLR 1545.
5 *R (MA and others) v Secretary of State for Work and Pensions* [2016] UKSC 58, [2016] 1 WLR 4550.
6 *Price v United Kingdom* [2002] 34 EHRR 53.

11 LGBTQ+ People Have Rights

1 *Preddy v Bull; Hall v Bull* [2013] UKSC 73, [2013] 1 WLR 3741.
2 *Lee v Ashers Baking Co. Ltd and others* [2018] UKSC 49, [2020] AC 413.
3 *Lee v United Kingdom*, Application no 18860/19.
4 *R (C) v Secretary of State for Work and Pensions* [2017] UKSC 72, [2017] 1 WLR 4127.
5 *MB v Secretary of State for Work and Pensions* [2016] UKSC 53, [2017] 1 CMLR 13.
6 *MB v Secretary of State for Work and Pensions*, EU:C:2018:492, [2019] ICR 115.
7 *For Women Scotland Ltd v The Scottish Ministers* [2025] UKSC 16, on appeal from [2023] CSIH 37, 2024 SC 117.
8 *R (Elan-Cane) v Secretary of State for the Home Department* [2021] UKSC 56, [2023] AC 559.
9 *In re G (Adoption: Unmarried Couple)* [2009] AC 173.

12 Workers Have Rights

1 *Hounga v Allen* [2014] UKSC 47, [2014] 1 WLR 2889.
2 *Onu v Akwiwu, Taiwo v Olaigbe* [2016] UKSC 31, [2016] 1 WLR 2653.
3 *Patel v Mirza* [2016] UKSC 42, [2017] AC 467.
4 *Matthews v Kent and Medway Towns Fire Authority* [2006] UKHL 8, [2006] ICR 365.
5 *O'Brien v Ministry of Justice* [2017] UKSC 46, [2017] ICR 1101.
6 *Chief Constable of the West Yorkshire Police v Homer* [2012] UKSC 15, [2012] ICR 704.
7 *Seldon v Clarkson Wright and Jakes* [2012] UKSC 16, [2012] ICR 716.
8 For example, *Autoclenz Ltd v Belcher* [2011] UKSC 41, 2011 ICR 1157.
9 *Pimlico Plumbers Ltd v Smith* [2018] UKSC 29, [2018] ICR 1511.
10 *Uber BV v Aslam* [2021] UKSC 5, [2021] ICR 657.
11 *R (Independent Workers Union of Great Britain) v Central Arbitration Committee* [2023] UKSC 41, [2024] ICR 189.
12 *Gilham v Ministry of Justice* [2019] UKSC 44, [2019] 1 WLR 5905.

13 Women Have Rights

1. *Dumfries and Galloway Council v North and others* [2013] UKSC 45, [2013] ICR 993.
2. *Hewage v Grampian Health Board* [2012] UKSC 37, [2012] ICR 1054.
3. *Shamoon v Chief Constable of the Royal Ulster Constabulary* [2003] UKHL 11, [2003] ICR 337.
4. *White v White* [2001] 1 AC 596.
5. *Miller v Miller, McFarlane v McFarlane* [2006] UKHL 24 [2006] 2 AC 618.
6. *R (Coll) v Secretary of State for Justice* [2017] UKSC 40, [2017] 1 WLR 2093.
7. *D v Commissioner of Police of the Metropolis* [2018] UKSC 11, [2019] AC 196.
8. *McFarlane v Tayside Health Board* [2000] 2 AC 59.
9. *Parkinson v St James and Seacroft University Hospital NHS Trust* [2001] EWCA Civ 530, [2002] QB 266.
10. *Rees v Darlington Memorial Hospital NHS Trust* [2003] UKHL 52, [2004] 1 AC 309.

14 Patients Have Rights

1. *Darnley v Croydon Health Services NHS Trust* [2018] UKSC 50, [2019] AC 831.
2. *Sidaway v Board of Governors of the Bethlem Royal Hospital and the Maudsley Hospital* [1985] AC 871.
3. Laid down in *Bolam v Friern Hospital Management Committee* [1957] 1 WLR 582.
4. *Montgomery v Lanarkshire Health Board* [2015] UKSC 11, [2015] AC 1430.
5. *R v Bournewood Community and Mental Health NHS Trust, ex parte L* [1999] 1 AC 458.
6. *In re F (Mental Patient: Sterilisation)* [1990] 2 AC 1.
7. *HL v United Kingdom* (2005) 40 EHRR 32.
8. *Cheshire West and Chester Council v P* [2014] UKSC 19, [2014] AC 896.
9. *Rabone v Pennine Care NHS Trust* [2012] UKSC 2, [2012] 2 AC 72.
10. *Aintree University Hospitals NHS Trust v James* [2013] UKSC 67, [2014] AC 591.
11. *R (Nicklinson and another) v Ministry of Justice and others* [2014] UKSC 38, [2015] AC 657.

15 Making Law in the Courts

1. *Holman v Johnson* (1775), 98 ER 1120, 1 Cowp 341.
2. *Tinsley v Milligan* [1994] 1 AC 340.

270   Notes

3   *Hounga v Allen* [2014] UKSC 47, [2014] 1 WLR 2889.
4   *Les Laboratoires Servier v Apotek Inc.* [2014] UKSC 55, [2015] AC 430; and *Bilta (UK) Ltd v Nazir (No 2)* [2015] UKSC 23, [2016] AC 1.
5   *Patel v Mirza* [2016] UKSC 42, [2017] AC 467.
6   *Donoghue v Stevenson* [1932] AC 562.
7   *Bamford v Turnley* (1862) 3 B & S 66.
8   *Fearn v Board of Trustees of the Tate Gallery* [2023] UKSC 4, [2024] AC 1.
9   [2019] EWHC 246 (Ch), [2019] Ch 369.
10 [2020] EWCA Civ 104, [2020] Ch 621.
11 *Ivey v Genting Casinos (UK) Ltd (trading as Crockfords Club)* [2017] UKSC 67, [2018] AC 391.
12 [2014] EWHC (QB) 3394, [2015] LLR 98.
13 [2016] EWCA Civ 1093, [2017] 1 WLR 697.
14 *R v Ghosh* [1982] QB 1053.
15 *R (Jackson) v Attorney General* [2005] UKHL 56, [2006] 1 AC 262
16 *R (Privacy International) v Investigatory Powers Tribunal* [2019] UKSC 22, [2020] AC 491.
17 *Anisminic Ltd v Foreign Compensation Commission* [1969] 2 AC 147.
18 *Semayne's Case* (1604) 5 Co Rep 91a, at 91b.

16 Making Law in Government

1   United Nations Security Council (SCR 1373).
2   *Ahmed and others v Her Majesty's Treasury* [2010] UKSC 2 and 5, [2010] 2 AC 534.
3   [2017] UKSC 51, [2020] AC 869.
4   *R (Dolan and others) v Secretary of State for Health and Social Care and another* [2020] EWCA Civ 1605, [2021] 1 WLR 2326.

17 Making Law in Parliament

1   *AAA v Secretary of State for the Home Department* [2023] EWCA Civ 745, [2023] 1 WLR 3103.
2   [2023] UKSC 42, [2023] 1 WLR 4433.
3   Dissolution and Calling of Parliament Act 2022, s 4.

Acknowledgements

When I planned to write about what goes on every day in our courts and tribunals, it would have been fun to turn up unannounced – and I did that in the Royal Courts of Justice, because surely the senior judges who sit there would not be put off their stride if the former President of the Supreme Court slipped into the seats for the public? But it didn't seem fair to do that in the other courts and tribunals I visited and I needed permission to observe the family courts. So I am very grateful to the lead judges in all of them, who welcomed me warmly and made sure that I could see what I wanted to see – which was nothing special, just their ordinary work on an ordinary day. I am also grateful to all the other judges and magistrates whose hearings I observed, and who also welcomed me into their courts and hearing rooms. I hope that, if they read what I have written about their work, they will feel that it gives a fair picture of the work they do and what goes on in courts and tribunals up and down the country every day.

Once again, I am very grateful to Stuart Williams and all the team at The Bodley Head. Writing books which I hope will reach a broader readership than the lawyers and would-be lawyers who read law books is much more challenging. Things which we take for granted have to be explained. Things which we think unremarkable can become remarkable. The whole idea is to tell a series of true stories and tell them as best one can. Stuart and the team have been invaluable in helping me to do that. If this book succeeds in persuading readers that the law can indeed be on our side – even if it sometimes is not – then much of the credit belongs to them.

Index

Accident and Emergency (A&E), 186–8
Ackerman-Livingstone, Jonathan, 133–5, 140
Acts of Parliament, 5–6, 166, 204, 205, 211, 214, 221, 225–9
   committee stage, 245, 250, 257
   reading stage, 245, 250, 253, 254
   report stage, 245, 250, 257
   Royal Assent, 245
   secondary legislation and, 6, 204–5, 232, 235–6, 239
actual bodily harm (ABH), 78, 81, 90–92
Advisory, Conciliation and Arbitration Service (ACAS), 55
Afghanistan, 258, 260
age discrimination, 161–3
Ahmed and others v Her Majesty's Treasury, 232–5
Al-Qaida and Taliban Order 2006, 232, 234, 235
All Creatures Great and Small (Herriot), 28
Anderson of Ipswich, David, Baron, KC, 255, 257, 260
anger management, 61, 105
Anisminic Ltd v Foreign Compensation Commission, 227–8
Anne, Queen, 245
appeals, 9–10, 211, 225, 229
   benefits tribunals, 35–7, 38, 40, 42–3
   criminal 12, 13–16
   right to, 229, 248, 254, 259, 264
Appellate Committee, 123, 210, 212, 228, 252

Appellate Jurisdiction Act (1876), 252
APT&C, 131–2
Archibald, Susan, 131–3, 140
Ashers Baking Company, 144–6
assault, *see* violence
assisted suicide, 200
Assizes, 86–7
asylum, 47, 206, 231, 245–64
Atkin, James Richard, Lord of Appeal in Ordinary, 217
atomic tests, 18
Attorney General, 93
austerity programme (2010–c. 2019), 135, 236
Australia, 150, 247
autism spectrum condition, 100, 101, 191–4

Baccarat, 208, 222–5, 230
backlogs, 2, 44, 55
bail, 76, 77, 80, 82, 84
Bamford v Turnley, 218
Baraitser, Vanessa, Judge, 94
barristers, 17, 24, 78, 83, 100, 108
Bedford, Bedfordshire, 177
bedroom tax, 135–7
Begum, Shabina, 120–24
benefits, *see* welfare
bereavement damages, 195–7
Bevan, Yasmin, 120–24
Bill of Rights 1689, 207
Bilta (UK) Ltd v Nazir, 215
Bin Laden, Usuma, 234

Bingham of Cornhill, Thomas, Baron, 13, 226
blameworthiness, principles of, 221–2
Blavatnik building, Tate Modern, 218–21, 229, 230
Blunkett, David, Baron, 255
Bolam test, 190, 195
Booth, Cherie, KC, 123
boundary disputes, 18
Bramwell, George, 1st Baron, 218
Braverman, Suella, KC, 250
Brexit, 149, 262
Bristol, England, 142–4
Bristol, Vivienne Faull, Bishop of, see Faull, Vivienne
British Empire, 207
Browne of Ladyton, Desmond, Baron, 258, 260
Buckland, Robert, Sir, KC, MP, 259, 260
Bull, Peter and Hazelmary, 142–4
bullying, 115
burglaries, 20, 90, 94–5, 209
Burnett of Maldon, Ian, Baron, 13
Butler of Brockwell, Robin, Baron, 254
Butler-Sloss, Ann Elizabeth, Baroness, 258
by-laws, 204, 205

Caesarean sections, 189–91
CAFCASS, 64, 66–9
Cameron of Chipping Norton, David, Baron, 251
Canada, 150
cannabis, 61–3, 105
Canterbury, Justin Welby, Archbishop of, see Welby, Justin
cardiopulmonary resuscitation (CPR), 197, 198
cards, cheating at, 208, 222–5, 230
Carlile of Berriew, Alex, Baron, KC, 255, 257
Carnwath, Robert, Lord, 228

Cash, William, Sir, MP, 250
catering, 33
CCTV, 53
Central Criminal Court, 4, 11, 87, 92, 93, 95, 96–109
Central London County Court, 11
Central London Employment Tribunal, 48
Central London Family Court, 56, 58, 70
Chakrabarti, Shami, Baroness, 256, 260
Chelmsford, Guli Francis-Dehqani, Bishop of, see Francis-Dehqani, Guli
child benefit, 36
Child Poverty Action Group, 257
children
    abuse of, 56, 57, 58–63, 103–7, 120, 133
    cases about, 56, 57, 58–69
    offenders, see young offenders
    rights of, 2, 113, 115–27
Children's Legal Centre, 123
China, 59–61, 222
chocolate box, 93
Christianity
    Church of England, 251, 255
    education and, 124–6
    LGBTQ+ and, 142–6, 152
chronic obstructive pulmonary disease (COPD), 197
Church of England, 251, 255
circuit judges, 10, 28, 58–63
Citizens Advice Bureau, 21, 36, 43, 49
Civil Contingencies Act (2004), 239
civil justice system, 2, 4, 9, 12, 16–19, 20–33, 56
    county courts, 10, 16, 20–33, 130, 131, 134
    fast-track trials, 28–33
    High Court, 16–19
    injunctions, 25–8
    small claims, 22–5

civil partnership, 142–4
Clarke of Nottingham, Kenneth, Baron, 256, 257
class action, 17
Cleverly, James, MP, 249, 259
climate change protests, 90, 92–3
Coaker, Vernon, Baron, 258, 260, 261
cocaine, 82–4, 88, 105
Coll, Isobel, 177–8
commercial courts, 17
common law, 5, 209–30, 237–8
    dishonesty, 221–5
    illegality defence, 213–16, 221
    private nuisance, 216–21
    rule of law, 225–9
compensation, 1, 2, 4, 21–5, 56
    bereavement damages, 195–7
    divorce cases, 176–7
    employment tribunals, 45, 46, 47, 54, 156–7
    fast-track trials, 28–33
    Foreign Compensation Act (1950), 227–8
    illegality defence and, 213–16, 221
    negligence and, 217
    rape victims, 180
    school exclusions, 117
    small claims, 22–5
    trafficking victims, 103, 156–7
Constitution, 5, 166, 203–8, 245, 263–4
    parliamentary sovereignty, 203–4, 244, 245, 253–4
    see also common law; legislation
constitutional courts, 203–4
constructive unfair dismissal, 52
contempt of court, 92–3, 138
Contracts of Employment Act 1963, 45
Cooper, Yvette, MP, 249
Coronavirus Act 2020, 239
corporal punishment, 124–6
Council of Europe, 150
county courts, 10, 16, 20–33, 58, 73–4, 130, 131, 134

Court of Appeal, 10, 210, 211
    Civil Division, 9, 10, 11, 130, 176, 183–4, 188, 192, 200, 219, 241, 247
    Criminal Division, 9, 10, 11, 12, 13–16, 88–9, 224
Court of Justice (EU), 149, 160
Court of Protection, 198
Court of Session, 210
Covid-19 epidemic (2020–22), 41, 48, 67, 70, 204, 208, 221, 231
Covid-19 epidemic secondary legislation and, 239–41, 243
criminal justice system, 2–3, 6, 9, 221
    Central Criminal Court, 4, 11, 87, 92, 93, 95, 96–109
    Crown Courts, 9, 10, 20, 85, 86–95
    magistrates' courts, 9, 10, 76–85
Crippen, Hawley, 99
Crockfords casino, London, 222–5, 230, 266
Cromwell, Oliver, Sir, 244
cross-bench peers, 252–3
Crown Courts, 9, 10, 20, 85, 86–95
Crown Prosecution Service (CPS), 77–8, 81, 82–4
curfew, 94
Curia Regis, 225

D'Souza, Frances, Baroness, 257
dais, 49
Daly, James, 136
Dar es Salaam bombing (1999), 234
Data Protection Act 2018, 98
Davies of Brixton, Bryn, Baron, 255
Davis, William, Lord Justice, 13
death penalty, 98
Deben, Baron (John Selwyn Gummer), 257
debts, 20–21, 138
degrading treatment, 3, 139, 180–81
delegated legislation, *see under* secondary legislation

Deliveroo, 164
demonstrations, *see* protests
Denbigh High School, Luton, 120–24
Department for Work and Pensions, 35–44, 147–50
Deprivation of Liberty Safeguards (DOLS), 194
diabetes, 188–91
disabilities, 2, 4, 5, 128–40
   accessibility and, 36, 77, 129–31
   discrimination and, 46, 48, 51–2, 128, 134, 136–7
   employment and, 48, 131–2
   welfare and, 36, 37–42, 135–7
Disability Discrimination Act 1996, 46
discounts, 79, 89
discrimination, 4, 128
   age and, 161–3
   disabilities and, 46, 48, 51–2, 128, 134, 136–7
   employment and, 45–6, 48, 51–2, 161–3, 172–4
   race and, 128, 172–4
   sex and, 128, 172–4
   sexuality and, 141–53
district judges, 10, 164–7
   county courts, 22, 25, 48, 73–4
   family courts, 57, 58, 63–6, 73–4
   magistrates' courts, 10
divorce, 57, 70–73, 174–7
Dolan, Simon, 240
domestic abuse, 57, 58, 65, 66, 73–4, 81–2, 105–6
Donoghue v Stevenson, 217
drugs, illegal
   child care cases, 61–3, 105
   conspiracy to supply, 88–90
   driving under influence, 82–4
Dubs, Alfred, Baron, 257
Durham Crown Court, 87

Earl Marshal, 251
edge sorting, 208, 222–5, 230

education system, 2, 4, 5, 6, 113, 115–27
   corporal punishment, 124–6
   exclusions, 115–18
   unauthorised absences, 118–20
   uniforms, 120–26
Ekweremadu family, 102–3
Elan-Cane, Christie, 150
elections, 205, 207, 238, 250, 251, 254, 261, 262
emergency regulations, 239
employment, 45–6, 55, 113, 154–68
   age discrimination, 161–3
   discrimination and, 45–6, 48, 51–2
   employment tribunals, 9, 45–55, 156, 160, 162, 163–4, 173
   freedom of contract, 154–5, 167
   part-time workers, 155, 158–61, 166
   redeployment, 131–3
   trafficked workers, 155–8
   unfair dismissals, 48–54
   whistle blowers, 164–7
   women's rights and, 169, 170–74
Employment Appeal Tribunal, 9, 46, 164, 211
Employment Rights Act 1996, 45
employment tribunals, 9, 45–55, 156, 160, 162, 163–4, 173, 211
   Fees Order 2013, 235–9
EncroChat, 88
Equal Pay Act 1970, 45, 169, 170
Equality Act 2010, 46, 51, 128, 134, 149–50, 178
Equality and Human Rights Commission, 143
Equality Commission for Northern Ireland, 145
Etherton, Terence, Baron, 255
European Convention on Human Rights, 117, 122, 125
   deprivation of liberty, 241
   disability rights cases and, 136, 137, 139

freedom of speech, 166
inhuman/degrading treatment, 3, 139, 180
LGBTQ+ rights cases and, 143, 145–6, 150, 151–2
right to fair trial, 229
right to life, 195–6
Rwanda scheme and, 247, 248, 250
sectioning case, 192, 193–4
European Court of Justice, 149, 160
European Union (EU), 149, 155, 166
ex turpi causa non oritur actio, 213

Falconer of Thoroton, Charles, Baron, KC, 165
family courts, 9, 10, 12, 56–75
children cases, 56, 57, 58–69
domestic abuse, 57, 58, 65, 66, 73–4
financial remedy cases, 57, 58, 69–73
fast-track trials, 28–33
Faull, Vivienne, Bishop of Bristol, 258
Fearn v Board of Trustees of the Tate Gallery, 219–21
Fife Council, 131
filibustering, 260
financial dispute resolution (FDR), 71
Financial Remedies Court, 57, 69–73
Fire Brigades Union, 159
firefighters, 158–60
First-tier Tribunal, 9, 35, 211
Ford Motor Company, 169
Foreign Compensation Act 1950, 227–8
France, 207, 246
Francis-Dehqani, Guli, Bishop of Chelmsford, 257
freedom of contract, 154–5, 167
freedom of speech, 166
Fry, Elizabeth, 96
funding, 2, 4, 21, 164–7
backlogs and, 2, 44, 55
closures and, 69, 85

legal aid cuts, 21
staff shortages and, 2, 33, 63
whistle blowers and, 164–7

gambling, 208, 222–5, 230, 266
gay marriage, 144–6, 148
Gender Recognition Act 2004, 147, 149–50
Gender Representation on Public Boards (Scotland) Act 2018, 149
general elections, 205, 207, 238, 250, 251, 254, 261, 262
General Medical Council, 191
Gilham, Claire, Judge, 164–7
Glastonbury, Somerset, 133–5
Glorious Revolution (1688), 207
Goddard, Ann, Judge, QC, 109
Goldsmith, Peter, Baron, KC, 253
Good Friday Agreement (1998), 256
government, 1, 245
bedroom tax cases, 135–7
budget cuts, 2, 21, 33, 55, 165–7, 236
legislation, *see* legislation
rule of law and, 3, 225–9, 245, 254, 263
Government Communications Headquarters (GCHQ), 226–9
Government of Wales Act 2006, 205
Gray's Inn Road, London, 36
Great Hall, Royal Courts, 12
grievous bodily harm (GBH), 103–7
guilty pleas, 78–9, 89

habeas corpus, 192
Hailsham, Douglas Hogg, Viscount, 256
Hall, Martyn, 142–4
Hamilton, Carolyn, 123
Harrogate Youth Court, 84
Harrow Crown Court, 87
healthcare, 6, 185–200
Hennessy of Nympsfield, Peter, Baron, 255

Henry II, King, 87
Henry VIII powers, 205
hereditary peers, 251
Herriot, James, 28
Hewage, Sumithra, 172–4
High Court, 10, 11, 16–19, 61, 86, 209, 221, 225–9
 Family Division, 107
 King's Bench Division, 16–19, 225
 rule of law and, 225–9
 Rwanda scheme and, 247
hijabs, 100, 121, 122
His Majesty's Courts and Tribunals Service, 166
Hodgson of Astley Abbotts, Robin, Baron, 260
Holroyde, Timothy, Lord Justice, 13
Home Office, 139
homelessness, 133–5
Homer, Terrence, 161–3
homicide, 86, 97, 103–7
homosexuality, *see* LGBTQ+
honours lists, 251
Hope of Craighead, David, Baron, 257, 259–60
Houghton of Richmond, John Nicholas, Baron, 258
Hounga v Allen, 155–8, 214–15, 216
House of Commons, 207, 242, 244, 245–50, 258–61, 262
House of Lords, 11, 70, 211–12, 250–53, 262
 Anisminic Ltd v Foreign Compensation Commission, 227–8
 Appointments Commission, 252
 cross-bench peers, 252–3
 elected chamber proposals, 263
 hereditary peers, 251, 263
 International Agreements Committee, 253
 Law Lords, *see* Law Lords
 life peers, 251–2
 Lords Spiritual, 251
 ping-pong, 258–61
 Rwanda scheme and, 250–64
 Select Committee on the Constitution, 253
House of Lords Act 1999, 251
housing, 133–7
Hull, East Yorkshire, 84
human rights, *see under* rights
Human Rights Act 1998, 3, 117, 128, 146, 249–50
 emergency regulations and, 239, 240
 European Convention and, 117, 240, 249–50
 inhuman/degrading treatment, 140, 181
 patients' rights and, 195, 200
 property rights and, 235
 Rwanda scheme and, 248, 249–50, 254
Human Trafficking Foundation, 258
human trafficking, *see* trafficking
Hunting Act 2004, 226, 262

If... (1968 film), 124
Illegal Migration Act 2023, 246–7, 259–60
illness, 4, 186–200
immigration, 2, 34, 47
 asylum, 47, 206, 231, 245–64
 trafficking, 59–61, 101–3, 155–8, 208, 214–15, 258, 259
Income Tax Act 2007, 165
Independent Sentencing Review, 2, 16
Industrial Relations Act 1971, 45
Industrial Training Act 1964, 46
industrial tribunals, 46
inhuman treatment, 3, 139, 180–81
Inner London Crown Court, 87–95, 97
Inns of Court, London, 11
insider trading, 213–16
Instrument of Appointment, 165
Insulate Britain, 90, 92–3

insurance motor insurance, 22–5, 28–33
International Agreements Committee, 253
international child abduction, 58, 59–61
International Civil Aviation Organisation, 150
International Labour Organisation, 157
intersex people, 150, 153
Investigatory Powers Tribunal (IPT), 226–9
Islam
    dress codes, 100, 121–4
    jihadism, 97–101, 232–5
Islamic State (ISIS), 97–9
Israel, 247
Ivey v Genting Casinos (UK) Ltd, 222–5, 230, 266

James II, King, 207
James, David, 197–200
Japanese knotweed, 218
Jenrick, Robert, MP, 249–50
jihad, 101
jilbabs, 121–4
John, King, 212
Johnson, Jeremy, Mr Justice, 101
Joseph, Wendy, KC, Judge, 109
judges, 10, 47–8, 107–9
    circuit judges, 10, 28, 58–63
    county courts, 22, 25, 48
    Court of Appeal, 10
    district judges (county courts), 22, 25, 48, 73–4
    district judges (family courts), 57, 58, 63–6, 73–4
    district judges (magistrates' courts), 10
    family courts, 48, 57–8
    hierarchy, 210
    High Court, 10, 11, 58, 86, 93, 209–10
    lay magistrates, 10, 57, 58, 66–9
    self-employment and, 46
    Supreme Court, 10, 46, 210
    tribunal judges, 10, 35–6, 37, 46
    woman judges, 109
    workers' rights and, 160–61
Judicial Appointments Board, 206
Judicial Appointments Commission, 44, 206
Judicial College, 31
judicial independence, 206, 245
judicial review, 225–9
junior barristers, 17
jury equity, 93
jury trials, 13, 20, 33, 85, 86–7, 90–93, 107–9
    Central Criminal Court, 100–109
    Crown Courts, 85, 86–7, 89, 90–93
juvenile offenders, *see* young offenders

Karu, Usha, Judge, 87
Kerr of Tonaghmore, Brian, Lord of Appeal in Ordinary, 229
Kerr of Kinlochard, John, Baron, 258
Kes (1969 film), 124
King's Bench, 16–19, 225
King's Counsel, 17
King's Court, 225
Kinnoull, Charles Hay, 16th Earl, 254
Kirkhope of Harrogate, Timothy, Baron, 256

Lady Chatterley's Lover (Lawrence), 99
land ownership, 209–10, 211
landlords, 3, 21, 25–8, 133–5
Law Centres, 36
Law Commission, 214
Law Lords, 123, 212, 252
    Appellate Committee, 123, 210, 212, 228, 252
    Bamford v Turnley, 218
    children's rights cases, 123, 125–6
    disabled rights cases, 132–3

280 *Index*

Law Lords (*Continued*)
  Donoghue v Stevenson, 217
  LGBTQ+ cases, 152
  patients' rights cases, 190, 192, 193–4
  Tinsley v Milligan, 214, 215, 216, 230
  women's rights cases, 174, 176,
    183–4
  workers' rights cases, 160, 174
Lawrence, David Herbert, 99
lay magistrates, 10, 57, 58, 66–9
Lee, Gareth, 144–6
Leeds, West Yorkshire, 129
legal aid, 21, 34, 47
Leggatt, George, Lord, 219
legislation, 5, 166, 203–5, 211–12,
  245–64
  delegated legislation, 6, 204–5, 206,
    211, 231–43
  equality legislation, 45–6, 51, 128,
    134, 149–50, 169, 170, 178
  primary legislation, 5–6, 166, 204,
    205, 211, 221, 225–9, 232, 245–64
  secondary legislation, 5–6, 204–5,
    206, 211, 231–43
  workers' rights legislation, 45, 235–6
Leonard, Anthony, Judge, KC, 100
Les Laboratoires Servier v Apotek Inc, 215
levelling up, 128
LGBTQ+ people, 5, 113, 141–53, 248,
  255
libel, 16
Life Peerages Act 1958, 251
life peers, 251–2
Lincoln, Lincolnshire
  County Court, 138
  Crown Court, 87
Lister of Burtersett, Ruth, Baroness, 257
Lisvane, Robert Rogers, Baron, 255
Lloyd Jones, David, Lord, 229
London, Sarah Mullally, Bishop of,
  see Mullally, Sarah
Lord and Lady Justices of Appeal, 10
Lord Chancellor, 166, 236, 252

Lord Chief Justice, 166
Lord High Chamberlain, 251
Lord Mayor of London, 99
Lord Speaker, 253
Lords of Appeal in Ordinary, 252
Lords Spiritual, 251
Lowry, Nina, 109
Lucraft, Mark, Judge, KC, 97
Luton, Bedfordshire, 120–24

magistrates' courts, 9, 10, 76–85, 86
  family courts, 58, 66–9
  remand courts, 84
Magna Carta 1215, 212, 238
malicious falsehood 17
Manchester, David Walker, Bishop of,
  see Walker, David
Mansfield, William Murray, 1st Earl,
  213, 214
Marazion, Cornwall, 142–4
Marlesford, Mark Schreiber, Baron, 256
Mary II, Queen, 207
McArthur, Daniel and Amy, 144–6
McFarlane, Catherine, 181–2, 183, 184
McFarlane v McFarlane, 176
Mental Health Act 1983, 40, 191–4
mental health, 2, 34, 81, 133–5, 165,
  191–7, 252
  housing and, 133–5
  sectioning, 40, 191–4
  suicide, 116, 194–7
Middlesbrough county court, 20–33,
  58, 73–4, 87
Middlesex Guildhall, London, 212
Mike Darnley, 186–8
Miller v Miller, 176
ministers, 245
Ministry of Justice, 33, 166, 178, 237
miscarriages of justice, 108, 165, 265
misogyny, 265
Montgomery, Nadine, 188–91
mortgages, 3, 21
motor insurance, 22–5, 28–33

Motor Insurers' Bureau, 40
Mullally, Sarah, Bishop of London, 255
murder, 86, 97, 103–7
Muslim Council of Britain, 121

Nairobi bombing (1999), 234
National Assistance Act 1948, 35
National Health Service (NHS), 6, 186, 196
National Institute for Health and Clinical Excellence (NICE), 189
National Insurance, 165
  Local Tribunals, 35
Nationality and Borders Act 2022, 246
Nauru, 247
negligence, 217
Neill, Bob, Sir, KC, MP, 259
Neo Bankside, London, 218–21, 229, 230
Neuberger, David, Baron, 213, 215
Neuberger, Julia, Baroness, 257
New Year's honours lists, 251
New Zealand, 150
Newgate Prison, London, 96
Nicklin, Matthew, Mr Justice, 16
Nigeria, 102–3, 155, 214–15
non-gendered people, 150
non-refoulement, 247–8
Norman Conquest (1066), 1, 225
Northallerton, North Yorkshire, 80
Northern Circuit, 165
Northern Ireland, 117, 144–6, 151–2, 256
  Assembly, 5, 205
Northern Ireland Act 1998, 205

O'Loan, Nuala, Baroness, 256
Obeta, Obinna, 102–3
obstetrics, 188–91
Offences against the Person Act 1861, 221
oil rigs, 18
Old Bailey, *see* Central Criminal Court
open justice, 14–15, 49

Orders in Council, 227
organ trafficking, 101–3

Palermo Protocol, 157
Parkinson, Scott, 182, 183
Parliament, 1, 5–6, 152, 155, 203–4, 211, 244–64
  rule of law and, 3, 225–9, 245, 254, 263
  Safety of Rwanda Act (2024), 206, 245–64
  secondary legislation and, 204, 231, 240, 242
  sovereignty of, 203–4, 244, 245, 253–4
Parliament Acts, 1911 and 1949, 255, 261, 262, 263
Parliament Square, London, 212
part-time workers, 155, 158–61, 166
passports, 150–52
Patel v Mirza, 213–16, 221, 230
patients' rights, 4, 186–200
Paulley, Doug, 129–31, 140
pensions, 34, 35, 36, 147–50
personal injuries, 18
Phillips of Worth Matravers, Nicholas, Lord, 233
Pimlico Plumbers Ltd, 163–4
ping-pong, 258–61
planning permission, 220–21
Police National Legal Database (PNLD), 161
Poor Law, 35
Post Office, 18
Potter, Beatrix, 11
precedents, *see* common law
Preddy, Steven, 142–4
pregnancy, 170, 181–4, 188–91
primary legislation, 5–6, 166, 204, 205, 211, 221, 225–9
  secondary legislation and, 6, 204–5, 232, 235–6, 239
prisons, 2, 96, 138–40, 177–8
Privacy International, 226–9

282 *Index*

privacy, 16–17
Private Eye, 92
private nuisance, 216–21
pro bono publico, 36
probation services, 2, 79, 94
property, 18, 209–10, 217–18
prorogation, 240
protests, 11, 90, 92–3
public funding (legal aid), 21, 34, 47
Public Health Act 1984, 239, 240, 241
public spending, *see* funding
Punto Banco, 208, 222–5, 230

al-Qaida, 233, 234
Quakers, 81
Quarter Sessions, 86–7
QueerSpace, 144–6

R (Jackson) v Attorney General, 226
R (Privacy International) v Investigatory Powers Tribunal, 226–9
R v Ghosh, 224
Rabone, Melanie, 194–7
Race Relations Act 1976, 46
racial discrimination, 46, 128, 172–4
Randall of Uxbridge, John, Baron, 258
rape, 86, 178–81
recorders, 87, 97, 99, 160
redeployment, 132
Redundancy Payments Act 1965, 45
redundancy payments, 45, 47
Reed of Allermuir, Robert, Baron, 229, 237
Rees, Anthony, 182, 184
refoulement, 247–8
Refugee Council, 257
Regulation of Investigatory Powers Act 2000, 226
Reid, James, Lord of Appeal in Ordinary, 228
Reid, Silas, Judge, 90, 92–3
remand courts, 84
reoffending rates, 90

restraining orders, 82
retirement, 161–3
    pensions, 34, 35, 36, 147–50
Retreat, York 81
Rexton Farm, Somerset, 174
Richard II, King, 244
Richmond, North Yorkshire, 79–80, 83
rights, 2, 3, 113–27, 128–40, 141–53, 154–68, 169–85, 186–200
    children's rights, 2, 5, 113, 115–27
    disability rights, 2, 128–40
    LGBTQ+ rights, 5, 113, 141–53
    mental health and, 2, 133–5
    patients' rights, 4, 186–200
    women's rights, 113, 169–85
    workers' rights, 45–6, 55, 113, 154–68
road traffic accidents, 28–33
Rolls Building, London, 11, 16
Roosevelt, Eleanor, 99, 118
Royal Bank of Scotland (RBS), 213–16
royal coat of arms, 13, 66
Royal Courts of Justice, 4, 11–19, 58
Royal Ulster Constabulary, 174
rule of law, 3, 225–9, 245, 254
Rule of Law, The (Bingham), 226
Runcorn County Court, 165
Rwanda scheme, 206, 245–64

Safety of Rwanda Act 2024, 206, 245–64
Saleem, Mohammed, 100
Sales, Philip, Lord, 220
Salisbury/Addison convention, 254
schools, *see* education system
Scotland Act 1998, 205
Scottish Parliament, 5, 149, 205
secondary legislation, 5–6, 204–5, 206, 211, 231–43
    Covid-19 epidemic (2020–22), 239–41, 243
    devolved legislatures, 5, 205
    Employment Tribunals Fees Order 2013, 236
    Terrorism Order (2006), 232–5

secret courts, 14
Secret Intelligence Service, 226
sectioning, 40, 191–4
Security Service, 226
Seeley, Martin, Bishop of St Edmundsbury and Ipswich, 255, 257
Select Committee on the Constitution, 253
self-employment, 46, 108, 154, 163–4
Semayne's Case, 229
sentencing, 2, 78–9, 86, 94–5
    appeals, 13, 15–16
    Crown Courts, 86, 90
    discounts, 79, 89
    guidelines, 95
    length of, 82, 86, 90, 95
    maximum sentences, 82, 86
    reoffending and, 90
    tariffs, 90
Sentencing Council, 90
separation cases, 57, 58, 63–9
separation of powers, 233, 253, 257, 263
    see also rule of law
sex discrimination, 128, 172–4
Sex Discrimination Act 1975, 46, 169
Sexual Offences Act 2003, 221
sexual offences, 14, 15–16, 20, 56, 86, 170, 178–81
shalwar kameez, 121
shared care orders, 68–9
Sharif, Sara, 120
Sharpe, Andrew, Baron, 256, 261
el-Sheikh, Shafee, 98
shoplifting, 80, 84
shoulder dystocia, 189–91
single-sex facilities, 177–8
slander, 16
slavery, 3
    see also trafficking
small boats crossings, 245–64
small claims, 22–5
Smith, Gary, 163–4

Social Entitlement Chamber, 35, 44
social media, 91
Social Security Appeal Tribunals, 35
solicitors, 17, 24, 71, 78
Southwark Crown Court, 87
Special Development Orders, 231
St Edmundsbury and Ipswich, Martin Seeley, Bishop of, *see* Seeley, Martin
staff shortages, 2, 33, 63
Stalybridge, Manchester, 129–31
Stewart of Dirleton, Keith, Baron, 254, 257
Steyn, Johan, Lord of Appeal in Ordinary, 193
stipendiary magistrates, 10
Stirrup, Graham 'Jock', Baron, 258
stoma, 197
Suez Crisis (1956), 227
suicide, 116, 194–7
    assisted, 200
Sumption, Jonathan, Lord, 213, 215, 216, 229, 240
Sun, Cheung Yin, 208, 222–5, 230
super majorities, 203
Supplementary Benefits Appeal Tribunals, 35
Supreme Court, 5, 9–10, 11, 14, 15, 46, 49, 203–5, 210, 211–30
    disability cases, 130, 135, 137
    dishonesty cases, 221–5
    establishment of (2009), 123, 212, 233, 252
    illegality defence cases, 213–16, 221
    LGBTQ+ cases, 141, 143–4, 146, 148–50, 151–2
    patients' rights cases, 188, 190, 196, 199
    private nuisance cases, 216–21
    rule of law cases, 225–9
    Rwanda scheme and, 247
    school attendance case, 119
    secondary legislation cases, 233, 237
    women's rights cases, 173, 178

Supreme Court (*Continued*)
  workers' rights cases, 160–61, 164, 167, 173, 214–15
Surrey Quarter Sessions, 87
Sweeting, Derek, Mr Justice, 103
Syria, 97–9

Tailor of Gloucester (Potter), 11
tariffs, 90
Tate Modern, London, 218–21, 229, 230
Tax Chamber, 35
taxation, 2, 34, 35
terrorism, 86, 97–101, 232–5, 256
Terrorism Order 2006, 232–5
thalidomide, 137–40
theft, 209, 222
Theft Act 1968, 221
Thewliss, Alison, MP, 260
Tinsley v Milligan, 214, 215, 216, 230
Tolstoy, Leo, 57
Tom Brown's School Days (Hughes), 124
tort, 21–2, 209, 216–21
torture, 3, 139
totalitarian states, 14
Toulson, Roger, Lord, 213, 215–16
trade unions, 47, 237
trafficking, 59–61, 101–3, 155–8, 208, 214–15, 258, 259
trans people, 141, 147–53, 178
Treasury, 212, 232–5
trial by jury, *see* jury trials
tribunal judges, 10, 46
tribunal system, 9, 10, 34–44
  benefits tribunals, 37–42, 49
  employment tribunals, *see* employment tribunals
  First-tier Tribunal, 9, 35, 211
  industrial tribunals, 46
  Upper Tribunal, 9, 35, 211
Tribunals, Courts and Enforcement Act 2007, 236
True, Nicholas, Baron, 261

Trump, Donald, 98
Tubman, Robert, 186–8
Turkey, 97–9, 102

Uber, 164
ultra vires, 204
unfair dismissals, 48–54, 155
UNISON, 237
United Nations, 157, 232–5, 246, 247
United States, 98, 203, 207
Universal Declaration of Human Rights, 170
unlawful detention, 191–4
Upper Tribunal, 9, 35, 211

vasectomies, 181–2
Victoria, Queen, 12
Victory House, London, 48
violence, 20, 86, 90
  actual bodily harm (ABH), 78, 81, 90–92
  child abuse, 56, 57, 58–63, 103–7, 120, 133
  corporal punishment, 124–6
  domestic violence, 57, 58, 65, 66, 73–4, 81–2, 105–6
  grievous bodily harm (GBH), 103–7
  terrorism, 86, 97–101, 232–5, 256

Wakefield, West Yorkshire, 138
Wales and Chester Circuit, 165
Walker, David, Bishop of Manchester, 257
war pensions, 34, 35
War Pensions and Compensation Chamber, 35
Warrington County Court, 165
Warsaw Convention, 157
weapons, possession of, 80–81
Welby, Justin, Archbishop of Canterbury, 255, 256
welfare, 2, 34, 35, 47, 49

disability benefits, 37–42
  fraudulent claims, 214
  housing benefits, 135–7
  over-payments, 42–4
welfare checklists, 68
Welsh language, 34
Welsh Senedd, 5, 205
Westminster Hall, 12
Wetherby, West Yorkshire, 129
wheelchair users, 36, 37, 77, 129
whistle blowers, 164–7
White, Martin and Pamela, 174
'will of the people', 250–51, 255
William II, King, 244
William III, King, 207
Wilson, Nicholas, Lord, 229
Wilson of Dinton, Richard, Baron, 254–5
Windsor Framework (2023), 256
woman judges, 109
women's rights, 113, 169–85
  discrimination, 172–4
  divorce and, 174–7
  equal pay, 45, 169, 170–72
  pregnancy and, 170, 181–4, 188–91
  rape victims, 178–81
  single-sex facilities, 177–8
Worboys, John, 178–81
workers' rights, 45–6, 55, 113, 154–68
  age discrimination, 161–3
  discrimination and, 45–6, 48, 51–2, 172–4
  employment tribunals, *see* employment tribunals
  freedom of contract, 154–5, 167
  part-time workers, 155, 158–61, 166
  redeployment, 131–3
  self-employment and, 154, 163–4
  trafficked workers, 155–8, 214–15
  unfair dismissals, 48–54
  whistle blowers, 164–7
Wright, Jeremy, Sir, KC, MP, 258–9, 260

York City Magistrates' Court, 58, 66–9, 76, 97, 99
YouGov, 250
young offenders, 14, 15–16, 84–5, 94–5
Youth Rehabilitation Orders, 94